FREIGHT CAR MODELS VOL. 1

Robert Schleicher, Editor

TECHNIQUES

COUPLERS and TRUCKS

PAINTING

UPGRADING and IMPROVING PLASTIC MODELS

ALTERNATIVE KITS

KIT-CONVERSION TECHNIQUES

Kadee Coupler Installation on Athearn Cars, part I (the basics)

It looks like a "drop-in" job, but adjustments are nearly always necessary to get both car and couplers working properly . . .

Joe D'Elia & Robert Schleicher

Two words often make the difference between someone playing with a Christmas toy train and a model railroader: "Athearn" and "Kadee". Those Athearn locomotives and rolling stock kits are nearly everyone's first step into the hobby in HO scale and, once there, step two is often the desire for a coupler that looks real and that actually operates — Kadee's.

It would seem that putting Kadee couplers on Athearn cars would be so simple you could do it in your sleep. Far too many of us assume that to be true and then wonder why the couplers don't operate the same every time. Yes, Kadee did design its no. 5 coupler to drop right into the coupler box on an Athearn car (or was it Athearn who designed . . .?). Fit and function, however, do not always follow . . .

The potential problem lies in the height of the coupler. Athearn uses trucks and bolsters that conform to the National Model Railroad Association's Recommended Practices and Standards, but there are tolerances that can push the final installation beyond an operable limit. Check **every** coupler installation. Virtually every pair I have installed in the past decade, on at least 50 Athearn and MDC cars, has required some type of shimming or trimming to obtain proper coupler height. The photos and captions show you how.

You should also read Kadee's instructions and follow them. Sure, 95 percent of the Kadee couplers will couple and uncouple without the need to burnish the coupler faces, but why take even that chance? Use a fine-tooth jewelers file to finish the coupler faces, and the amount of "nudge" it takes to couple will be reduced considerably. There's no point in buying a locomotive that will crawl along at ¾ of a scale mile an hour if it has to speed up to 20 smph just to get the couplers to engage. Burnishing does reduce needed coupler impact.

While you're at it, consider building stability into your freight cars with the "three-point" suspension system. Real railroad cars often rock violently as they roll down the track, but that's one element of the prototype that looks more realistic **not** modeled. To eliminate the rocking on your models, simply shave about 1/64 inch from the inner washer on **one** of the bolsters on each car. When you install that truck's mounting screw, twist it tight, then back it out about a half turn so that truck is free to swivel but not rock. Install the second truck and screw in the conventional manner so that truck can **both** rock and swivel. The result is that one end of the car has what amounts to two steady points (the right and left pairs of wheels, while that second truck really has only one point of stability (its pivot). The system allows the trucks to follow undulating rails smoothly without setting up their own rocking action. It'll work with any car whose trucks are installed with screws, but you need to shave that Athearn (or MDC) inner pivot so it will not prevent the truck-mounting screw from being tightened enough to allow only pivoting movement in the truck.

Personally, I prefer metal wheelsets. My mind has convinced me they roll better because they sound better — a clickety-clack much like the real thing. In fact, I file light notches every 30 scale feet or so to simulate the rail joints of non-welded rail to enhance the sound. There are several brands, but Bowser, Kadee, North West Short Line, Old Pullman and Precision Scale seem to be the most readily available metal wheelsets, and all have styles designed to snap into Athearn trucks. Check the wheel spacing with the NMRA Standards Gauge regardless of whose wheelsets you use. Twist the wheels to move them in or out to match the notches in the metal NMRA gauge.

Tools-of-the-trade, for foolproof Kadee coupler installation include ***two*** *of Kadee's number 205 Coupler Height Gauges mounted on a piece of ½ x 1½ wood with 14 inches of track — long enough to clear the couplers on both ends of an 80-foot passenger car or 86-foot Trailer Train flat. You'll also need a pair of needlenose pliers with serrated jaws, a screwdriver and (not shown) a hobby knife and some Kadee no. 209 .010-inch-thick truck spacer washers, plus the "intended" car.*

The bottom of the Athearn coupler pocket is about .005 inch narrower than the Kadee coupler spring. Use a jewelers screwdriver as a chisel (or a no. 11 blade in an X-Acto knife) to remove about a paper-thickness (.005 inch) from each inner edge of the Athearn coupler pocket. Scrape the inside corners square. If there's a small nub (visible just beyond the tip of the screwdriver) it, too, must be removed.

REPRINTED FROM RAILMODEL JOURNAL — June 1989

Drop the Kadee no. 5 coupler centering spring into the now wide enough pocket in the draft gear box, then install the coupler. If you try to press the metal Athearn coupler box (draft gear box) cover straight on, the metal will simply shear-off the plastic pegs. Start the cover on just one side of the pocket to catch that peg, then push it or rock it across the width of the car to snap it over the opposite peg.

Install the trucks on the underframe and roll the car up to the coupler height jig. One end of this particular car was about 0.20 inch too high.

To **lower** the car (or coupler), file material from the top of the truck bolster. Be sure to keep the file square and flat so you don't create a leaning car.

To **raise** the car (and coupler), you must add spacer washers between the truck bolster and the top of the truck. This coupler is about .010 inch too low and, believe-it-or-not, it is a common problem with most of Athearn's kits that I have inspected. A too-low coupler can allow the coupler hose to drag over switch points and frogs to cause derailments. It is also possible for just the coupler pin to be too low so it won't clear the small pad on the Kadee 205 jig. Here, however, the coupler face itself is too low (as is the coupler pin).

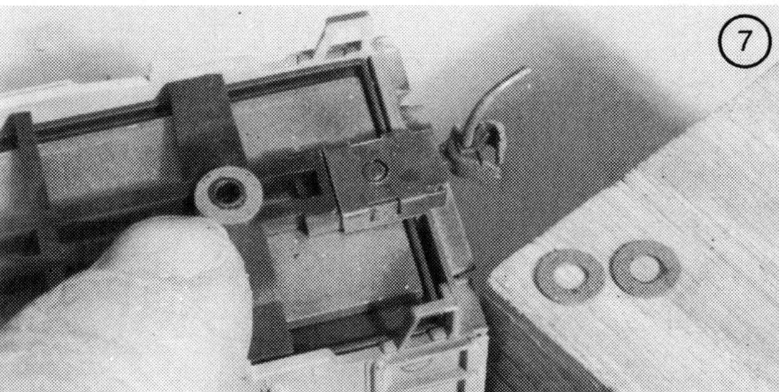

I simply place one of Kadee's no. 209 gray truck spacer washers around the Athearn bolster pin as shown. In most cases, this is enough to raise the coupler to the proper height. Usually, a washer must be added to **both** bolsters, but I have encountered cases where just one bolster needed the washer.

Recheck the coupler height. This one is just right, with the hose just clearing the pad on the 205 gauge and the coupler faces in alignment.

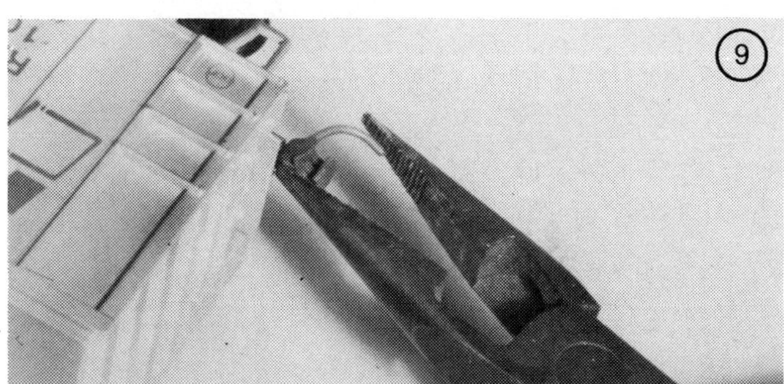

If the coupler pin happens to be too low, you can raise it by bending it upward. Grip the coupler so the tip of the pin that's in the coupler rests against the pliers' jaws so you are moving **only** the pin and not prying against the cast coupler. If in doubt, use two pairs of pliers and grip the pin just below the bottom of the coupler.

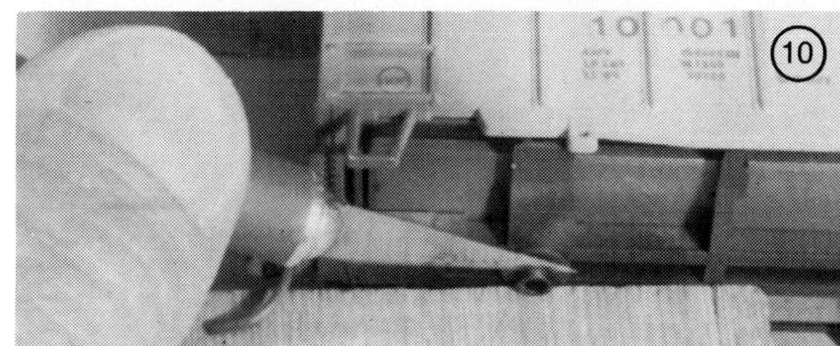

The "Three-Point Suspension System" won't make the cars couple any better, but it will prevent them from rocking from side to side and it can help solve some derailment problems. Simply slice 1/64 inch from the **inner** truck pivot pin on the Athearn bolster. By removing that material, you can later tighten the truck-mounting screw just enough to allow the truck to pivot without rocking. Leave the opposite bolster alone so that truck can both pivot and rock from side to side.

Kadee Coupler Installation on Athearn Cars (and others), part II

Part I, in the June 1989 issue, described the basic installation. Here are some additional tips to make Kadees perform the way you expect them to on **any** car or locomotive.

Joe D'Elia and Robert Schleicher

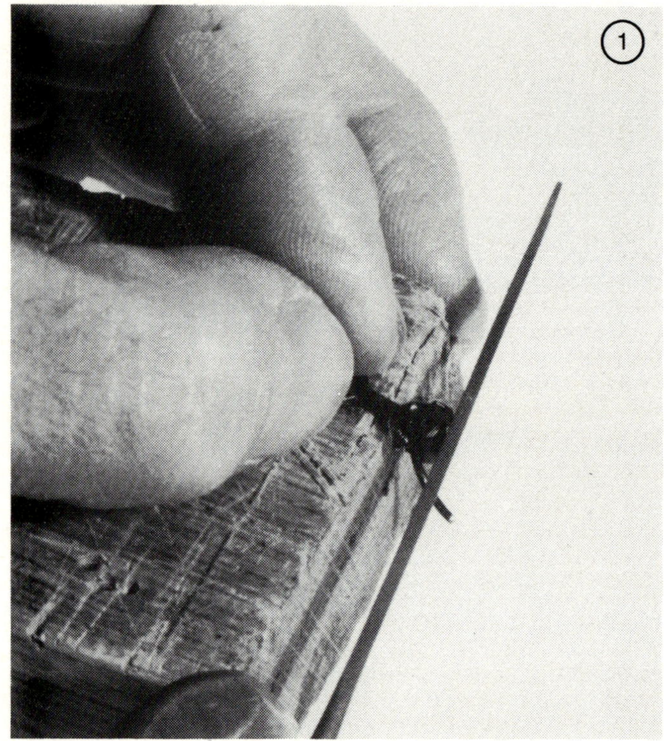

*The most important secret about virtually perfect operations with Kadee couplers is to read the instructions inside each package and perform **every** step listed **every** time you install a pair. It's also wise to gently file the face of the coupler with the fine-tooth jeweler's file, working across the coupler face as shown.*

Fill a small paint bottle with powdered graphite or Kadee's own "Grease 'Em" and store a few pairs of couplers submerged in the powder. Remove the coupler when you are ready to install it.

For better coupler performance, remove the coupler pocket from an Athearn (or MDC or Front Range or Details West or ConCor) underframe and install the Kadee no. 5 coupler and pocket. First, mark the location of the coupler pivot post, then remove the underframe and cut off the pocket with a razor saw.

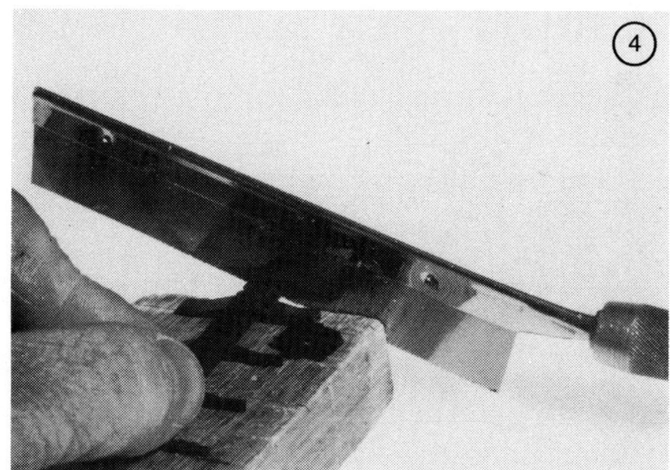

Mark the location of the Kadee coupler pocket with its pin and pin in the underframe's pocket aligned. Cut just enough off the original frame (with a razor saw) that the frame just clears the back of the Kadee coupler pocket.

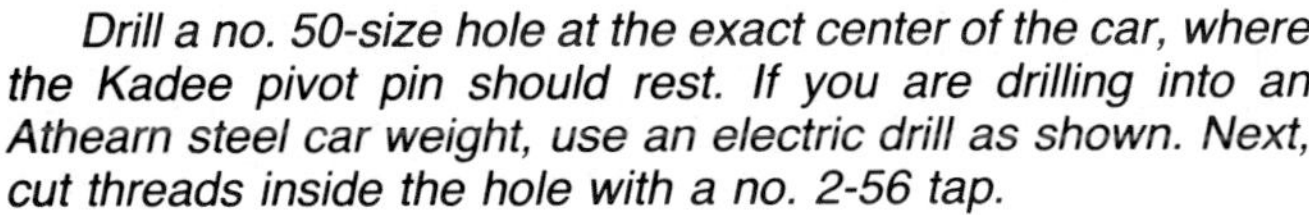

Drill a no. 50-size hole at the exact center of the car, where the Kadee pivot pin should rest. If you are drilling into an Athearn steel car weight, use an electric drill as shown. Next, cut threads inside the hole with a no. 2-56 tap.

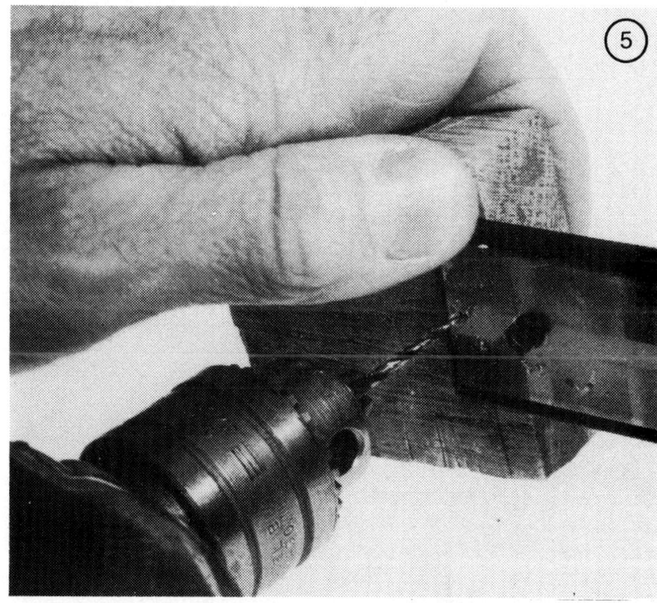

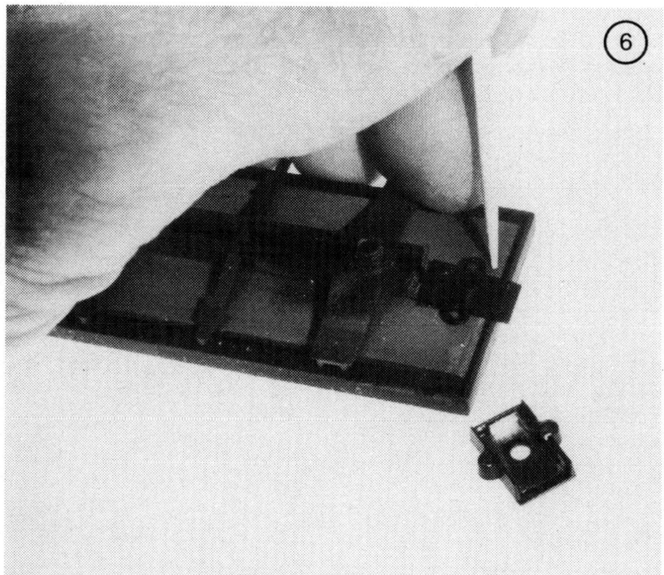

Attach the coupler pocket to the frame with thickened hobby-type cyanoacrylate cement (like Super Jet or Super T) so the attaching screw does not have to be over-tightened. Some modelers find that the Kadee no. 5 (and similar style) couplers operate more reliably with the flat coupler spring mounted upside down in the pocket ***cover*** *as shown (with a no. 5 pocket).*

Use a ¼-inch 2-56 screw (Woodland Scenics sells them to dealers) to hold the coupler pocket cover in place, but do not over-tighten the screw. Check the coupler and pin heights as shown in the June 1989 issue.

Authentic Railroad Color Chips — Matched to Model Paints

Colors and paint chips from ACF Industries, courtesy Ed Hawkins, Pat Wider and Ray Long

Hawkins, Wider and Long discovered actual paint chips in the files of ACF Industries, the firm that builds real railroad cars, and they matched model paints to those chips. To mix your own, use an eye dropper, and simply count drops. For their modelers' code F11, mix 80 drops of Floquil 110186 Oxide Red and 20 drops Floquil 110175 Southern Freight Car Brown. Be sure to thoroughly mix the original paints with a wood ice cream stick, then shake the bottle. Repeat the process with the mixed colors.

The box cars were painted with colors from the thin paint chips to the right of the longer color chips (left to right): Code A02, Accu-paint no. 54, Rich Oxide Brown, straight from the bottle; Code F11, mix of 80% Floquil no. 110186 Oxide Red and 20% Floquil no. 110175 Southern Freight Car Brown; and Code SO1, Scalecoat no. 2 Oxide Red, straight from the bottle. It is impossible to perfectly reproduce colors in photos, so we would suggest you compare the straight-from-the-bottle colors to these photos to see if your colors are a bit more red or more brown or lighter to give you a "control" base as a match for your mixed colors.

Freight Car Colors

Baltimore & Ohio Box Cars, circa 1947-1951

When built, these were the colors applied to these cars by the builder.

All photos and data from ACF Industries, courtesy Ed Hawkins, Pat Wider and Ray Long

One of the benefits of being part of a long-established hobby like model railroading is that the products and information become more sophisticated as the hobby develops. We benefit from technical advances such as improved motors for locomotives and better electronic controls. We also benefit from the increased availability of historical knowledge as research data for new kits that are closer to their prototypes.

That historical knowledge also applies to paint and lettering schemes, and on which cars, in which time period, those markings and colors appeared. Now, thanks to the efforts of some dedicated enthusiasts, we have actual paint color chips that were used on many of the freight cars produced by American Car & Foundry in the Forties and early Fifties, and in some cases, earlier. Ed Hawkins, Pat Wider and Ray Long found the chips shown in these photographs in ACF Industries files and carefully matched the chips to available paints (as shown on the previous page).

Unfortunately, we do not always know how long these colors were applied to freight cars; determining that is a chore being undertaken by many of the real railroad historical societies. Several of the societies have already produced color chips, and more are under way. It is not just a specific color that these historians seek, but the correct colors for particular time periods. Many railroads made major changes in freight car colors during the Sixties (and, often, during earlier time periods), from colors near Floquil's no. 110074 Box Car Red to darker shades closer to Floquil's Tuscan Red.

What we do know for certain is what colors were used by American Car & Foundry on cars built during the Forties and early Fifties. Some of those colors are shown here, and we'll present more later for other railroads.

Please, do not feel that you need to mix precise formulas for every freight car or that your existing fleet of models does not match prototype colors or that some of the model kits may be the "wrong" colors. For one thing, these colors faded fairly quickly and were soon altered by true "earth" colors as the dirt and grime surrounding the railroads was blown onto the cars and washed into the surface by rain and wind. This "weathering" is "real world" stuff, and that's what most of us are modeling — not the outgoing end of a freight car paint shop. The general shades, however, are visible in color photographs from the Fifties and later.

We see, for instance, that Union Pacific,

C&BT Car Shops has contacted each of the historical societies that represent the prototype railroads for C&BT's new HO scale box car models to try to obtain correct markings and colors for the kits. Their success and close-calls are typical of the difficulty both modelers and manufacturers have in duplicating real railroad colors. Before you judge them too harshly, remember that these real colors soon faded in use and were discolored by the blown and rain-washed soils to much different shades.

The long color chips below each car are paint mixes matched to actual colors used by American Car & Foundry (now ACF Industries) during the 1947-1951 period when they built cars for the B&O. Later or earlier colors may have been different from these. Each chip has sections sprayed with Testors Glosscote (the third nearest the car), with Testors Modelmaster Semi-Gloss clear (the middle third of the chip) and straight from the bottle with no clear cloating (the third furthest from the camera). These clear coatings can effect your ***perception*** *of the color by several shades. Note, for example, that we also sprayed the left half of the Santa Fe box car (the half with the herald) with Testors Dullcote. Also, earlier color mixtures of Floquil and other brands of paint differed considerably in color. We used the current 110XXX series Floquil for all of these color chips, but we have seen that some of these shades can vary.*

"The type of lighting makes a pronounced impact on how the colors appear to the eye. Under bright incandescent lighting, such as floods, the box car red shades appear quite brilliant. These same colors under normal fluorescent lights, however, appear somewhat drab. Keep this important fact in mind when you are selecting your layout lights."

C&BT Car Shops is actually mixing the color pigment into the plastic so there is not a thick layer of paint to obscure the detail. In our perception, however, there is still a slight translucence to the material, but the cars truly look painted if you spray them with Testors Dullcote after all the parts are in place. As always, the Dullcote blends the different reflectivity of the lettering with the overall color to produce a more realistic model. Some of these C&BT cars are only available from dealers who ordered custom-printed batches of cars. Those dealers' names are in parentheses beside the car (and their addresses are in the dealer directory in the back of this issue). Here are the C&BT cars/colors and the nearest match to actual American Car & Foundry paint chips:

Western Maryland (M.B.Klein, Baltimore, MD) SMP-Accu-paint A02, Floquil F11 and Scalecoat S02 paint.

Baltimore & Ohio (A. B. Charles & Son, Pittsburgh, PA) Floquil F03, F14 and F15 Paint.

Note: C&BT matched its B&O color to a shade very close to Floquil's no. 110074 Box Car Red. The Hawkins/Wider/Long research in color-matching assigned code F03 to this out-of-the-bottle color. Similar box car red colors used by ACF were F14, a mix of one part Floquil 110074 Box Car Red and three parts 110175 Southern Freight Car Brown, and code F15, a mix of equal parts of 110074 Box Car Red and 110175 Southern Freight Car Brown. This color is being used so far by C&BT on New York Central and Wabash cars as well as B&O. Anyone have proof that B&O actually used this brownish shade rather than a redder color close to the Western Maryland shade (as shown by ACF's color chips of B&O-specified paints in the 1947-51 era)?

Santa Fe (cars available to any hobby dealer) Floquil FO4 paint.

Note: C&BT colored its Santa Fe car in a reddish-brown shade closer to a mix of Floquil Tuscan or Box Car Red than Floquil's no. 110179 AT&SF Mineral Brown, which itself is a close match for the colors found by the Santa Fe Modelers group. But C&BT Car Shops did match a late Forties color chip in obtaining its color.

Southern (The Hobby Shop, Birmingham, AL) Floquil F02 paint.

Note: C&BT's car is a close match for this Floquil no. 110175 Southern Freight Car Brown (but the actual color is identical to the B&O car — the Southern herald makes it appear more brown).

Pennsylvania (A.B.Charles & Son, Pittsburg, PA) Floquil F07 paint.

Note: C&BT's car is also a close match

for Floquil's no. 110184 Tuscan Red #2 and the paint chip (shown here) supplied a few years ago to members of the Pennsylvania Railroad Technical & Historical Society.

Western Maryland, WABASH and (maybe — the paint chips say so) Baltimore & Ohio cars were more orange than the brownish-red cars of the New York Central, Santa Fe, Southern Pacific, Missouri Pacific, etc. The best this magazine, as an outlet for research material, can offer is specific examples of specific real railroad colors — it's up to you to blend them into a "fleet" with subtle weathering.

The double-door car below was painted light grey with black markings ***only*** *for its builder's photo. The ACF Industries files show it as part of lot 3197, painted a shade close to SMP Accu-Paint's no. 54 Rich Oxide Brown model paint with white lettering.*

Models —

HO Scale: Kit-convert the Front Range no. 5000 (it has the correct number of panels, but no rivets) with one 8-foot and one 7-foot door and the ends from the C&BT Car Shops 40-foot cars (or settle for the Front Range 5120 car kit's slightly wider panels, two 8-foot doors and more modern improve Dreadnaught ends).

N Scale: Con-Cor's model is similar.

O Scale: Kit-convert two of the Atlas 40-foot sliding door box cars with doors from Locomotive Workshop.

S Scale: Kit-convert the Pacific Rail Shops 50-foot single door kit the Pacific Rail Shops 50-foot single door kit as described for HO scale.

ACF Industries Data

(by builder's lot number)

Lot No.	Car Photo No.	No. Series	Length	Car Type	Date Built
3197	B&O 297094	297000-297499	50′	Box	10/47
	Riveted construction, intermediate improved Dreadnaught ends, 15-foot door, class M-58A. Pittsburgh Synthetic Red (A02): Sides, ends, roof Black: Underframe, trucks, AB brake White: Lettering APEX TRILOK running board (499 CARS), MORTON (1 CAR) AJAX hand brake				
3499	B&O 297803	297800-297849	50′	Box	3/51
	Riveted construction, improved Dreadnaught ends, 8-foot door, class M-60. Thresher Varnish Co. Freight Car Red (F11): Sides, ends, roof Black: Underframe, trucks White: Lettering Morton running board Miner hand brake				
3499A	B&O 282118	282000-282149	50′	Box	3/51
	Riveted construction, improved Dreadnaught ends, 8-foot door, class M-61. Thresher Varnish Co. Freight Car Red (F11): Sides, ends, roof Black: Underframe, trucks White: Lettering Morton running board Miner hand brake				
3545	B&O 282358	282150-283149	50′	Box	7/51
	Riveted construction, improved Dreadnaught ends, 8-foot door, class M-61. DuPont Freight Car Red (first 500 cars) (A02): Sides, ends, roof Pittsburgh Freight Car Red (last 500 cars) (F09): Sides, ends, roof Black: Underframe, trucks, AB brake White: Lettering Morton running board Miner or universal hand brake (500 cars each)				

Car 297803, from lot 3499, is also identical to the other 50-foot single-door cars but is from B&O class M-60 and carries words:

"TEST BEARINGS
RETURN DEFECTIVE BEARINGS AND AXLES
TO ENGINEER OF TESTS B&O RR CO.
MT. CLAIRE SHOPS BALTIMORE MD."

beneath the herald.

Models —

HO Scale: Front Range 5000 with rivets added, the improved Dreadnaught ends from C&BT Car Shops' 40-foot cars.

N Scale: Con-Cor's model is similar.

O Scale: None available, but it would be possible to kit-convert the car from two Atlas 40-foot single door models.

S Scale: Pacific Rail Shops, 2260 Sherman Ave., No. Bend, OR 97459, has a new kit for a similar car, but the side sills must be notched and the ends are the similar later-style improved Dreadnaught.

Car 282118 was part of American Car & Foundry's builder lot no. 3499A. The general shape and details of all of these single-door cars are virtually identical, with 8-foot-wide door openings, 16-panel sides with riveted ends, diagonal panel roofs and 3/4 interim improved Dreadnaught ends with a rectangular top rib (nearly identical to the ends on the Atlas O scale 40-foot box cars). The B&O classified this and car 282358 as M-61 cars.

Decals for Baltimore & Ohio Box Cars, circa 1947-1951 —

HO Scale Decals: Walthers 934-26100 or CDS HO-35 dry transfers
N Scale Decals: Northeast B&O-09 or CDS N-356 dry transfers
O Scale Decals: Walthers 936-26100 or CDS O-356 dry transfers
S Scale Decals: CDS S-356 dry transfers

There is no apparent difference between car 282358 from lot 3545 and the cars in lot 3499A except a slight change in the color. Accupaint rich oxide brown (#54) for first 500 cars and floquil zinc chromate primer (#110601) for last 500 cars.

Authentic Railroad Color Chips, Matched to Model Paints

Part I, with specific paint-mixing tips, appeared in the August 1989 issue. Here are the complete color-match charts from ACF.

Colors and paint chips from ACF Industries, courtesy Ed Hawkins, Pat Wider and Ray Long

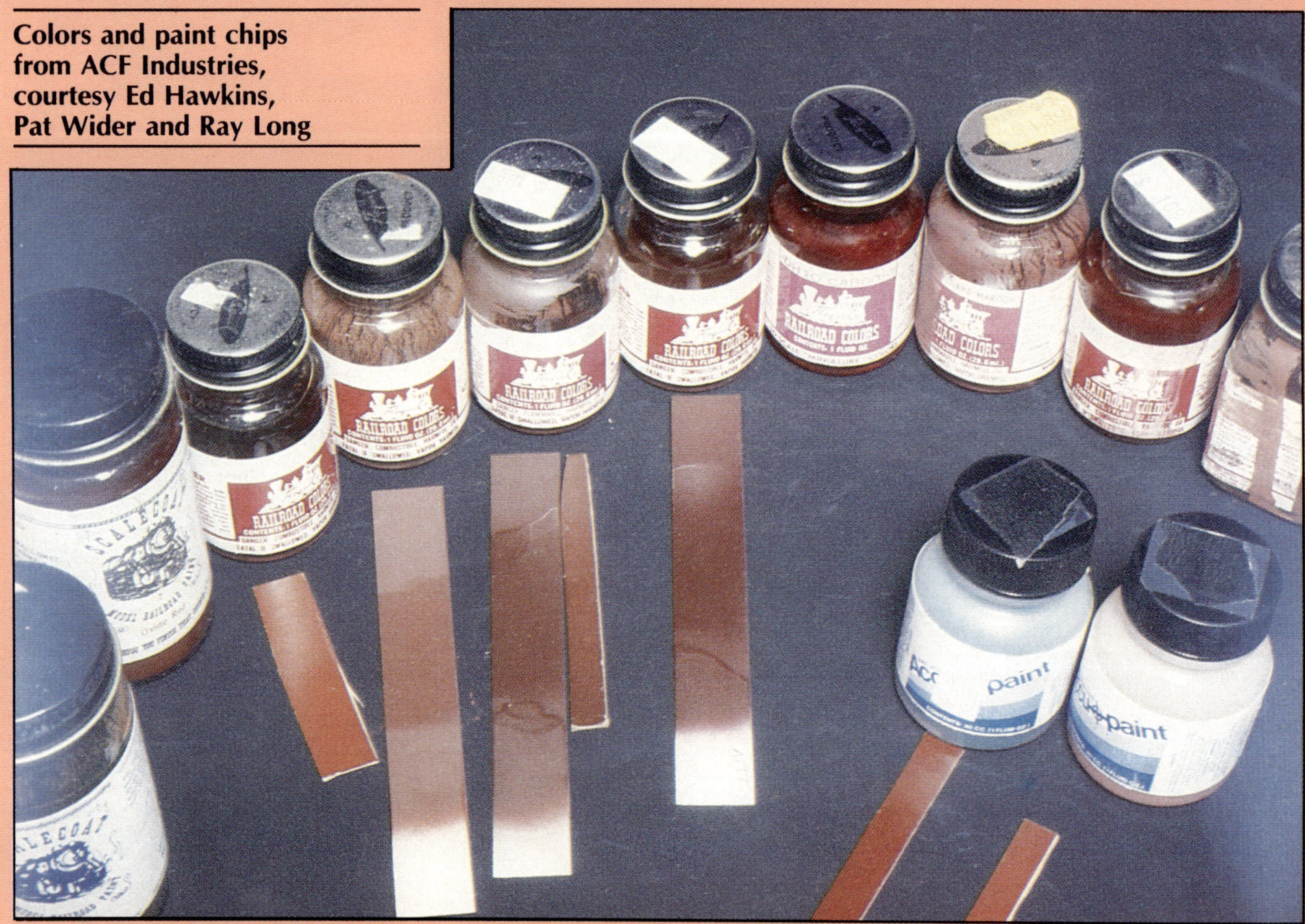

Ed Hawkins, Pat Wider and Ray Long have matched the actual paint chips from the ACF Industries files to the nearest possible shades of Floquil, Scalecoat I and SMP Accupaint colors, as there are substantial differences between the three brands of brown/red colors. The numbers in parenthesis are Hawkins/Wider/Long codes. The paints and their samples are (left to right): Scalecoat I no. 1 Oxide Red (SO1) and no. 13 Box Car Red (SO2) and Floquil no. 110186 Oxide Red (FO1), no. 110175 Southern Freight Car Brown (FO2), no. 110074 Box Car Red (FO3), no. 110179 ATSF Mineral Brown (FO4), no. 110088 D&H Caboose Red (FO5), no. 110160 RI Maroon (FO6), no. 110184 Tuscan (FO7), no. 110601 Zinc Chromate Primer (FO9) and SMP Accupaint no. 12 Oxide Brown (AO1) and no. 54 Rich Oxide Brown (AO2). The other colors on the chart are mixtures of these pure out-of-the-bottle colors.

Some historical data from real railroading is nearly impossible to obtain. One of the mystery areas has been authentic real railroad colors from the Fifties and earlier. Plenty of black and white photos exist, but color photography was in its infancy and what photos were taken often faded or shifted colors, thus providing unreliable sources of color.

Now, thanks to literally thousands of hours of research by a three-man team from the Midwest — Ed Hawkins, Pat Wider and Ray Long — some perfect color matches have become available to modelers. These three obtained permission from ACF Industries to enter the ACF (and predecessor American Car & Foundry) files to copy photographs and data. What they unearthed were actual color chips and paint makers' numbers for many (but not all) of the freight and passenger cars ACF constructed. Since ACF has always held a large proportion of the real railroads' freight car business, the ACF material can be considered representative of standard real railroad colors. At last, modelers have a source of authentic colors.

The team of researchers has gone a step further, however, to aid modelers; they have actually matched these color chips to paint samples from the model railroad paint suppliers. So far, most of their efforts have been focused on the elusive "box car red" family that ranges from an oxide primer red to the nearly maroon shade modelers call tuscan red. The team discovered that no two brands matched, and that turned out to be a blessing because it broadened the choice of colors.

Eventually, they matched 14 different pre-mixed paint colors to the actual ACF paint chips, but they also had to mix another 30(!) colors to create precise color match

COLOR-MIX: ACF FREIGHT CAR RED

PAINT-MIX FORMULAS:

FLOQUIL BASIC PAINTS
- *F01 Oxide Red (186)
- F02 Southern Freight Car Brown (SFCB) (175)
- *F03 Boxcar Red (074) — non Rev 1, browner shade
- *F04 ATSF Mineral Brown (179)
- F05 D&H Caboose Red (088)
- F06 RI Maroon (160)
- F07 Tuscan (184)
- *F08 Boxcar Red (R74) — old version no longer made, see F19 for equivalent
- *F09 Zinc Chromate Primer (601)

SMP (ACCUPAINT)
- *A01 Oxide Brown (12)
- *A02 Rich Oxide Brown (54)
- *A03 50/50 Oxide Brown/Rich Oxide Brown (12/54)
- *A04 Alkyd Brown (39)

SCALECOAT
- *S01 Oxide Red (2)
- *S02 Boxcar Red (13)
- *S11 75/25 OXIDE RED/BOX CAR RED (2/13)
- *S15 50/50 OXIDE RED/TUSCAN (2/12) DT&I ONLY

FLOQUIL MIXES
- *F11 80/20 Oxide Red/SFCB (186/175)
- *F12 50/50 Oxide Red/SFCB (186/175)
- F13 50/50 D&H Caboose Red/Boxcar Red (088/074)
- F14 75/25 SFCB/Boxcar Red (175/074)
- *F15 50/50 SFCB/Boxcar Red (175/074)
- *F16 50/50 Oxide Red/D&H Caboose Red (186/088)
- *F17 50/50 D&H Caboose Red/SFCB (088/175)
- *F18 75/25 Boxcar Red/SFCB (074/175)
- *F19 50/50 Boxcar Red/Oxide Red (074/186)
- *F20 75/25 SFCB/Oxide Red (175/186)
- *F21 75/25 Oxide Red/SFCB (186/175)
- *F22 75/25 Oxide Red/Boxcar Red (186/074)
- *F23 75/25 Boxcar Red/Oxide Red (074/186)
- *F24 75/25 Boxcar Red/D&H Caboose Red (074/088)
- *F25 75/25 D&H Caboose Red/Boxcar Red (088/074)
- *F26 75/25 Oxide Red/D&H Caboose Red (186/088)
- *F27 75/25 D&H Caboose Red/Oxide Red (088/186)
- *F28 75/25 SFCB/D&H Caboose Red (175/088)
- *F29 75/25 D&H Caboose Red/SFCB (088/175)

Code numbers are those established by Ed Hawkins. Pat Wider and Ray Long's research in ACF Industries files. Numbers in parenthesis are model paint makers numbers.

*Colors match one or more ACF paint chips.

The overspray of clear protective colors will alter the perceptible shades of the colors. Here, an acutal color chip near Box Car Red (Floquil no. 11074) is next to the Floquil shade, followed by (left to right) Floquil no. 110186 Oxide Red, no. 110175 Southern Freight Car Brown, no. 110179 ATSF Mineral Brown and no. 110184 Tuscan. Each color, however, has been sprayed with Testor s Model Master Semi-Gloss across the top one-third, Testors Dullcote across the middle third and no coating at all on the bottom third of each color sample.

samples to recreate the freight car colors of the Forties and Fifties. Their exact formulas are reproduced on the "Fact File Card" in this issue. In later issues we'll show you other colors, including grey, that the team has color-matched.

There's more to matching colors, however, than merely mixing paint. Modelers usually need to protect the finish and decals or dry transfers of their models with a coat of clear, flat-finish paint. The clear finish itself, however, alters the perceptible color. The team of researchers made no direct attempt to alter its color formulas to reflect how an overcoat of, say, Testors Dullcote might effect, say, a model painted with Floquil's no. 074 Box Car Red. The team's efforts produced semi-gloss paint surfaces to match the semi-gloss paint chips. If those paint chips were faded (the effect produced by spraying a model with Dullcote or a similar clear non-gloss paint), the assumption was that the prototype color chip would be affected about the same as the model paint. You'll see samples here of a selection of paints as-mixed and with Testors Dullcote and the semi-gloss Modelmaster series of Testors paints applied by spraying over the paint. The semi-gloss produces less "fade" on the paint chips than the Dullcote, so a model of relatively new (or freshly repainted) equipment might consider protecting decals or dry transfers with the Modelmaster semi-gloss and producing faded effects with thinned flat finish paints applied with an air brush or powdered pastel chalks to dull out the finish.

Finally (for this issue), Ed Hawkins had some comments on the August 1989 **Railmodel Journal's** first article on his group's efforts:

*Thank you for the August 1989 **Journal** containing the article on B&O colors. In general, I thought it was very good and I hope enjoyed by many readers. A couple of points should be mentioned about the article: For ACF Lot 3545, the color chip codes on page 16 call out A02 and F09 (DuPont and Pittsburgh Freight Car Red, respectively), but the photo caption on page 14 erroneously calls out S01.*

I would also like to address the Floquil paint color discussion per the first column on page 15. You mention of hearing about color inconsistency, but then point blame on the modeler for improper mixing and shaking. Please see the enclosed two bottles of Floquil 110074 Box Car Red which are very different. Both of these bottles were bought within the last few months from local hobby shops. One is on the brown side and the other is closer to 110179 ATSF Mineral Brown. As you can see, the color inconsistency is in the bottle, not the modeler. This has been our biggest problem trying to match the ACF color chips, since 110074 is such a basic color and is used for mixing with other colors. When you see code F03 used in our data, we are using the browner shade.

As you described the various C&BT precolored plastic cars on page 15, you make mention of several of our color code lists be published as a handy look-up table. I can just visualize someone going to the hobby shop and asking for a bottle of F04 or A02 or S01. Also, it should be explained that this coding business is done purely as a shorthand method for computerization purposes. As new colors are added in the future, I will provide you a periodic update of the list.

American Car & Foundry Colors, circa 1953

Here are three color photographs, taken directly from ACF Industries color transparencies, with the actual colors based on the color chip-matching done by Ed Hawkins, Pat Wider and Ray Long. No, the photos don't exactly match the color chips, but the differences in the colors will provide some idea of how far off a color photograph might be as compared to the actual car color.

ACF Industries photographs

Here are some actual ACF Industries color photographs of cars built in the Fifties. The color may have shifted slightly over the years, but the photos are useful to compare to one another and to paint samples you can mix with the formulas on the previous pages. These cars are from series later than any that Hawkins/ ***Wider/Long could match. The car was*** *built in May 1953 with a 7-foot-wide door opening as part of number series 20500-20999.*

Models—HO Scale: C&BT Shops with rivets sanded off and weld lines scribed.

N Scale: Con-Cor.

O Scale: Atlas/Roco (but kit has 8-foot door).

Decals—HO Scale: CHAMP HB25A, Microscale 87-309, Walthers 934-33001 or CDS HO-127 dry transfers.

N Scale: Microscale 60-309 or CDS N-126 dry transfers.

O Scale: Walthers 936-33001 or CDS 0-126 dry transfers.

This Pennsy car is similar to the other two shown here in having a 7-foot-wide door opening, welded side panel seams, interim improved Dreadnaught ends with a rectangular top rib and diagonal panel roof. It was built in November 1950 as ***part of number series 602000-603499.***

Models—HO Scale: Middle Division, P.O. Box 332, New Cumberland, PA 17070, has specific decals for this series lettering. Send aa stamped, self-addressed envelope for a price list. Walthers 934-77001 is also similar.

N Scale: Northeast PRR-05 or Walthers 938-77001.

O Scale: see Middle Division, above or Walthers 936-77001.

We'll have a series of articles, beginning in the July 1990 issue of ***Railmodel Journal****, on modeling these cars from Eastern Car Works and MDC kits in HO scale, and from V-Line, Arnold and Atlas kit-conversions in N scale and Weaver and Gloor Craft kits in O scale in later issues. This car was built in July 1953 as* ***part of DT&I number series 11000-11099. For painting, use S15 paint mix. Formulas on page 12.***

Decals—HO Scale: Champ HC319 plus HC408.

N Scale: None known.

O Scale: Champ C319 plus C408.

Authentic Railroad Colors: Pennsylvania RR "Freight Car Red"

The reality of matching real railroad colors, as researched and authenticated by Pennsy modelers.

Curt La Rue, Ralph Gutowski and Brady McGuire of The PRRT&HS Cincinnati Division

Note: Paint mixing and matching tips appeared in the August 1989 issue and ACF color-mix formulas (matching model paints to real paint chips) appeared in the June 1990 issue.

Some railroads specialized in hauling coal or ore, and some timber. All but a few carried passengers. But for many railroads, the bills were paid by hauling general freight — box cars and box cars of freight. The web of tracks called the Pennsylvania Railroad stretched out from New York on the east to Washington, D.C. on the south, Chicago and St. Louis on the west, and the Great Lakes on the north. As the Pennsy wound its way through America's industrial heartland, it moved the nation's products and goods to market via its own extensive trackage and through interchange with other railroads. By the late 1940s and early 1950s, the Pennsylvania's freight cars comprised over 10 percent of the national freight car fleet, and PRR cars could be seen rolling over most railroads throughout the country. Both prototype and freelance modelers should consider including a representative number of PRR freight cars in their consists, depending upon their home road's proximity and relations with the Pennsy.

Painting the Prototype

An important facet of modeling PRR freight cars is replicating the correct color. A popular misconception is that PRR freight cars were painted Tuscan Red, probably because Tuscan was the color of Pennsy passenger equipment. (When painting Pennsy passenger equipment, Floquil "Tuscan Red" by itself does not produce the right color; it should be mixed in equal parts with "Caboose Red"). The "P" company specified that all revenue-producing freight cars be painted "Freight Car Enamel." Maintenance-of-way equipment was originally painted grey, then yellow after the mid-1950s. Pennsy modelers now refer to this color simply as "freight car color." The original color formulation specified in the 1920s was for "iron sesquioxide." This was basically an iron oxide shade with a light tint of orange. The color became increasingly darker and more brownish in the 1950s and 1960s. All PRR freight cars that were painted common schemes, including cabin cars (cabooses), were painted freight car color. Exceptions were introduced for covered hoppers (painted grey sometime after late 1953 or early 1954), open hoppers (black after March 1957), and cabin cars (Focal Orange after June 1965). Pennsy ore jennies, classes G38 and G39, were also painted black.

The following paint scheme was used on new freight equipment:

— Car body (sides and ends): Freight car color.

— Roof: Freight car color. There is some doubt about new galvanized steel roofs. Specifications call for two coats of an asphaltum compound, which is thought to be dark grey or black, but painted over with freight car color.

— Underframe: Freight car color.

— Trucks: Black on new cars; freight car color on re-shopped or repainted cars.

Painting Models

The difficulty in painting PRR models an accurate shade of freight car color is that there are no existing color samples or pigments to match paint from the 1920 through 1950 era. An article titled "Painting and Lettering Pennsylvania Railroad Cabin Cars" in the December 1974 issue of *The Keystone*, journal of the PRR Technical & Historical Society, sparked the interest of our Cincinnati area PRR modeling group to experiment to find colors that "looked right" when compared to color photos or movies from this era. We discovered that freight car color darkened rather quickly after exposure to weather and the elements. We have adopted several color mixtures, depending on the brand of modeler's paint used and the time period being replicated.

1920s and 1930s Era:

Freight car color had an orange-ish cast. The numbers in parentheses are the color formulas that appeared in the June 1990 **Railmodel Journal** (page 62), matched to actual 1950-era color paint chip samples by Ed Hawkins, Pat Wieler and Ray Long. There is a slightly off-color photo of a Pennsy X43A box car from 1950 in this same article. Use the following mixtures to achieve the approximate color:

Scalecoat — Oxide Red (SO-2) according to the above *Keystone* article, is a bit dark; however, it can be used for a slightly weathered shade of freight car color.

Floquil — Zinc Chromate Primer (FO-9) is the best choice for a base coat of freight car

color, but is a lighter orange-ish shade compared to the Scalecoat Oxide Red.
Floquil — Oxide Red (FO-1) is a darker shade than Zinc Chromate Primer and can be used for a more weathered and darker shade of freight car color.
Floquil — D & H Caboose Red (FO-5) is a good choice for weathered wooden cabin cars because freight car color tended to weather to a greyish-red tint on wooden cabin cars.

Late 1940s and 1950s Era:

Freight car color of the late 40s and 50s was a darker, more brownish shade of the color seen in the 1920s and 1930s. The following mixtures can be used to approximate this shade:
Scalecoat — Equal parts of Oxide Red and Box Car Red. (No ACF equivalent).
Floquil — Equal parts of Zinc Chromate Primer and Box Car Red. (No ACF equivalent).

1960s Era:

Freight car color of the 1960s became even darker, with a more brownish hue. This shade can be approximated by starting with either of the basic mixes given above for the 1940-50 era and adding slightly more Box Car Red so that the mix becomes six parts Box Car Red to five parts of the other color. Accupaint brand's Rich Oxide Brown is also a good choice for the late 1950s to 1960s era. James Hunter, former modeling editor of *The Keystone*, has suggested a mixture of four parts Box Car Red and one part Caboose Red to replicate freight car color in this period.

To paint a model of a PRR freight car, select the color mix that best fits the era in which the prototype was originally built and painted or re-shopped and repainted. The following format will produce a realistic car for your layout.

— Car body (sides, ends, roof): Freight car color.

— Underframe: Freight car color with a light overspray of Grimy Black or dirty brown to represent road grime.

— Trucks: new cars — black with a light overspray of Rail Brown; re-shopped cars — freight car color, then weathered; older cars — Roof Brown or Rail Brown, then weathered.

Color Variation

After viewing countless color slides, photos, movies and videos, we have noted distinct deviations in color from car to car within a train. Paint coloration varied from light bleached-out to very bright to very dark shades of freight car color, depending upon the amount of use and weathering a particular car might have experienced. When you paint your freight cars, don't be concerned if there is some color variation from one batch to the next. For realism, your trains should not be made up of cars of all the same shade. This can best be achieved by weathering your cars using any of the popular air brush and chalk weathering techniques.

A note of caution is in order. The mixtures given in this article apply to HO scale cars. The amount of light reflected by S scale and larger or smaller N scale models can alter the appearance of the color. That is why the chip of turquoise paint looked so much different in the store where you picked it out than when you finally saw it on the bathroom walls at home. Modelers in other scales may have to experiment somewhat with the basic paint mixtures given above to find the shades of PRR freight car color that look best on their models.

Lastly, as Pennsy modelers, we are interested in operating authentic versions of cars from other prototype railroads, too. We want our consists to look as much like the real thing as possible. We invite other prototype modelers to share with us their techniques and formulations for building, painting and lettering prototypical rolling stock that found its way onto the tracks of the "Standard Railroad of the World."

Lettering Arrangements

For accurate information regarding PRR freight car lettering arrangements, we suggest the following publications:

The Keystone, Vol. 21, No. 2, Summer 1988, "Lettering Schemes For PRR Boxcars: 1876 to 1968," by Brady McGuire, is an excellent article with photos and lettering arrangement drawings. It can be obtained from: PRRT&HS, Box 389, Upper Darby, PA 19082. The price is $8.00, including postage and handling.

Pennsylvania Railroad Compendium, Vol. 1, "PRR Freight Car Lettering Arrangements: 1954-1968," covers variations in the Shadowed Keystone and Plain Keystone schemes for many classes of PRR freight cars, with 115 pages of large, high quality lettering diagrams. It is published by: The Middle Division, P.O. Box 332, New Cumberland, PA 17070.

In addition, many lettering diagrams have also appeared in various issues of *Rails Northeast* and *Pennsy Journal*. Unfortunately, both of these publications are now out of print, and back issues are hard to find. To help narrow your search, *The Keystone* article by Brady McGuire, referenced above, contains a listing of issues and lettering diagrams. **RMJ**

Sources

The Keystone, Vol. 7, No. 4, December 1974, "Painting and Lettering of Pennsylvania Railroad Cabin Cars."

The Keystone, Vol. 20, No. 1, Spring 1987, p. 10, description of "freight car color."

The Keystone, Vol. 20, No. 2, Summer 1987, p. 8, date open hopper color changed to black.

The Keystone, Vol. 21, No. 2, Summer 1988, pp. 13-46, article on PRR box car paint schemes.

The Keystone, Vol. 11, No. 4, December 1978, Pennsy Modeling Notes: "Notes on Painting PRR Freight Cars," by James R. Hunter.

Acknowledgements

The authors wish to express their appreciation to fellow Pennsylvania Railroad Technical & Historical Society members Rich Burg, Andy Hart, Don Hess and Walt Keely for their assistance.

Honorarium for this article is being donated to the PRRT&HS restoration project of the Pennsylvania Railroad station at Lewistown, Pennsylvania.

Decal Application

Decals are supposed to make the lettering and heralds appear as though they were actually painted on the car sides, not like they are clear plastic stick-ons. These are the techniques you'll need to make decals appear as though they weren't decals at all.

Richard Hendrickson
Photos by Robert Schleicher

The Evolution of Model Railroad Lettering

The Dark Ages

Back in the infancy of model railroads, locomotives and cars were lettered by hand with a fine-tipped paint brush or a pen. Needless to say, this approach was very laborious, and the results usually left a lot to be desired, so in the 1930s, lettering began to appear in the form of decals (decal is short for "decalcomania," a a process for making decorative designs on clear film and then transferring them onto glass, wood, metal,

*If you are going to the trouble of applying decals to a model, start with accurate prototype information — a photograph of the car or locomotive you are recreating, from the era you wish to simulate with your models. Shown is the March 1990 issue of **Railmodel Journal.** You will also need the decals (which we list with every prototype car or locomotive for which a decal is known to be available), a bottle of decal-softening solution (Microscale's Micro-Sol, Walthers' Solvaset or Champ's Decal-Set), a small paint brush, a cup of warm water, some soft paper towels or facial tissues (not shown), scissors and Testor's Dull Cote flat finish paint (available in aerosol cans). Paint the model with glossy paints (ours was painted in flat to make the decal-softening fluids and water more visible), or spray the finished model with Testor's Gloss Cote or Floquil's Barrier glossing shield, and let it dry for 48 hours before applying decals. The decals adhere better to glossy surfaces, and there's less chance of air being trapped beneath the decal (leaving the clear portion looking frosted, like tissue paper, rather than being invisible).*

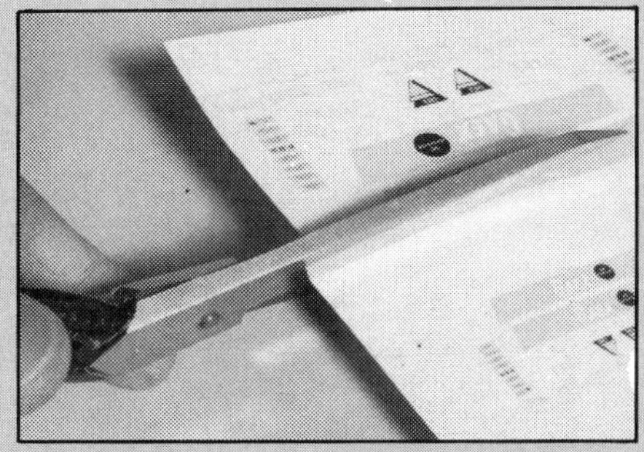

Cut the decals as close to the printed image as possible. Microscale has thin clear film only near the colored portion of the decal (Champ, Walthers and Herald King cover the sheet with clear film), but you will be able to handle and position the decal more accurately if there is as little clear around the edges as possible.

Use tweezers to handle the decal from now on. Dip the decal in water for 10 to 20 seconds, then place it on a folded paper towel to soak.

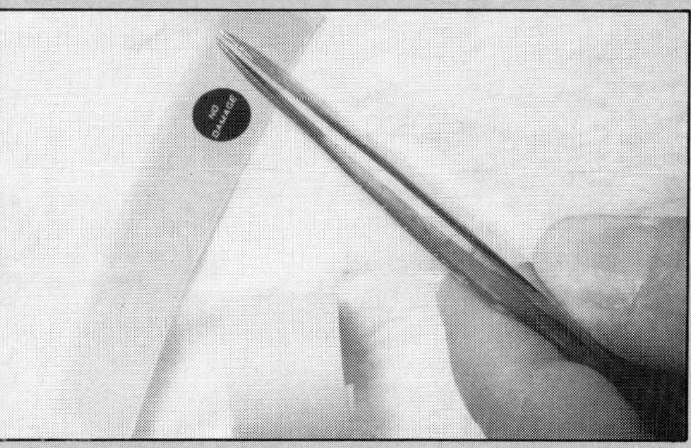

The decals should begin to unroll as the water soaks completely through the paper. Use the paint brush to help flatten the decal and to test the smaller decals to determine if the decal itself can be moved without moving the paper backing — that's when the decal is ready to be applied. Dip only enough decals for one car side at a time.

The finished model was produced by cutting up two C&BT Shops 40-foot box cars to make a precise match for the side rivet patterns, end corrugations and roof of the prototype cars built by General American/Evans in late 1950. The kit-conversion techniques, step-by-step, were shown in the March and April 1990 issues, with prototypes for these cars in the March 1990 issue. Prototypes for later cars, as repainted in a darker green with markings similar to the Walthers 934-77130 HO scale decals were shown in the March, April, June and September 1990 issues. Decals for this 1955 era car were bound into the March 1990 issue, and Champ has a similar set, no. HB162, for a 40-foot car.

Modeling the GAEX Cars in HO and S Scales

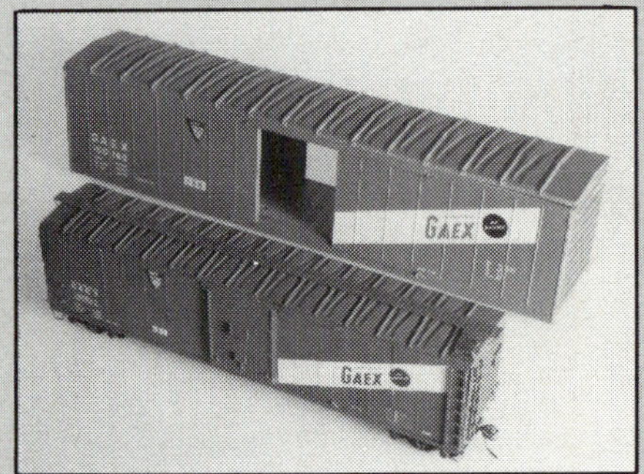

S DeSignS, 37 Snow Dr., Mahwah, NJ 07430, is lettering the Pacific Rail Shops' S scale 50-foot cars in the GAEX scheme. This model is closer to the prototype than either HO or O scale models. That's our HO scale C&BT Shops 40-to-50-foot kit-conversion car in front.

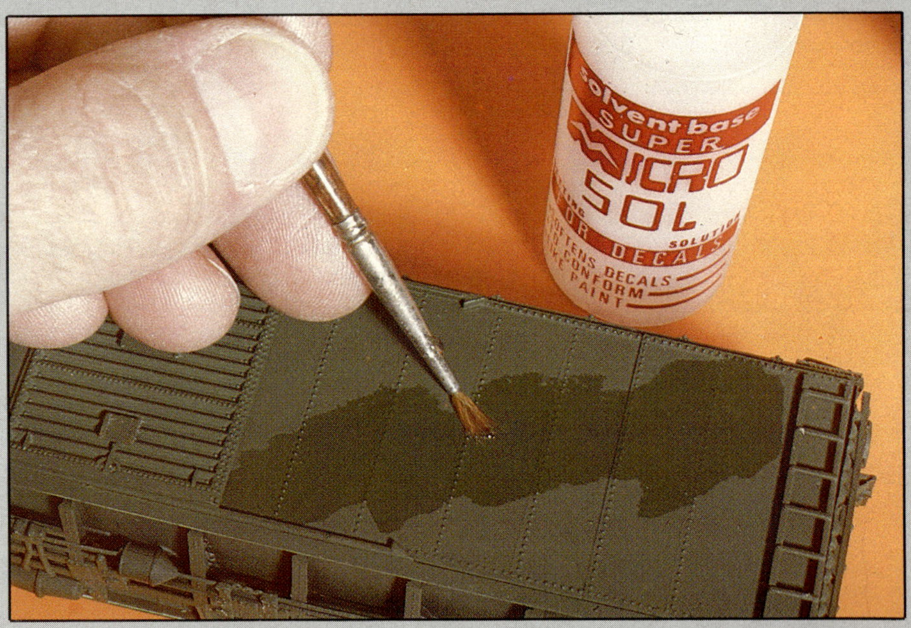

Coat the area where you are going to apply the decal with the clear decal-softening solution just before you apply each decal. The fluid makes the car appear darker here because we are using flat finish paints; it won't be this visible on a gloss surface.

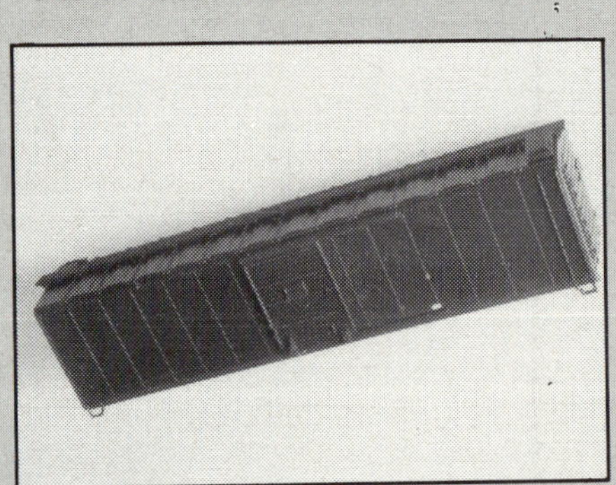

Athearn's 50-foot car (no. 5050 — undecorated) has the proper proportions, but the roof is an earlier style without the diagonal panels; the ends are also older, with a 5/5 rib pattern and smaller ribs, and it has 14 side panels rather than the prototype's 16 panels — the effect makes the car appear a bit lower than it should.

The kit-conversion shown in the March 1990 issue requires two 40-foot box car kits and, frankly, is difficult to complete with all the parts fitting properly.

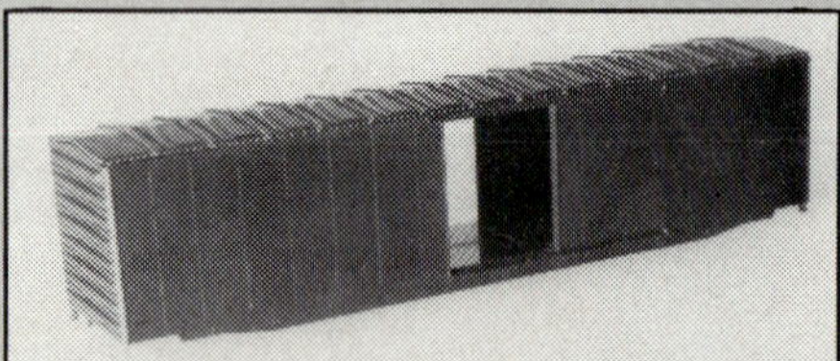

The Front Range 50-foot car has the more modern ends that were used on the GAEX cars with the horizontal seam down the length of both sides. If you can accept the absence of that seam (or want to add a strip of .005-inch-thick Evergreen styrene to simulate it, this car, with a new lower sill, is very close to the GAEX cars built in 1955.

Position both decal and paper backing precisely where you want the decal. Hold the decal with the paint brush while you gently pull at the decal and paper backing with a very light grip on tweezers — the tweezers should snag just the paper backing — if not, use the tips of your thumb and index finger to grip the very corner of the decal and, with a light rubbing motion, pull the paper from beneath the corner of the decal. Now you can pull the paper from beneath the decal with tweezers. If the decal won't move off its paper backing, dip both in water again and let them soak for a few more minutes on the paper towel.

Dip the brush into the decal-softening solution and cover the surface of the decal with the fluid. Use the brush, too, to move the decal into precise position. Keep the model flat on the workbench until all the decals on one side are in place and the decal-softening solution has dried overnight. You can then proceed to the opposite site, followed in successive days by each end. If you are in a hurry, you can plan brief morning decal application periods to begin work one evening on one side, to apply decals to one end the next morning, to the opposite side that evening and to the opposite end that next morning and to finish the car with clear flat paint the evening of the third day.

Hold a bright light over the decal to see if air bubbles are trapped. The decal will be a slightly different color where the bubbles appear — usually around rivets or seams in the surface of the model. Use the brush to push down firmly on the decal to work the bubble out and "walk" it over to the edge of the decal. If the bubble won't move, prick the surface of the decal with a pin or the tip of a hobby knife blade to release the air, then apply more decal-softening solution. In cases of larger rivets (or thicker decals), it may take as many as 12 applications of decal-softening solution to make the decal to conform to the surface of the model. ***Do not*** *attempt to move a decal that has been treated with decal-softening fluid, because the decal is nearly as soft as wet paint — the softening solution should not, then, be applied until you are certain the decal is precisely where you want it.*

Gently scrub the surface of the model with warm water and a cotton swab to remove any traces of the decal's glue or leftover softening fluid. Let the model dry overnight, then spray it with a light coat of clear flat to blend the reflective surface of the decal to the model (so the decal doesn't shine more than the model). If the edge of the clear film is visible after the clear paint dries, sand the edge very lightly with no. 600 sandpaper, and apply another coat of clear flat.

etc., which dates back to the 19th Century). The earliest decals were printed with a letterpress on film that was relatively thick and inflexible, and the type fonts that were available frequently bore only a vague resemblance to prototype stenciling. In spite of these shortcomings, though, they were a vast improvement over hand lettering.

Decal Lettering

Decal Sources

Walthers pioneered decal lettering over a

half-century ago and still offers an extensive line of decals in both HO and O scales, as well as some decals in N scale. The Champion Decal Co., now in its 51st year, offers a large variety of decal lettering in HO and O scales, with the emphasis on lettering of the '30s through '60s. Both Walthers and Champ have been upgrading their more popular lettering sets and discontinuing outdated ones in recent years. More recently, Microscale has developed an extensive line of O, HO and N scale decals covering everything from billboard reefers of the '20s to the most modern diesel locomotives. Another good source of HO scale lettering for locomotives and cars of the '60s through '80s is Herald King.

All these manufacturers offer comprehensive catalogs, the Walthers decal catalog, also covers Microscale and several smaller manufacturers. Walthers also publishes four prototype lettering diagram books, each covering a somewhat different era, and Champ offers two freight car lettering plan books.

In addition to these major decal sources, other model manufacturers, as well as model railroad clubs and prototype railroad historical associations, market custom decal sets from time to time, often on a limited-run basis. There are also several decal markers offering custom-printing services to small companies and individuals. All told, literally thousands of different decal sets are available, especially in HO scale. Of course, there are still many more thousands of prototype variations in lettering than there are decals to reproduce them, but most of these variations can be modeled by combining parts of two or more sets — and if worse comes to worst, custom decals in modest quantities are surprisingly inexpensive, provided you're willing to devote the time and effort required to create your own artwork.

Surface Preparations

For proper adhesion and to prevent air bubbles from being trapped under the film, decals *must* be applied to a shiny surface. Some model railroad paints (Accu-Paint, Scalecoat) have a gloss finish, but others (Floquil, Pactra Scale Model enamels, Testor's Modelmaster enamels) have a flat, microscopically grainy finish when dry. Making these flat paints shiny can be accomplished either by adding liberal amounts of clear glaze to the color coats or by spraying a clear gloss finish like Testor's Gloss Cote or Floquil glaze or barrier glossing shield over the color coats after they have set.

Make sure that all the paint on a model is completely dry before attempting to apply decals. Low-temperature baking (around 140-150 degrees) will accelerate drying, and a makeshift oven for this purpose can be created by placing a couple of 60-watt light bulbs in a home-made wood or metal enclosure (make sure the bulbs are located some distance away from the model and several inches away from any adjacent surface). *Never* use a kitchen range or toaster oven for this purpose, as the temperature settings on such appliances are often wildly inaccurate, and the peak temperatures as they cycle on and off are high enough to distort plastic — or even melt solder! Also, *never* use heat on a model made of urethane or polyester resin, as even a little heat may soften and deform parts made of these materials. (For that matter, never leave such a model exposed to direct sunlight or enclosed in a car trunk on a hot day.)

Decal Application

In cutting out decals, the backing film should be trimmed as close to the edges of the lettering as possible, so that the film won't show beyond the edges of the lettering; a metal straight-edge and a single-edge razor blade are useful for this purpose. For heralds, slogans and other irregular shapes, a sharp pair of small nail scissors can often be used to advantage. As each piece is cut out, it should be soaked in water for 10-20 seconds (or more, if the decals are old) and then placed on the model near where the lettering is to be located. Let the decal stand until the water has soaked completely through the backing paper and only a gentle nudge is needed to slide the film off the paper. Then maneuver the lettering into position with tweezers and a modeling knife or paint brush. If it doesn't want to slide into place easily, add a drop or two of water; if too much water is causing it to float around, soak up some of the water with a cotton swab.

When the decal is positioned about right, apply some diluted setting fluid around the edges with a small brush — cheap nylon paint brushes work well for this purpose — but make sure you experiment with a piece of scrap decal first. Setting fluids vary widely in strength, and there's no way to know in advance how they will affect a particular variety of decal film. Undiluted Champ Decal-Set, for example, is especially potent and will cause some delicate decal films to shrivel up into a shapeless mass almost instantly (on the other hand, it's the only setting fluid that's strong enough to work effectively on some of the heavier films). Note, too, that not all the decals in a set may have been printed on the same film, so you may need to test each piece in the set, especially if the pieces are different in color or appearance.

Several successive applications of decal solvent are often required to eliminate air bubbles and make the film conform to the shape of rivets or other surface irregularities; good results require patience! Except on Microscale decals (which are discussed in the next paragraph), my usual practice is to make an initial application of Decal-Set cut with 50 percent water. After the decal has set, I then slit any air bubbles with the point of a sharp modeling knife and apply 50/50 Decal Set again. Only when the decal conforms completely to the surface do I make a final application of full-strength Decal-Set, after which the decal film is virtually welded to the paint.

Microscale decals require special handling, owing to their very thin, discontinuous film. In theory, each section of a Microscale decal is supposed to have its own film which tapers to a feather edge, so it isn't necessary to trim along the edge of the lettering. This doesn't apply when using lettering from Microscale's general data sets, however, and some trimming may also be required on other lettering to avoid interference with adjacent details. In addition, Microscale film is *very* fragile, especially if the set has been around (either at your dealers or in your decal file) for several years, and must be maneuvered very carefully from the backing sheet to ther model. Using lots of water to literally float it into place is highly recommended.

Sometimes decal film disintegrates no matter how carefully you handle it; especially if a set is known to be old, test a scrap piece first. Even decals that are "over the hill" can often be salvaged by applying a coat of Microscale's liquid "Super Film" over them before you cut them out. Once Microscale decals are in place on the model, it's advisable to use only Microscale Micro-Set setting fluid, followed by a final application of their more potent Micro-Sol; the effect of other setting fluids is unpredictable at best.

With the decals firmly in place on the model and all air bubbles eliminated, you may wish to remove any spots left by the setting fluid by wiping gently with a cotton swap moistened in a little diluted setting fluid — but be careful not to disturb the decals in the process, and note that swabs are prone to shed tiny fibers which will mar your final finish unless you make sure to remove them from the surface of the model.

Concealing the Film

The next step is a coat of clear flat finish to hide the decal film and dull the glossy paint. A number of satisfactory flat finishes are available, but make sure that the one you use doesn't lift or craze the paint that's already on the model; when in doubt, try a little first in some inconspicuous location, as nothing is more disheartening than watching the paint and lettering you're painstakingly applied to a model shrivel up and turn into ugly mush when oversprayed with clear finish. If you want an absolutely flat finish, apply a wet coat of clear flat and let it dry completely (at least a day or two); then fog on a final coat which is just wet enough to penetrate the surface of the first coat but not completely dissolve it. Acceptable results are possible with aerosol cans, but thinner coats and a much smoother surface can be achieved with an air brush.

If your model should have a semi-gloss surface, you can mix dull and glossy coatings in suitable proportions to get the desired effect — but always apply a uniform layer of flat finish first as a base coat. Even a model that's supposed to look shiny should have a clear coating with some flat finish mixed in, as a completely glossy finish doesn't "scale down" realistically. **RMJ**

Your Top Tips

Earn $20.00

We'll pay you $20.00 each for any idea we publish. Just send us your tip, preferably with a sketch (photos are optional) and enough of an explanation that we can photograph a recreation of the idea or redraw it. Keep the tips simple; a minimum of one step and a maximum of three steps must complete the technique. (More than that and you should consider a full-blown article. If it's that complex, write and ask if we're interested before proceeding.

The ideas, sketches or photographs **will not,** ever, be returned, and their use, as illustrations or as part of ideas, is our option. You may, of course, incorporate them into future articles for us or any other magazine. We pay **approximately 45 days after publication. Be sure your name and address** are on each idea, photograph or sketch you submit. Mark the envelope "Top Tips" when you submit your ideas. We reserve the right to reprint the material, in any form, without further payment. Please let us know if you do **not** want your city and state mentioned (we never provide addresses). Come on, share 'em!

Use a "Bright Boy" or similar track-cleaning eraser to remove unwanted lettering from a car side. Work carefully, and just the letters or numbers can be removed. It works best when just changing a single number or two to renumber a car. — Jim Barsballe

Drafting supply stores sell stainless steel eraser guards similar to this one. The guard is designed to be placed over a drawing so you can erase just what appears in the hole, but none of the surrounding material. For modelers' uses, the holes provide patterns for "weathering" streaks and spots using an aerosol can for the paint. You must, however, mask any surrounding areas with paper and tape. Apply the tape to the metal mask, not the car, so you can move the mask and tape to repeat or enlarge the pattern. — Robert Occhiogrossi

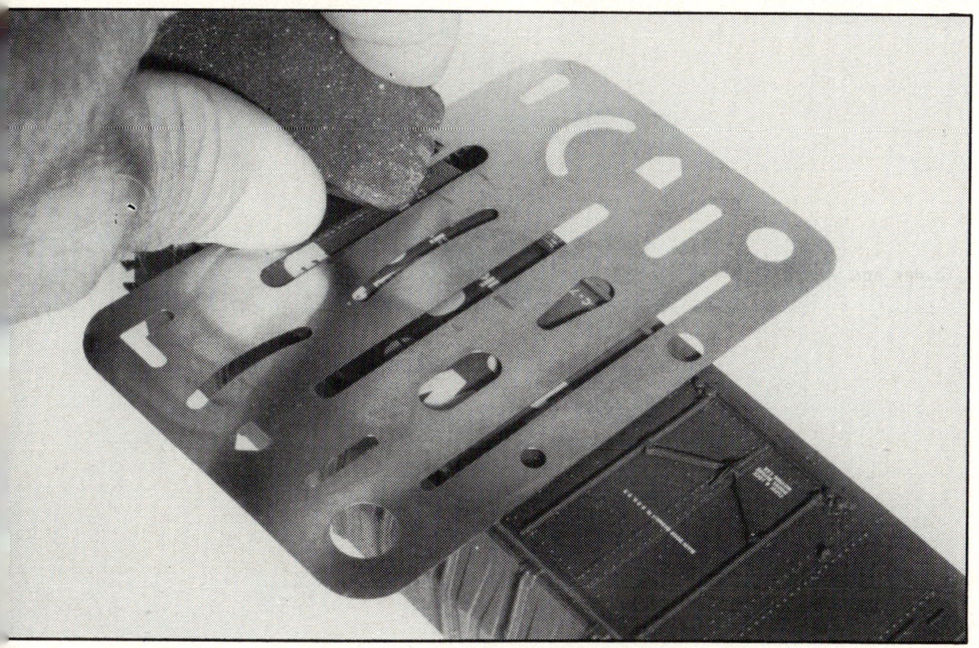

Work a bit harder with that "Bright Boy," and you can remove spots of paint to provide black (assuming the molded body is black) weathering spots or streaks. The effect can be similar to what you would achieve spraying on a thin coat of black paint to simulate kicked-up or rain-washed soot and cinders. Use that eraser guide to control the area's shape. — Albin Burroughs

How to Apply Dry Transfers

"Rub-on" lettering allows you to avoid many of the pitfalls of decals, including decal softeners to get the letters to snuggle down around rivets and seams and the need to wait hours for softeners and setting fluids to dry (all shown in the April 1991 issue). There are several tricks and special techniques, though, that you'll need to learn about applying dry transfers.

Richard Hendrickson
Photos by Robert Schleicher and Richard Hendrickson

There are, at present, two major sources for dry transfer lettering, Clover House and CDS. Clover House specializes in turn-of-the-century and early 20th Century lettering but also makes a variety of sets for rolling stock of the '30s, '40s and '50s. CDS offers more modern ('50s through '70s) lettering for many railroads and, since the firm is located in Canada, it has an unusually complete line of lettering for Canadian railroads of all eras. Clover reprints the diagrams included with each set in its catalog; CDS publishes its diagrams separately in booklet form. Both companies have good reputations for painstaking research, so their lettering sets as well as the prototype data included with them are generally quite accurate. Woodland Scenics also offers some dry transfers, but diagrams are not included, so you'll need a photograph of a prototype (or a diagram from a set of decals) to select the proper sets and position the lettering. A few kits now include custom dry transfer lettering, and custom-made dry transfers are available from other sources on a limited production basis.

Surface Preparation

The good news here is that dry transfers require no special surface preparation. The adhesion problems modelers once encountered with dry transfers that weren't manufactured specifically for use on scale models are a thing of the past, and dry transfer model railroad lettering now sticks reliably to almost any surface, whether glossy or dead flat (in fact, it usually transfers somewhat better to matt surfaces than to glossy ones).

Dry Transfer Application

(1) In one important respect, dry transfers are completely unlike decals; you can't slip and slide them into position. Consequently, it is essential that you have the lettering located exactly right before you start applying it and keep it that way until you're finished. Fortunately, Clover and CDS both go out of their way to print large chunks of lettering in the correct arrangement and spacing, which greatly simplifies the process

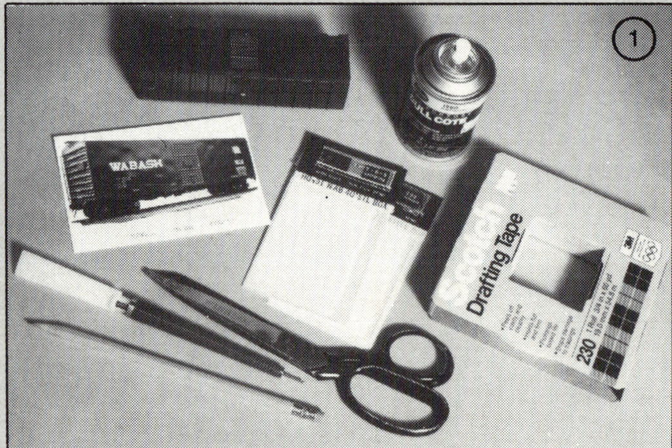

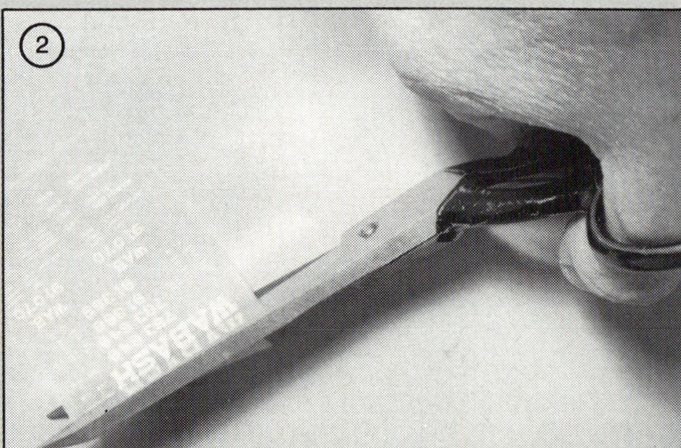

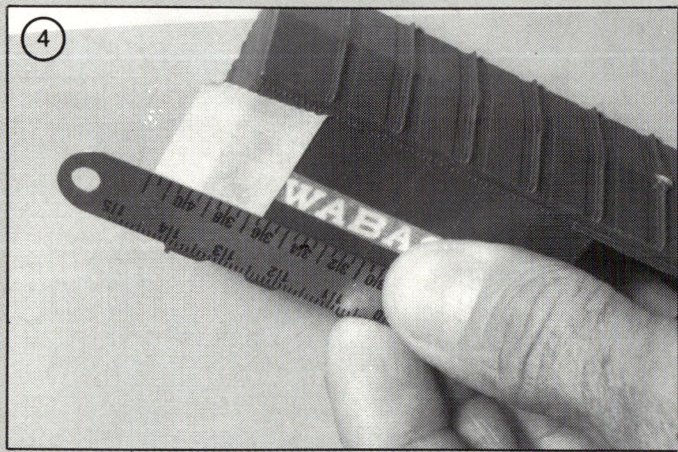

of getting it properly aligned. (2) Start by cutting the lettering set apart into easily managed pieces. (3)(4) Then take one piece at a time, line it up in exactly the right position on the model, and hold it in place with a piece of drafting tape. (5)(6) While holding the opposite edge of the transfer down with your fingers, press firmly on the backing paper with a stylus or burnishing tool, and work it back and forth over the entire transfer, paying special attention to any areas where there are rivets or other surface irregularities.

(7) Next, begin at one corner to slowly lift up the backing paper, checking to make sure all of the lettering transferred from the back-

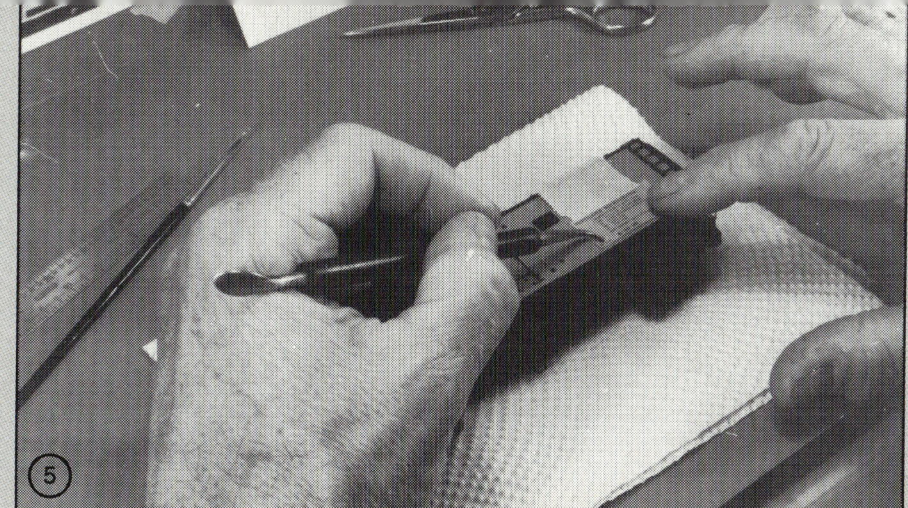

5

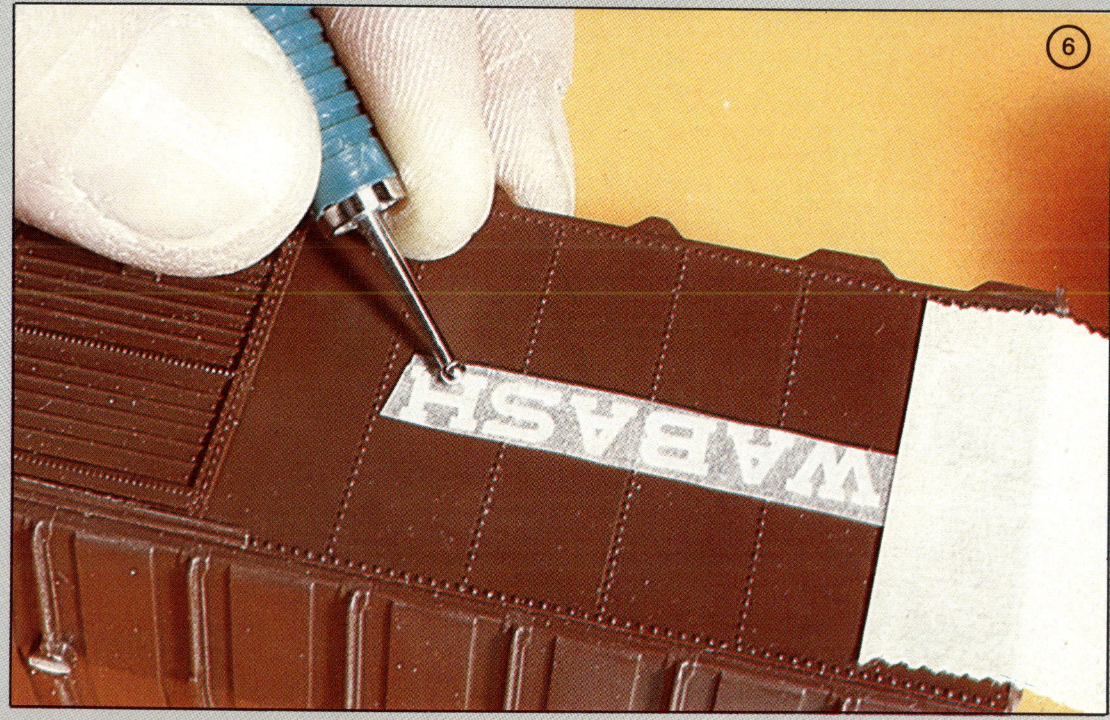

6

7

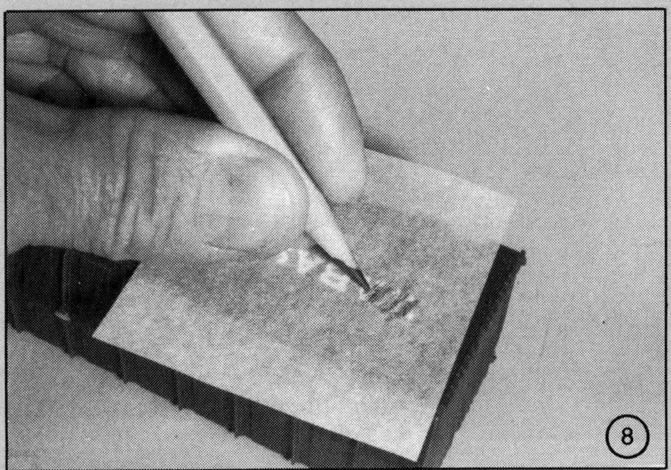

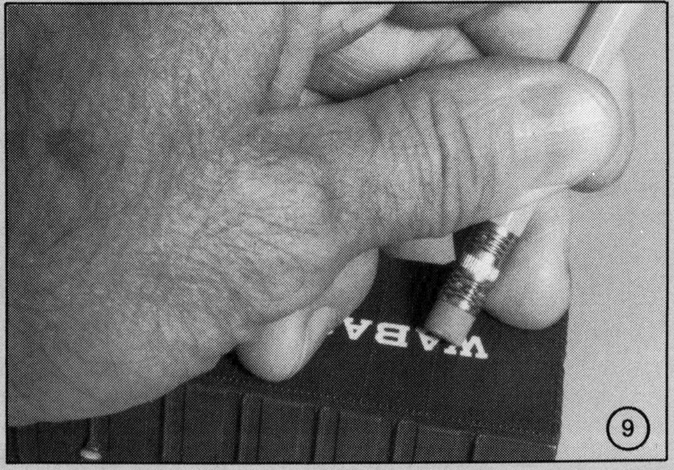

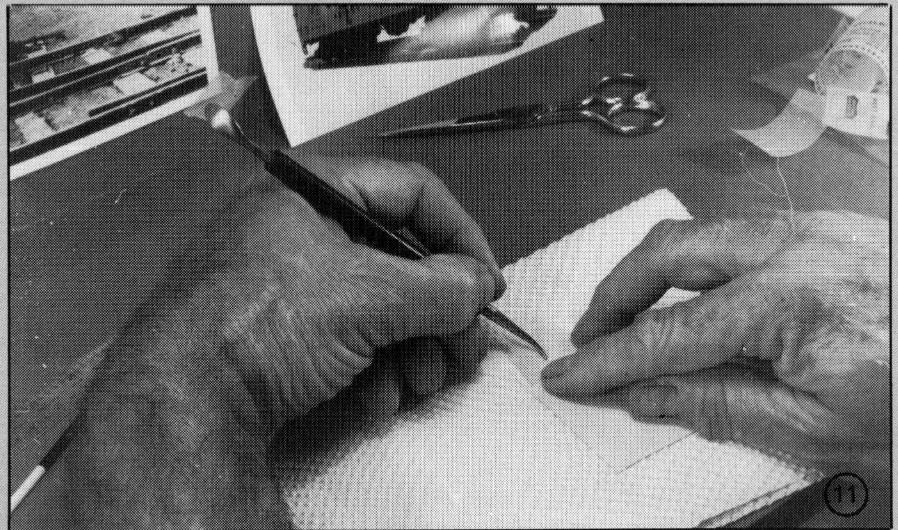

ing paper to the car side. If any part of the lettering failed to transfer, go over it again with the stylus, meanwhile making sure the backing paper hasn't moved. When you have confirmed that all the lettering has transferred to the car side, remove the backing paper. Now take a piece of the waxy protective paper that comes in the lettering set, place it over the lettering you've just applied, and burnish the entire surface to make sure the lettering adheres firmly to the model. (8) If you're applying one part of the transfer close to where you've just applied another part, cover the lettering that's already on the car with a piece of the protective paper so you won't accidentally lift it off or get some unwanted lettering stuck to it. (9) Direct dabs downward with a soft eraser can be used to force letters down around larger rivets.

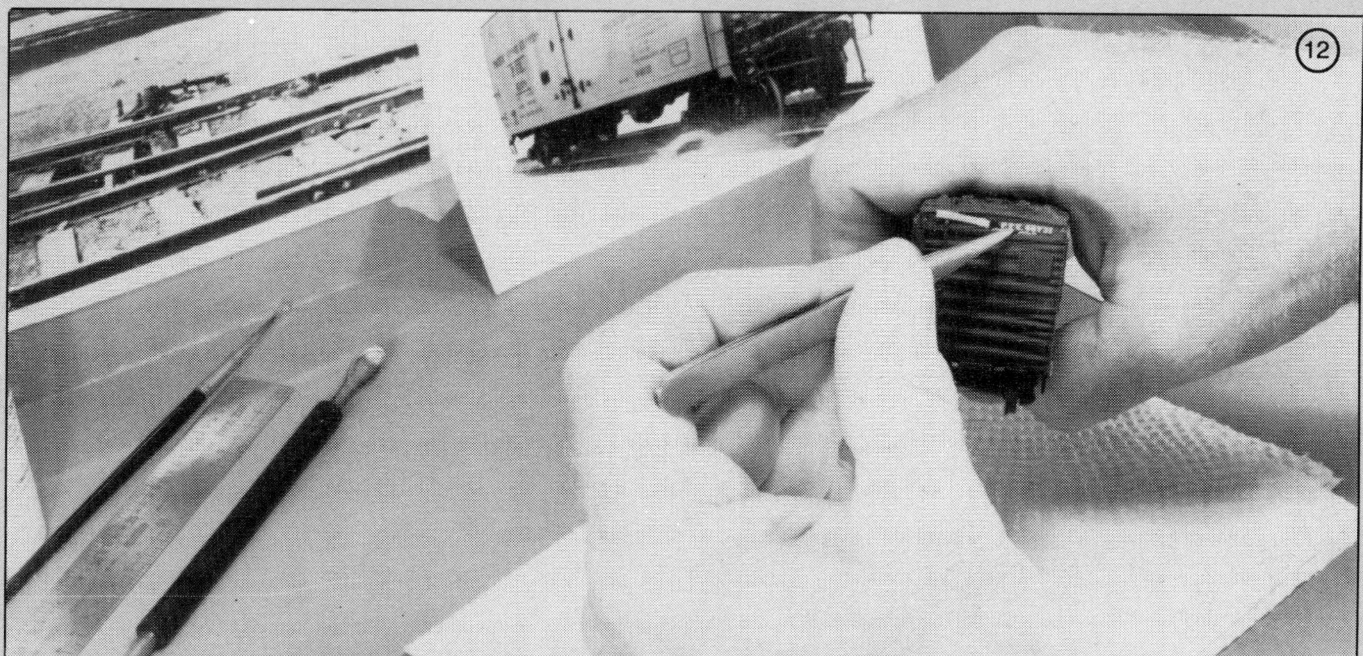

Continue adding lettering, progressing from one end of the car to the other to avoid as much as possible, working on top of lettering you've already applied; being lefthanded, I go from right to left, but if you're righthanded, you should start at the left end of the car and work toward the right end. (10) If the lettering set includes more than one color, it will specify the order in which the colors should be applied. Be sure you seal the first color, and each subsequent color, with clear flat finish and let it dry thoroughly so that what's already in place won't lift when you add the next color. (I'll admit that I have applied several layers, one right after the other, without sealing between layers and gotten away with it, but that's obviously risking disaster and can't be recommended.)

This model of a Pacific Fruit Express R-40-20 reefer, built from an Athearn-based Westrail conversion kit, was lettered with Clover House dry transfers. Note the three-color UP herald, which was applied in three separate layers. With multiple colors, insuring that each layer is aligned exactly with the others is especially important.

How do you apply dry transfer lettering in recessed areas on car ends or between side braces or stake pockets, where it's very difficult to line up the transfers correctly and get them to hold still? Byron Rose suggested to me a "why didn't I think of that?" solution to this dilemma: Simply apply the transfers to a piece of blank decal paper and then apply the lettering as a decal. ⑪ ⑫ Be careful, though, to keep the decal clean while you're working with it, because the waxy coating around the dry transfer lettering tends to collect dust and dirt.

Final Finishing

⑬ Once all the lettering is in place, final finishing is as easy with dry transfers as the surface preparation is; you simply spray on a good coat of any clear flat finish that's compatible with the paint on the model, and your lettering job is complete. **RMJ**

The lettering on this Westrail flat car wraps around the stake pockets and other protruding details, so the CDS dry transfers were first applied to a sheet of blank decal paper and then cut out and applied to the model in decal form — a neat way to avoid problems when applying dry transfers in difficult locations.

Also built from a Westrail conversion kit, this model represents a 1945-vintage Canadian National box car; lettering is from a CDS dry transfer set. With today's CDS and Clover House dry transfers, even the smallest lettering is sharp and legible.

Painting with Aerosol Cans, part II

The Basics

SKILL LEVEL

You can achieve a paint finish with aerosol cans that is as smooth as that attainable with an air brush — if you follow these basic steps. Part I, "Weathering with Aerosol Cans," with Frank Forest's techniques, appeared in the February 1990 issue.

Robert Schleicher
Models and techniques
by Frank Forest

There's more, much more, to applying paint to a model using an aerosol can than simply pushing the button until the model has "color." Just as there are specific steps to follow beyond simply dunking decals in water (see the April '91 **Journal**) or rubbing dry transfers (see the May '91 issue), there are some specific techniques that will make paint applied with an aerosol can as smooth as if applied with an air brush.

1. — Work in a completely lint- and dust-free environment. A spare bathroom with the vent fan on and the door closed to avoid actual air (and dust) flow is a possible location, but you must be certain the vent fan has an explosion-proof motor. It's possible, especially when working with quick-drying synthetic paints and acrylics, to work outdoors on a still day. Proper ventilation of the toxic and (sometimes) explosive fumes is essential, but you don't want currents of airborne dust flowing over the tacky paint.

2. — Heat the can under warm (not hot) water to room temperature (about 70 degrees F.), and shake the can thoroughly for at least one minute. It helps to move the can in a swirling motion so you can hear the mixing balls (inside most cans) roll around the perimeter of the can.

3. — Hold the model between 6 and 12 inches from the spray nozzle. Start the spray off to the side of the model and move the model, not the can) under and through the

Frank added coupler cut bars from bent wire and Kadee couplers (with the "hoses" cut off for automatic coupling and manual uncoupling using a toothpick placed between the knuckles and twisted). The kit itself, however, is a stock Details West model.

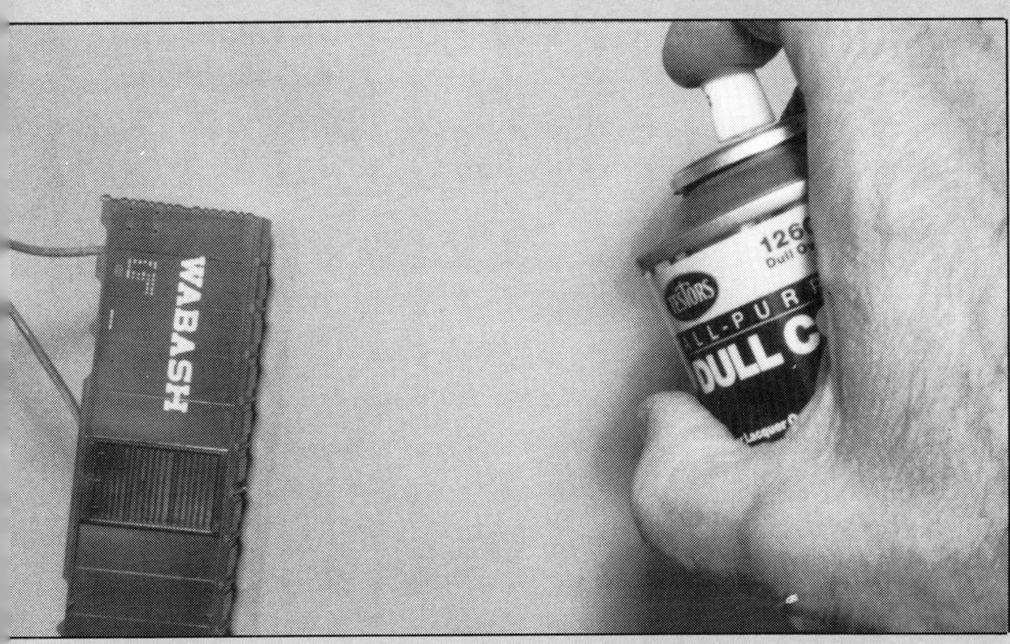

Hold the model on a bent coat hanger. Move the model under the spray pattern as described in the text.

Frank Forest uses aerosol cans and paint brushes exclusively in painting and weathering his models. This Details West insulated plug-door 50-foot box car was repainted with glossy enamel matched to a color photo of PC green and purchased in a hardware store. The model was decorated with Champ (HB-388) and Microscale decals and lightly weathered.

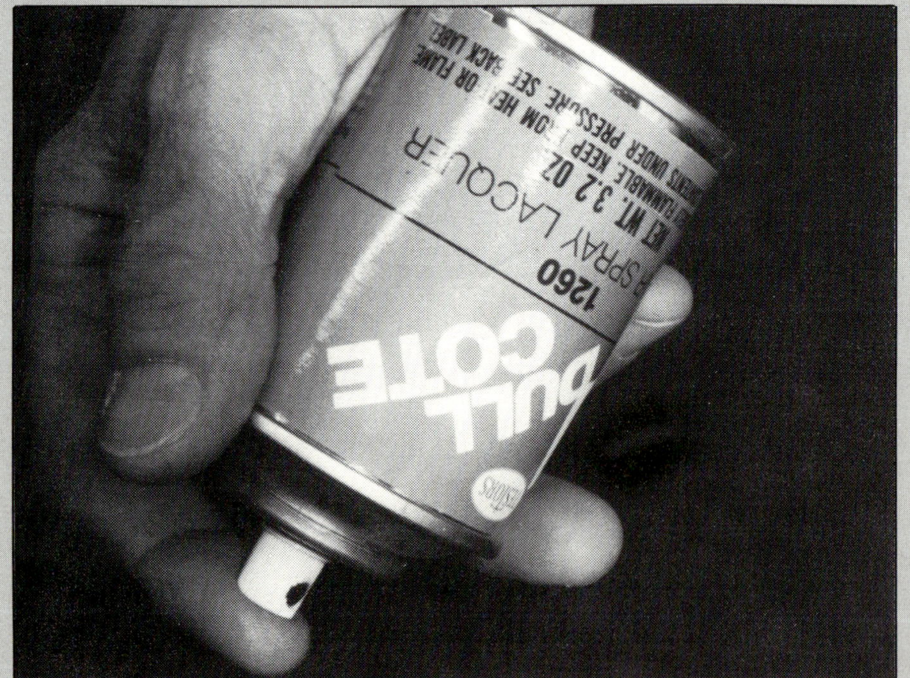

The final step when painting with an air aerosol can is to turn the can upside down immediately after use and before the paint can dry. Press the nozzle and allow the paint to spray just long enough that the color disappears and only gas escapes, then release the button. A quick burst of the gas from the can will clean the nozzle. If you hold the button down too long, however, so much gas will escape that there won't be enough pressure to completely empty the can.

spray pattern. Keep spraying until the model is clear of the pattern, then release the button. With practice, you can do this almost as quickly as you can push and release the button.

4. — The first spray coat provides a rough grip or "tooth" for the subsequent coats, so make that first coat quick and light so it barely covers the model with a see-through coat of color. Let that first coat dry for at least 20 minutes before applying the second coat. Let that coat dry for at least an hour. The final coat can be the heaviest, but it cannot be applied so thick that it runs. The only way to learn how much is too much is to practice on an old model or an empty box lid to see what the paint looks like when it is too thick. You'll soon learn to judge how quickly to move the model beneath the spray pattern. The model can be moved back and forth rapidly without releasing the spray button to aim the paint slightly upward to cover the underside of the eaves and ladders, then slightly downward to cover the tops of the ladder rungs or other raised details.

5. — If you do find runs or trapped dust or lint, try to smooth out the run with a paint brush while the paint is still wet. If you find large pieces of lint or hair, remove them with tweezers, smooth area with a brush, and let it dry. If there are visible marks after the paint has dried to a hard finish, sand the surface with no. 400 grit wet-or-dry sandpaper soaked in water. Apply another coat of paint.

6. — When the model is painted, cover it with a box at least a foot square with a few 1-inch holes cut for ventilation. The box will help keep dust and lint from settling on the model.

7. — When the painting is complete, turn the spray can upside down and depress the button just long enough for the paint to stop flowing and the gas from the can to blow the nozzle clean. **RMJ**

Weathering . . . with Aerosol Cans

Who says you need an air brush to produce realistic models?

Robert Schleicher
Models and techniques by
Frank Forest

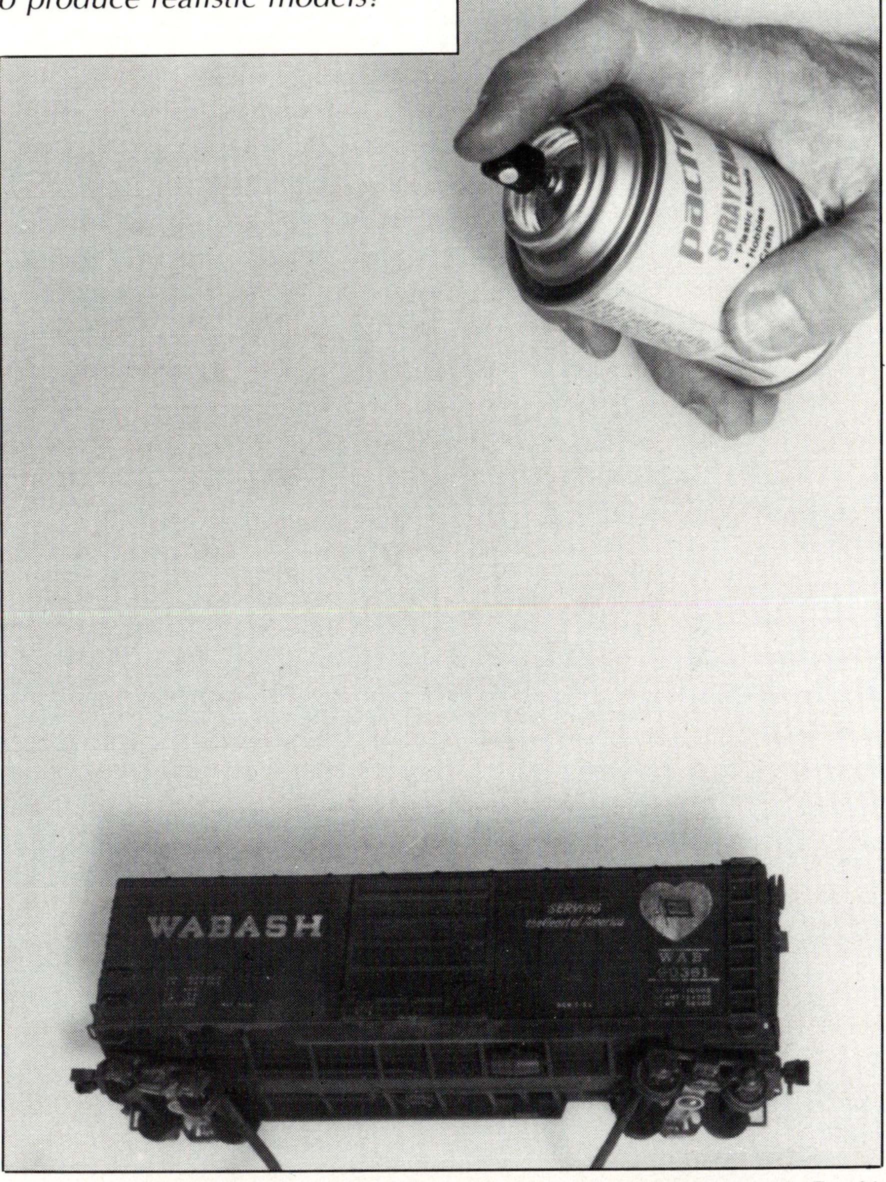

Bend a wire coat hanger to hold the trucks of the car while you paint it. For this superdetailed Life-Like tank car (Walthers now has a similar version with body-mounted couplers), the model was lightly dusted with zinc chromate (reddish brown) primer as a mist to produce the dusty effect that hints of rust. Flat black is then misted lightly over the dome area in three or four applications to reproduce the oil spill effect.

When you can't afford an air brush, but you're gritting your teeth in envy at the color shots of model locomotives and cars painted and weathered by experts, the aerosol spray can can be the tool to recreate those painting effects. The lowly spray can of paint, if used judiciously, can be nearly as versatile as an air brush.

There are a number of techniques you can use with aerosols to produce results that are at least as realistic as those you can achieve with an air brush. These same techniques can also be used, by the way, with an air brush.

An aerosol can lacks two important control functions available with an air brush: (1) You cannot adjust the flow or spray of the paint with an aerosol, while you can adjust some air brush spray patterns so fine they'll reproduce the period at the end of this sentence. (2) You cannot mix thinner or clear coatings with the paint in an aerosol can to provide see-through or lighter color applications.

These are, however, techniques that can overcome both of these shortcomings, and there are examples on these pages. We'll present more ideas in later issues, but these two basic techniques will get you started. Both provide alternatives to shortcoming 2 above. The tank car has been weathered by very quick direct passes with an aerosol can to leave just a fine mist of paint behind. For darker colors, make more quick passes. The trick here is to resist the temptation to make a darker weathering shade by holding the spray pattern over the model for a longer period. For a darker color, make more passes. Always hold the model at least 12 inches from the can, further with some colors. Move the model beneath the spray pattern, not the can. Above all, make several test-painting attempts on a scrap of cardboard to see how the pattern will appear. The tank car has been weathered with about four passes (from about 18 inches) with a can of primer to produce the rusty, dirty effect, followed by two vey quick passes (from about 9 inches) with flat black primer to produce the oil spills around the dome.

The box car was weathered with a less obvious technique that begins with an unpainted model. For this one, you must be willing to apply decal or dry transfer lettering to the painted model. Here, the basic model was painted with a primer or undercoat using an aerosol can of flat white primer. The box car red is Floquil's aerosol, but the color was applied just thick enough to cover the white while allowing some of the white to show through. The result, a box car red that looks as though it had been faded in the sun. The effect is similar to that you would achieve by mixing about one part white in one part box car red if you were using an air brush. You are, then, applying just enough of the darker box car red color to make it slightly translucent (see-through) to expose the undercoat as a "tint."

This same technique can be used to produce slightly darker colors (using a black undercoat or primer) or to add a reddish tint (using zinc oxide primer as an undercoat). One of the advantages of the system is that a "family" appearance can be provided, through color, so a string of, say, Cotton Belt box cars look more sun-faded than a string of Conrail or Pennsy box cars.

Caution: many brands of aerosol paints will attack the plastics used in models. The paints may simply craze the plastic surface, but that alone can destroy rivet details. Some paints may even warp and bend the plastic. Test-paint some leftover scraps of the kit's plastic with thick coats of the paint you want to use to see if the paint destroys the plastic. You may need to buy several different brands before you find one that won't damage the plastic. Floquil makes a paint called

The bent wire coat hanger holds the model. Move the model, rather than the spray can, for better control over the paint pattern and to avoid paint splashes and splatters that can occur when the spray can is started or stopped.

Etched running boards and wire handrails and steps were added to superdetail this Life-Like tank car. The new Walthers kit would provide a better starting point because the underframe has the coupler pockets on the frame rather than on the trucks.

Barrier that can be used to protect the plastic, but that adds yet another coat of paint, and some of the aerosols may even attack the Barrier. It's best to find an aerosol that won't attack the plastic. Be sure to test each type of plastic with the paint because there are some major differences in the plastics in various kits. Also, test each color you intend to use because the mixtures of colors or primers of the same brand of paint often contain different chemicals.

The most important thing to remember when using aerosols is to try to find the color you want in a flat finish. The flats will cover with a much thinner coat than the glossy paints. The glossy colors contain a large proportion of clear (to achieve the gloss or shine), and that often means a very, very thick coat of paint is needed to cover the model. Above all, experiment and practice on scrap material so you're sure of the effects you can achieve before painting the model itself. **RMJ**

This McKean box car was painted with a white undercoat or primer coat. Floquil Box Car Red was then sprayed over the dried white with just enough of the darker color to produce an even shade — the white shows through enough to produce a sun-bleached or faded effect. After the decals and their protective coat of clear flat paint were applied, a light mist of zinc oxide primer was applied to blend the white decals into the model.

Weathering . . .

with Aerosol Cans and Brushes, part II

Some very serious weathering and distressing tips for load-weary gondolas.

Robert Schleicher
Models and techniques
by Frank Forest

There's much more to creating a realistic model than simply spending the money to obtain a complex kit, then assembling said kit properly. Most of the model kits, even many of the toy train models, have truly incredible detail right out of the box. A modeler can enhance the three-dimensional appearance of those details by removing molded-on grab-irons, ladders, steps and brake pipes and substituting thinner roof walks and, on many box cars, taller doors without grossly oversize slide devices. Kadee couplers in place of the horn hooks on the inexpensive kits and ready-builts are another helpful 3D details.

That detailed model, however, is only the beginning. On a real railroad, the rolling stock is only new until it gets rained on once or twice. From then on, the appearance of the car is altered as diesel exhause (or steam smoke in earlier eras) settles onto the surface and wind-blown dirt, dust and ballast are clouded onto the car and retained by rain and more exhaust or steam. The sun bleaches and powders the paint, and the rain washes some of it down the car, and, of course, a bit of rust begins to gather here and there. The inside of the car is also subject to another kind of "weathering"; abuse by the crews loading and unloading or simply by the

Frank assembled this Westerfield box car as suggested by the kit instructions. He painted the model with Krylon gloss brown from an aerosol can purchased at a hardware store. The gloss finish if far better than dull for applying decals and, once the decals are protected with a coat of Testors Dullcote (also from an aerosol can), the overall model is flat brown. The decals are Walthers 934-78060 plus Champ HB-33.

Frank uses Testors Model Master series of both bottle and aerosol paints for many of his models. The rust streaks and spots on this car were applied with a cotton swab dipped lightly into Model Masters "Rust."

After the rust color dried, this model was dipped in a pan filled with a mixture of water and about 5 tablelespoons of common baking soda. The model was then turned upside down and allowed to dry overnight. The baking soda left a light grey residue that effectively simulated sun bleaching. The odd drip marks were brushed away with a paint brush dipped in water and dabbed dry.

This GTW car began life as a ICG bright orange car with black lettering. Frank removed the paint with automobile brake fluid and old tooth brushes but some of the orange remained after the lettering was gone. He used an aerosol can of Testors regular series of Gloss Brown and to paint the model but he deliberately used a thin coat in some areas to allow the orange to show through as rust. He had replaced the plastic ladder rungs with .010 wire and he built the Superior door from Evergreen styrene sheet and strips before painting the model. The decals are Champ no. HB-142.

Frank lettered this model with Champ BH-42 decals and sprayed them with Testors Dullcote to blend them into the car side and, in the process, to give the entire model the same dull finish. A few dabs of Testors Model Master series "Rust" were applied to simulate areas where the rust had eaten right through the paint.

impact of shifting loads as the car moves down the track. This type of abuse or ''distress'' is, naturally, most visible in an open-top car, and particularly in a gondola that might be loaded with scrap metal or other rough and heavy commodities (as opposed to relatively smooth sand or coal).

The real railroads' rolling stock displays an infinite variety of weathering, too, from brand new or freshly repainted cars to near-derelict and rusty equipment. For maximum realism, your rolling stock should display this same spectrum of the effects of age, weather and general abuse.

Frank Forest considers painting and weathering to be one of the most enjoyable aspects of the hobby. Certainly, it is one of the most creative and artistic aspects, aside from scenery. In truth, frank considers rolling stock to be as much a part of his railroad's scenery as the surrounding hills, the ballast or the structures — and he is absolutely right. If you look at real railroad rolling stock with the eye of an artist, as he does, you'll soon begin to notice the subtle effects of weathering. Do not, however, trust your eye! Take color print photographs of sample rolling stock with weathering effects you want to duplicate. The cars you photographs certainly do not need to match your model's shape or style — one steel gondola is likely to weather in a manner similar to another. One dark blue box car is also likely to weather to about the same shade and pattern as another, even though one may be lettered for a southern road and the other for a northwestern owner. Do bear in mind (or, better, in your mind's eye) that geography does have an effect on weathering. Cars that spend most of their life in the industrial Northeast tend to be blacker, and/or more rusty, while cars that spend most of their life in the Southwest tend to be beige or sun-bleached, and so on . . .

Frank's most significant advice is simply to **do it!** Try weathering on a car, and if you don't like it, repaint it and try again. Experiment with these techniques and any you may think of as you work with these ideas. Remember, its the final result that matters, now how you achieve it. **RMJ**

Both Life-Like and Bachmann have gondolas like this one. Frank mounted the couplers on the frame, using McKean Models couplers. He also shaved off the grab irons and brake lines and replaced them with .010 wire pieces.

The model was painted with FIVE colors, allowing a full week for each color to dry. The first color is Testors aerosol "Gloss Brown," followed by Testors Model Master aerosol "Rust," then a brush-on mixture of Grumbacher's artists' acrylic red, yellow and white to make three brownish shades, Testors aerosol "Gloss Black" and, after the decals were in place, Testors aerosol "Dullcote."

Frank distressed and warped the plastic BEFORE the model was painted. He wrapped the end of an X-Acto hobby knife with a layer of lead foil from a wine bottle (four or five layers of aluminum foil should work as well). The foil was heated over a candle flame and immediately pressed into the inside of the car body as shown. The edges were warped and large lumps were forced into the sides. The blade end was also used to gouge out the floors and sides.

The five coats of paint and decals were applied after the body was dented. The gouges, however, were forced into the body after all the paint had dried so some of the paint edges would help simulate the thin and broken edges of metal.

Frank poured a thimble-full of Floquil "Box Car Red" into an old bottlecap and allowed to dry completely. He then cut up the dried paint with a hobby knife and crumbled it into a powder of simulated rust. This powder was then brushed onto the car a drop of thinner applied to "set" the powder so it looked like loose rust but was firmly affixed to the car body.

For the final touches, Frank dabbed on some Testors Model Master "rust" right from the bottle. He also rubbed most of the interior of the car with a brown broad-tipped felt-tip pen to give the interior a patina of rust.

Basic Air Brush Weathering

Contrast the effects of wind and water-born dirt and grime ("weathering") applied with an air brush to those applied within a cotton swab on page 15 of the September 1989 issue of ***Railmodel Journal****...*

Robert Schleicher

We used one of MDC's HO scale no. 1802 modern-era "waffle-side" kits for the photos, but the procedures are the same for any car of any era.

There are two basic "secrets" to achieving successful weathering effects, whether with an air brush, a cotton swab or a brush: (1) Thin the paint with about nine parts thinner to one part paint, and (2) Have a photograph of a prototype of at least a similar color at hand as your inspiration or guide.

Here, we're using the inexpensive Binks Wren air brush where only the air pressure, not the paint flow, can be regulated. With that 9:1 mix of paint and thinner, however, the quantity of paint is not so critical, because only a small amount of actual color is being sprayed.

I usually start with a flat black like Floquil's Grimy Black to spray the couplers and areas where the wheels would splatter water and oil onto the lower edges of the car.

The third significant weathering color should be a beige, brown or reddish-brown that would match the soil (or the loads) that might be blown onto the car in its travels. Expect beige on cars from the far West, brown on cars that travel mostly in the Midwest and East and reddish brown on cars from the Southeast, because those are the predominant soil colors in those areas. Again, the color would likely be most obvious on the lower portions of the car, but it can also appear on the roof and in streaks down the car side — check that photo of the prototype again.

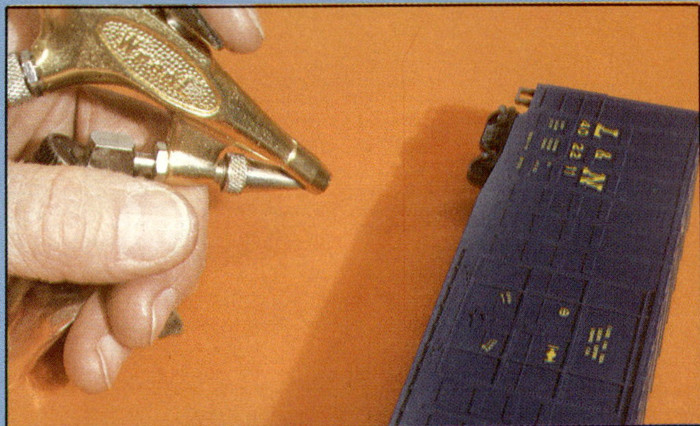

For lighter weathering effects, I use a light grey for "generic" dust. Floquil's Grime or Concrete colors are suitable, here, again mixed 9:1, thinner to paint. Look at that photo of the prototype to see where the grey tones occur, but expect them near the eaves and beneath white numbers or letters where the paint has dissolved and been washed down the side of the car.

The fourth significant weathering color should be a mixture of a color close to that of the car (medium blue, in this case) mixed about 2:1, color to white paint. That mix should then be thinned with nine parts thinner. This is the color that will blend the previous weathering effects and produce the effect of sun-bleached paint. Be very cautious here to apply just a trace of the color to soften any color changes in the previous weathering. For your first attempt, consider thinning the paint 19:1, thinner to paint, to minimize the chances of applying too much "bleach." This color can be effective, too, on a brand new car to slightly blend the lettering into the car side, which helps eliminate the toy-like appearance of the lettering.

Airbrush Painting, part II Basics and Weathering Techniques

▲ SKILL LEVEL

It is possible to achieve some of the weathering effects shown here with paint brushes, aerosols or even cotton swabs, but the airbrush makes it so much easier to achieve the wind-blown effects that weather produces on railroad equipment.

The equipment is all out-of-the-box Athearn with subtle weathering on the locomotive (it's "near new") and more extensive weathering on the cars. Even the rusty rails and bleached ties were created with paint from an airbrush.

Robert Schleicher

The airbrush is a miniature version of the spray guns used to paint automobiles and by commercial painters for painting houses. Inexpensive spray guns are available at hardware stores for use in the home, but the pattern of spray produced by spray guns is far too large for use on models, and the spray gun itself is awkward to manipulate. Hobby shops sell a wide range of airbrush outfits ranging in price from $30 to $500.

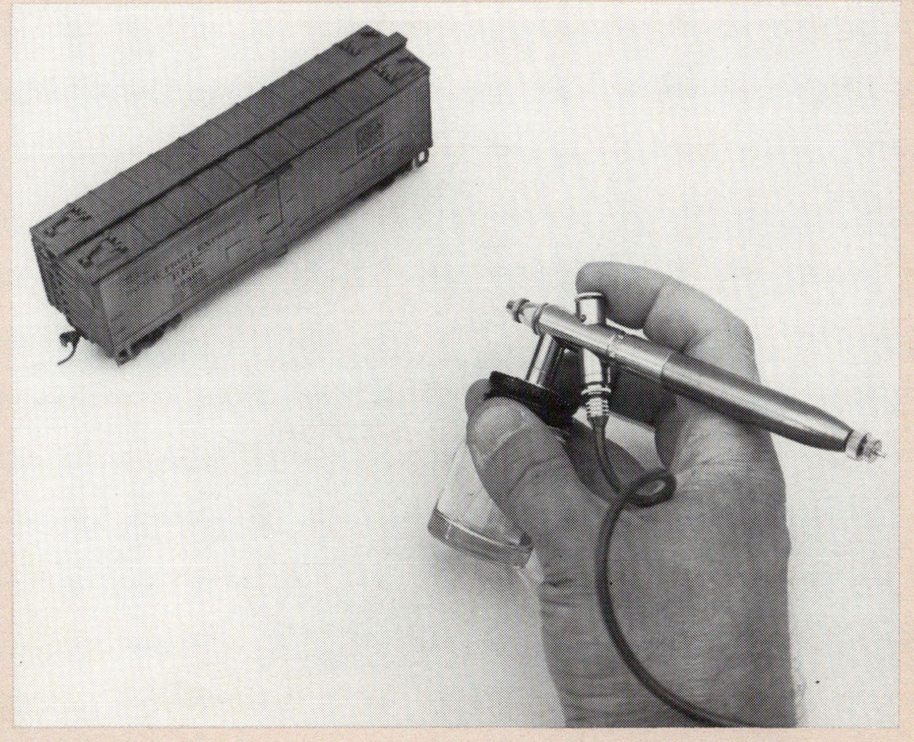

Air Supply

The most important part of an airbrush outfit is the air supply. Badger, Binks, Paasche, Testors and Tamiya offer aerosol cans of propellant that can be used as an air supply. These can sell for about $5 to $9, and some are even "ozone safe." The supply, however, will only last about a fifth the time of a similar size can of aerosol spray paint because you will be using more "air" and less paint with an airbrush. I consider these cans to be simply a stopgap that will allow you to discover the advantages of an

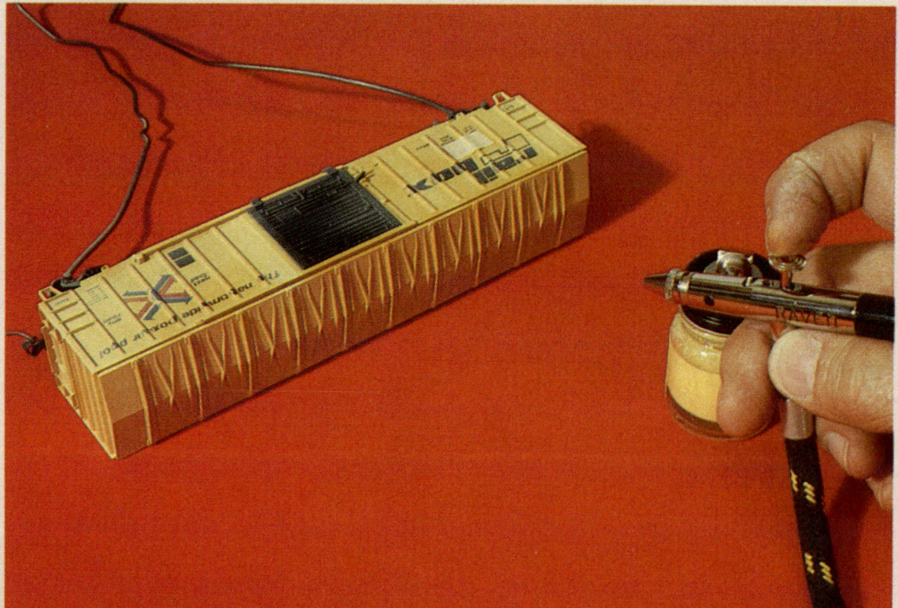

When mixing "weathering" colors, use about four parts thinner (80%) to two parts paint. A basic "bleaching" color is a light beige to simulate sun-faded paint. Here it's being applied lightly to the top of a box car, with less on the sides. For this work, the air pressure was set at 20 psi.

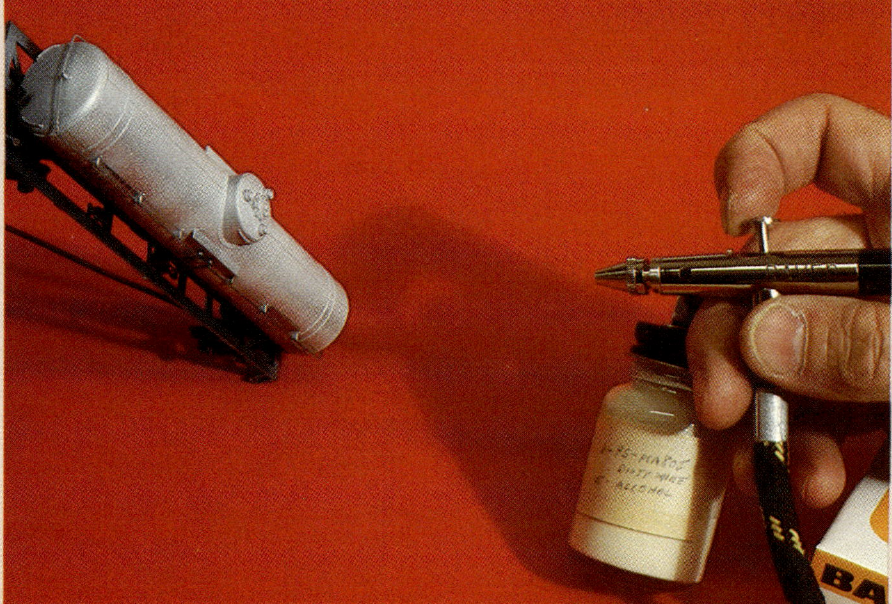

The bleaching color was applied only to the top of the tank car so it faded the silver color to a dull grey on the top, allowing more and more of the silver to show through as the tank sides appear. Here, move the work only back and forth along the length of the car, beneath the spray pattern. Use as many as a dozen light coats to "work up" to the effect you wish. When weathering, always, always, always have a photograph of a similarly colored car (if not the precise road or style) at hand as a reference so you match real world colors.

The dark grey dust and exhaust that settles on the track is swept up onto the bottom edges of the cars and along the edges of any vertical posts. Set the air pressure at 15 psi and work about an inch away to blacken the posts: use 20 psi and work about 2 to 3 inches away to gently shade the lower edge of the car side and to deaden the shine on the plastic trucks.

airbrush before spending more bucks on a reliable, and of more importance, adjustable air supply system.

I use a reclaimed CO_2 tank purchased from a fire extinguisher company with a pressure-check and guarantee. They fitted it with Badger's no. 50057 CO_2 regulator and gauge ($60.00), and the tank was another $50.00 plus labor to install the gauge. The same fire extinguisher company refills the tank for about $20.00, and a refill lasts me a year, enough to paint several dozen locomotives or perhaps a hundred cars. For me, the major advantage of the rig is that it is silent; air compressor noise drives me crazy.

A relatively silent air compressor will run between $400 and $500, so most of us will be willing to put up with a little noise. Diaphragm-style compressors suitable for airbrush use sell for as little as $250, piston-types for as little as $110. I would not recommend any compressor without the addition of a pressure regulator and gauge (about $30 to $45). The compressor (or CO_2 tank) is not much better than the aerosol cans if you have no means of adjusting the air pressure — that's the purpose of the pressure regulator — 15 to 25 psi (pounds per square inch) is the most effective pressure for spraying a model, and most compressors deliver an erratic 35 psi.

A Place to Spray

You will also need a "safe" place to spray, even if you are using acrylics. The paint must be thinned with solvent for enamels, and alcohol works best with acrylics. Both thinning agents are toxic and easily inhaled. The easiest "safe" place to work is outdoors with a 5-mile-an-hour wind behind your back and no dust. There are more of those moments than you might realize. Also, of course, the spray must be kept well away from any open fire or flame, for the spray is explosive, too — another good reason to work outdoors. If you must paint indoors, buy one of the indoor spray booths like Badger's ($200) and use household dryer vent hose to duct the spray outside. Regardless of where you spray, however, I'd advise the wearing of a respirator (another $35 to $50 from Badger or Norton, but it could save your life).

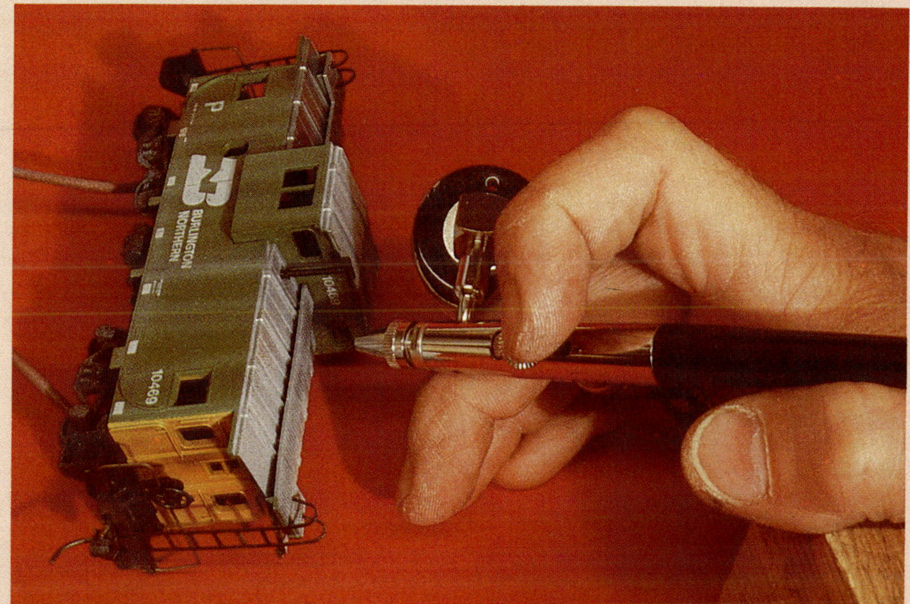

Use a thinned "wash" of flat black paint and 80% thinner to blacken the holes in roofwalks and running boards so the surface looks more like "see-through" screen. Use about 15 psi of air pressure and hold the airbrush about an inch away so the paint is blown from the upper edges and pushed down into the cavities. Work directly over the roofwalk with the airbrush at 90 degrees to the car.

A B C D

A

B

C

D

E

Actual samples of airbrush patterns. Patterns A, B, C and D were produced with the same combination of thinner/paint, air pressure, air flow, paint flow and with the same airbrush. The text explains the differences in the patterns.

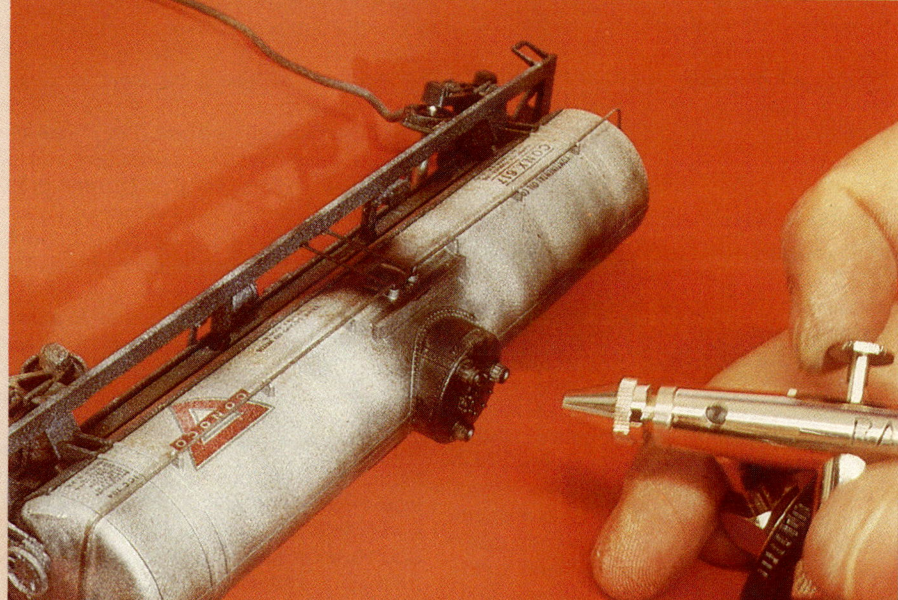

Use gloss paint, again thinned with about 80% thinner, to simulate oil spills. Hold the airbrush about an inch away, and keep the paint flowing until it runs down the sides of the dome.

Airbrushes

Oh yes, the airbrush itself. . . I have my own opinion here, so I'll get it over with: I prefer a single-action, internal-mix airbrush with a bottle, not an open cup. The Badger 200 is $55, and the Paasche H31 is $64, both with hoses and extra bottles. The single-action airbrush has no adjustment for air flow at the brush, you just push down for paint. Double-action brushes are favored by most professional model painters, and Badger's 152 ($110), Binks Raven II (about $160), W.R. Brown's Pro-Airbrush ($100), Polk's no. 113 ($49.95) or Paasche's VL ($97) are typical double-action airbrush sets with spare bottle and hose. You might want to try the double-action airbrush; the air feed levers can be locked into position so the airbrush functions like a single-action model.

These single- and double-action airbrushes have what is called "internal mix," because the paint is sucked up a tube inside the airbrush itself and atomized internally into a spray pattern. This method provides the best control over the spray pattern and will allow you to adjust the paint and air so the brush will actually spray a dot no larger than a period or, if held correctly, spray a pencil-thin line. This fine and precise adjustment capability is what makes internal-mix airbrushes worth the money.

The least expensive airbrush outfits (an airbrush, extra jar and hose, at least) are single-action, external-mix. With these airbrushes, the paint is sucked up a nozzle just in front of the air nozzle so the air and paint mix externally. The spray pattern can be adjusted down to a dot as small as 1/16 inch with some, others go down only to 1/4 inch or so. The flow of paint at such small and close settings (you must spray about an inch or so from the model) is more difficult to master than with the internal-mix airbrushes. External-mix, single-action airbrushes sell for between $20 and $50 from Badger, Binks, Paasche, Polk's, Tamiya and Testors.

Painting with an Airbrush

If you can paint with an aerosol can, you'll have no trouble learning to paint with an airbrush. In fact, the airbrush has adjustments that overcome nearly all the potential problems that can occur when using aerosol spray cans. If you are using one of the external-mix, single-action (inexpensive) airbrushes and a simple aerosol can for an air supply, you will still have a couple of advantages of painting with aerosol cans. First, you can adjust the size of the spray pattern from thin to broad coverage. Second, you can thin the paint so more and thinner coats can be applied to reduce runs and sags. You cannot, however, adjust the volume of paint and air that flows through the airbrush with this least expensive setup. That means you must still move the model very rapidly through the paint pattern of the airbrush, just as you must when painting with aerosol cans. You must be both skillful *and* quick to achieve good results. Always start with the spray aimed off to the side of the model because the external-mix airbrushes often sputter and provide spatters when they first spray.

If you use a compressor or CO_2 tank with a pressure regulator valve and gauge, you can control the amount of air that will reach the airbrush. The single-action, external mix airbrush still has limitations, however, because it takes about 30 psi of air to atomize the paint. If you must purchase an airbrush outfit on a budget, I'd suggest starting with an inexpensive external-mix airbrush and aerosol cans, then adding an air compressor with regulator and gauge and, finally buy a better quality internal-mix single- or double-action airbrush.

With an internal-mix airbrush, you can adjust the flow of paint by turning an adjuster knob or needle. The paint flow must be balanced with the airflow; you can spray with as little as 15 psi, but the paint must be adjusted to a very small amount. If you are spraying larger patterns, on a building, say, you may need as much as 35 psi of pressure, and the paint flow needle or knob must be adjusted for more flow. Experiment with both the pressure (at the air supply — by turning the value on the pressure regulator to adjust the air pressure) and the flow of paint to see the differences. While you are experimenting, try holding the airbrush closer or further from the work. Pattern A shown here can be produced with either 15 psi and minimum paint, with the airbrush about 2 inches from the work, or using about 30 psi with minimum paint flow and the airbrush held 4 inches from the work — but with the work moved much more quickly past the spray pattern.

One of the advantages of an airbrush is that you can experiment to find the methods that work best for you. Remember the variables: (1) air pressure, (2) paint flow, (3) distance from work to airbrush nozzle, (4) air flow, (5) the speed the work is moved past the airbrush and (6) the amount of thinner mixed with the paint. The samples of airbrush spray patterns shown here can be produced with several different combinations of the above six variables. Pattern C is the ideal, although the paint could be mixed with a bit more thinner and/or a bit more air pressure and/or air flow used to better atomize the paint. Pattern A is produced with either too much paint, too much pressure, too close a distance between nozzle and work or from holding the work in place too long. Pattern B results from the nozzle being too close to the work or from too much air pressure, and pattern D results from too much air pressure. The lines D and E vary in width an intensity because D was held closer or longer near the pattern and/or from more paint flow than E.

I am a lazy modeler. I often use Floquil paint right out of the bottle. I've even made some Floquil-size paint caps to fit my airbrush so I can simply open a bottle of paint, stir it, then shake it well and apply it to the airbrush for painting. I only add thinner for weathering effects. If the model's surface is too rough for decals (a rare occurence, usually with darker colors), I simply spray the model with a thin coat of clear gloss before applying decals. Most professional modelers, however, follow Floquil's instructions to mix 75% color, 25% Glaze and 20% Dio-Sol. I do have to follow instructions for adding about 20% thinner to Scalecoat or SMP paint and 40% thinner to Polly S and other acrylic paints.

I'm also lazy about cleaning my airbrush. I simply "back-flush" the airbrush after every color change by putting on a bottle of thinner and holding the tip close enough to a rag so the air is forced back down the paint tube to produce bubbles in the thinner. I quickly move the rag on and off the nozzle to force the paint back and forth through the airbrush orifices. I do use two bottles of thinner, one clean, the other a bit murky, but I only disassemble the airbrush (as all manufacturers recommend) about once a year to clean the parts in thinner.

I use inexpensive paint thinner for everything but acrylics, and alcohol for thinner and cleaner with acrylics. Remember, both are toxic and explosive, so work with adequate ventilation, away from any open flame, and wear a respirator. I'd also suggest wearing rubber gloves to both protect your model and to make it easier to clean or hold the model.

One last tip: Let the painted model dry for at least a week beneath a shoe box or whatever size cover will clear all the parts. Punch a dozen or so 1/2-inch holes in the sides of the box for ventilation. The box will keep dust from settling on the fresh paint, and it can actually be removed after about 12 hours. For quicker work, I often turn the vent fan on after the model has rested under the box for six hours and let the air flow dry the paint for 12 hours. I know dozens of modelers who use ovens to dry models, especially brass models, by turning the oven on to medium heat for a quarter hour, then turning it off before placing the model inside to cure for a few hours. I've never wanted to take the risk of damaging a model myself, so I'm certainly not going to recommend the procedure to you. But it does produce a smoother and harder surface faster than drying in the air. **RMJ**

Your Top Tips

Earn $20.00

We'll pay you $20.00 each for any idea we publish. Just send us your tip, preferably with a sketch (photos are optional) and enough of an explanation that we can photograph a recreation of the idea or redraw it. Keep the tips simple; a minimum of one step and a maximum of three steps must complete the technique. (More than that and you should consider a full-blown article. If it's that complex, write and ask if we're interested before proceeding.

The ideas, sketches or photographs **will not**, ever, be returned, and their use, as illustrations or as part of ideas, is our option. You may, of course, incorporate them into future articles for us or any other magazine. We pay **approximately 45 days after publication. Be sure your name and address** are on each idea, photograph or sketch you submit. Mark the envelope "Top Tips" when you submit your ideas. We reserve the right to reprint the material, in any form, without further payment. Please let us know if you do **not** want your city and state mentioned (we never provide addresses). Come on, share 'em!

One of the least expensive ways to accelerate the curing or setting of hobby-type CA cement is to simply add a drop of water to the seam between the parts where you have just applied the cement. Hold the parts in place and use an eyedropper to apply the water on the seam — the CA will set almost instantly. Just remember to keep the water (or that "kicker", in the other "Top Tip") away from the parts until they are in perfect position. — Richard Wendel

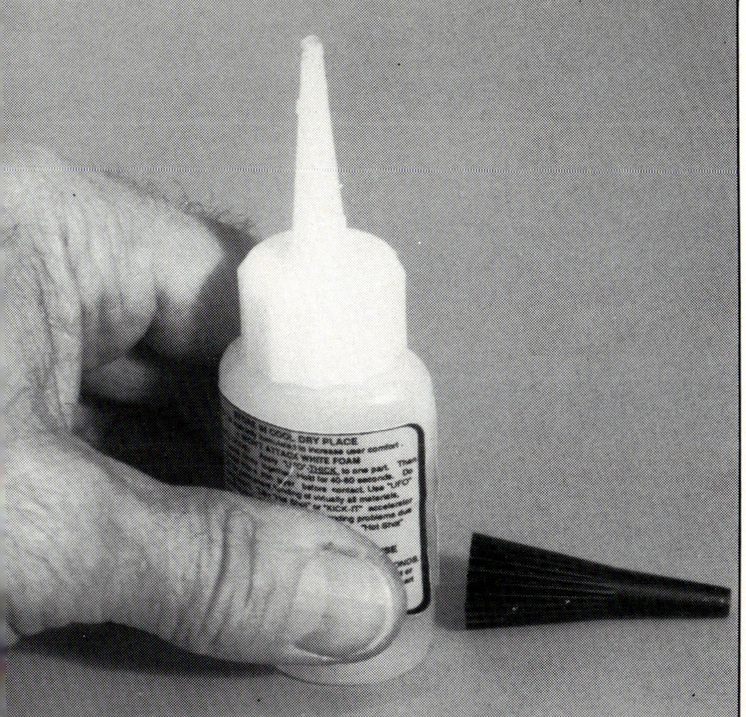

When you're working with hobby-type cyanoacrylate (CA) cement, especially the thickened types, the cement has a tendency to clog the tip of the bottle. When you're finished squeezing out a drop on a scrap of plastic bag (see a previous "Top Tip"), place the bottle down on the table for about a minute to let the cement drain down, then gently squeeze the bottle until air hisses out the hole — that should clear the nozzle for the next application. Put the cap on and store the bottle. — Bill Wright

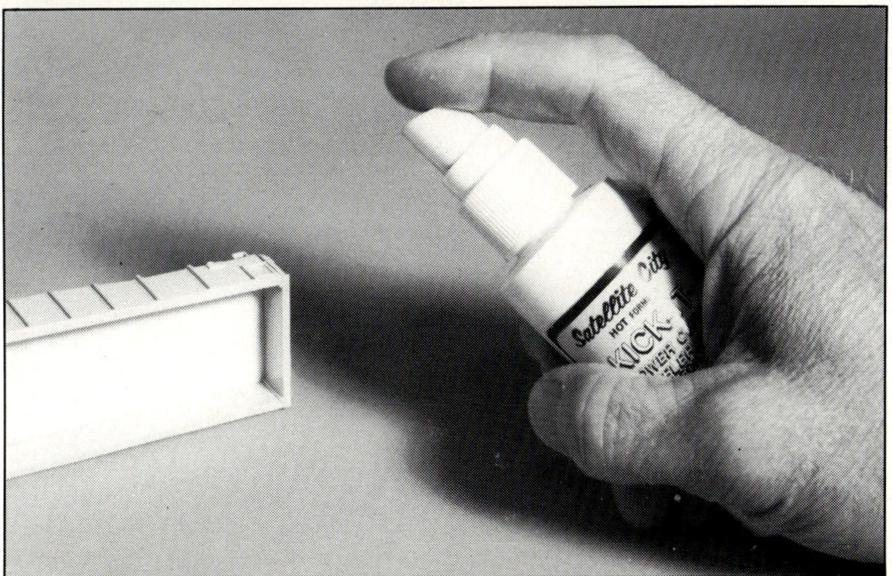

Ask your hobby dealer to order one of the "kickers" for cyanoacrylate cement (if he doesn't already carry two or three brands). The pump-pressure bottle sprays a fine mist of fluid that instantly sets the cyanoacrylate cement, even the thickened kinds. It makes the work far quicker when you are using the thickened type of CA cement. Work in a ventilated area and test the spray on a scrap of plastic, especially if the model is already painted as the fluid may attack some paints, and it could etch some clear plastic parts. — Bill Wright

TECHNIQUES

That "Used and Abused" Look for Plastic Hoppers and Gondolas

The dents and scrapes that make steel cars so obviously steel can be simulated on any plastic model, in any scale, to make that plastic look like dented and distressed steel.

Ed Bley and Ralph Gutowski

Honorarium for this article is being donated to the Pennsylvania Railroad Technical and Historical Society restoration project of the Pennsy station in Lewistown, Pennsylvania.

Whether you model a prototype railroad or freelance one, build craftsman kits or run models right out of the box, the technique described here can be used to make your hoppers and gondolas have that realistic used and abused look. Virtually every railroad has hauled hoppers and gondolas at one time or another. Hopper cars were and still are used to transport coal, ore, limestone, coke and other minerals from mine or dock to electric power plants, steel mills, foundries and industrial facilities. Gondolas most often see duty hauling irregular loads of scrap metals, pipe and steel coils.

Both hoppers and gons receive heavy abuse. Loads are dumped or dropped into them, those loads often contain corrosives, and they are open cars exposed to all types of weather and extremes of temperature and moisture. Gons in particular receive a lot of heavy, visible damage from being bashed by swinging crane hooks and magnets, shifting loads, hot metals and corrosive chemical residues eating into raw steel. To look realistic on a modeler's pike, hoppers and gons should be severely distressed to reflect the abuse they receive in real life.

The technique described in this article is quick and easy to perform. It does not require special skill or artistic talent, and it will produce cars that will have visitors to your railroad ''Ooo-ing'' and ''Ahhh-ing.'' Although we both use this technique for cars on our layouts of the Pennsylvania Railroad's Monogehela Division, these methods can be applied to any modeler's railroad. In addition to the cars themselves, you will need a 25-watt soldering iron with a pencil tip, a small hobby screwdriver and/or a hobby knife blade holder, a coarse file, a fine file, some Testor's *liquid* cement for plastic, an old stiff bristle brush, model paints, pastel artist's chalks and a spray can of Testor's Dullcote.

First, using a small 25-watt soldering iron, lightly touch or stroke the tip on an area inside the car to create dents, which normally go from inside to outside.

Once the plastic is softened, use the tip of a screwdriver or the round end of a hobby knife handle to push the softened area outward, thus forming a bulge.

Step 1: Creating Dents and Bulges

Dents and bulges can be applied to out-of-the-box painted cars or to undecorated cars. If you are using a craftsman kit, build the model first, but wait to paint it until after the dents and bulges are applied. Unpainted cars are preferred, but we have used pre-painted Athearn or Con-Cor cars. We have *never* tried this technique on models made from cast resins, such as older Westerfield kits (dark resin material) or car kits by Funaro & Camerlengo. Proceed at your own risk on these materials.

First, use a small 25-watt soldering iron and lightly touch or stroke the tip on an area *inside* the car. Dents and bulges typically go from inside to outside. No need to press, just warm and soften the plastic by moving the tip back and forth gently, depending on size of dent or bulge desired. Be careful not to hold the iron on the area too long — about 15-30 seconds is right — just long enough to soften the plastic. If you get it too hot, it will melt the plastic and possibly burn a hole through the side. If this does happen, don't worry; you can patch the hole just like the prototype railroads do.

Once the plastic is softened, use the tip of a screwdriver or the round end of a hobby knife blade holder to push the softened area outward to form a bulge. *Do not use your finger tip*; you can easily burn your finger on the hot plastic. Hold the tool for about five seconds or so until the plastic cools. Try not to make every dent or bulge the same. Stagger them. You should locate them in the more damage-prone areas between the car's side ribs.

Next, use the tip of the soldering iron to warm a small spot along the top edge, then lightly touch the softened spot with the tip of a screwdriver to create a dent simulating something being dropped or banged on the top edge. Sometimes cars show an upward pull of the top lip caused by a crane hook getting caught on the lip; be sure to simulate one of these now and then.

The next step after distressing both sides and top edges is to use a fairly coarse modeler's file to go over the distressed area to remove any plastic "wisps" which form when the tool is removed. This also blends the effect and removes that melted plastic look. It makes for a more natural looking dent or bulge. Follow the coarse file with a fine-grained file or an emery file (a disposable fingernail file works well) to remove any heavy filing marks.

Gondolas are often seen with their ends bulged outward, both fore and aft. Apply the same technique as above to the ends of gondola cars to create an outward bow simulating overloading or the wild, errant swing of a crane's electromagnet. At this point, you might apply small squares of 0.005-inch-thick Evergreen styrene sheet to the car's sides, placing them at odd angles to simulate patches over holes in the sides of the hopper or gondola.

Step 2: Painting and Weathering

If you are using a pre-decorated car, after the car has been distressed, *lightly* overspray the entire car with a weak, diluted solution of a similar color. If you used an undecorated car kit, now paint the model with the intended car color of that railroad (Pennsy cars get freight car color, B&O get black, etc.), decal the model, and allow it to dry thoroughly. Next, overspray the lettering using a very thin wash of the same color as the car to simulate paint bleed-through.

Some cars have been exposed to the elements for quite awhile and undergo paint distress. This step is to simulate paint distress or rust that has come through the paint. After the car has been painted, decaled and has dried thoroughly, make sure the model is lying flat on its side, then drip a drop or two of Testor's liquid plastic cement along the

Next, use the tip of the soldering iron to warm a small spot along the top edge.

Lightly touch the softened spot with the top of a screwdriver to create a dent simulating something being dropped or banged on the top edge of the car.

After the car has been painted and decaled, apply a drop or two of Testor's liquid plastic cement to spots on the car side, and allow it to sit for a minute or two to eat into the pan. Then use a stiff-bristled brush to jab or poke the softened area to create the stippled effect caused by deterioration from rust.

side of the car and allow it to sit there for a minute or two to eat into the paint and the side of the car. After the plastic has softened, use an old (the older the better), very stiff (the stiffer the better) bristle brush to jab or poke into the softened area to create a stippled effect that deterioration from rust causes. This seems to work best on prepainted Athearn cars.

After the liquid cement solvent evaporates, let the model sit for several hours to allow the plastic to harden again. Then use an air brush to spot-paint the "rusted" areas. Here, we like to shoot Floquil roof brown with a mixture of either engine black, weathered black or grimy black, varying the mixtures to get color variations. Our personal opinion is that Floquil rust color paint looks too new and too orange, and the rust we want to simulate is older, weathered, darker rust. Also, make runs and streaks down the sides of the car to simulate the effects of rain washing down the rust.

This is a good time to paint the inside of the car. Hoppers get grimy or weathered black, and gons get a dirty, dirty brown with heavy rust pigment. Vary each car and the finish within each car. The idea is to simulate different cars having served for different lengths of time in the open, under different loads and seasonal conditions. Paint the inside of some cars with mixtures having more black, some with more brown, and some with more white. Don't forget to do the car's underside, trucks and couplers, too.

Once the car is dry (overnight), use artist's pastel chalks to weather the entire car. We prefer to use orange, brown, black and light grey and blend them. First, we mix black and brown, and dust the car all over. On top of this, we then apply orange in spots to bring out rusted highlights. The chalks are "fixed" in place with a quick shot of Testor's Dullcote spray. Heavily dust the inside of gondolas with the chalks so there is a large powder build-up. Dullcote will soak much of this and bond it to look like a buildup of industrial dirt and grime, especially in the corners.

Vary the distress technique for each car so your rolling stock does not all look uniform. Some cars might look fairly new, while others should have the appearance of being "trashed" by years of hard revenue service. In several hours of fun, you can add a million miles and decades of hard use to your hoppers and gondolas. **RMJ**

After the "rust" spots have dried for several hours, the "rusted" areas can be spot-painted with a mixture of Floquil roof brown and either engine black, weathered black or grimy black. Once that paint is dry, use artist's pastel chalks to weather the entire car. Work with shades of black, brown, orange and light grey. Fix the weathering with a final coat of Testor's Dullcote.

The completed car has the prototypical appearance of one that has seen years of service.

Ed Bley's HO Scale Con-Cor Pennsy G-31 54-foot Gondolas

The Con-Cor (ex-Revell) gondolas are very close to the prototype Pennsy cars. Ed added some details and "distressed" the models as described on the previous pages.

Model photos by Ed Bley and Ralph Gotowski
Prototype photo by John C. LaRue

Modeler: Ed Bley
Car: Class G-31C gondola numbered 371200 to 371949.
Era: Built in 1950 and in service until the merger in 1968.
Basic Kit: Con-Cor 54 foot mill gondola.
Modifications:

Side sill: Cut approximately 2 scale feet from bottom of side sill and reshape the taper to each end per prototype photo.

Underframe: Discard the underframe and body weights which come with the kit. From the underside of the car, remove the bolster pin around which each truck pivots. Stretch an Athearn 50-foot box car underframe and bolsters to fit, but cut off the coupler pockets molded into this frame before cementing it in place. Cement BB shot along the center length of the new underframe to add weight.

Ends of Car: Notch the car's end sill to receive a Kadee coupler box flush with car floor, and install a Kadee no. 5 coupler assembly. Add scale 4x10-inch styrene filler strips along the end sill between the coupler pocket and car sides.

Steps: Remove the stirrup steps and replace with A-line style "A" stirrup steps.

Ladders: Shorten Detail Associates no. 6207 freight car ladders to four rungs, and cement in place on the right and of each side of car, per photo.

Grabs, Side: Shave off the molded grabs,

(Continued on Page 98)

Upgrading HO Scale Plastic Freight Car Kits

from Athearn, MDC, McKean, Con-Cor, Life-Like, Accurail, Walthers, Model Power, or Stewart

Use these techniques to improve the appearance of any HO scale hopper or other freight car kit so it looks as good as the imported brass models.

Bill Wright and Ed Hawkins
Based on Ed Hawkins' MDC hopper car on the previous pages

I decided to enhance the detail on this MDC hopper with a few basic modifications. All molded on grabirons/ladder rungs on the sides and ends are removed using a no. 17 X-acto chisel blade for shaving/smoothing. The right side of the end ladders need to be shortened to a point just above the slope sheet. Using a no. 79 bit, carefully drill holes to accept wire grabirons. In all cases, the top grab is a Detail Associates no. 6210 straight type while the others are drop steps, Detail Associates no. 2202 grabirons. Two straight wire grabs are used on the bottom of each end on either side of the coupler pocket. Another straight wire grab is installed on the far left of the car side, where the hopper bay meets the corner post. Just below this, the heavy plastic "cross braces" are removed and replaced with .015-inch brass wire, simulated long grabirons. Simply cut to size and fasten with hobby-type cyanoacrylate.

Ed Hawkins' HO scale MDC hopper is an accurate replica of an American Car & Foundry-built prototype on the Texas & Pacific Railroad (see previous pages). He used these techniques to remove the molded-on detail and to add the wires and lines that can make an inexpensive plastic kit seem as realistic as the imported brass models. This "project" utilizes the MDC three-bay hopper, but the details on the Athearn, McKean, Life-Like, Model Power, Walthers, Con-Cor and Stewart models are similar and all will benefit from these changes.

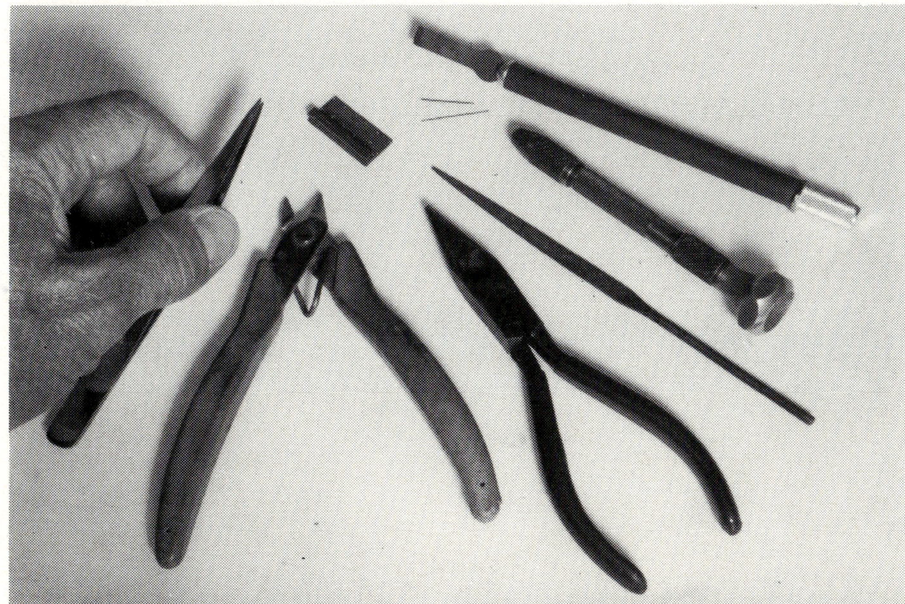

The basic tools to upgrade any HO scale plastic kit include (l. to r.): tweezers, flush-cut diagonal cutters, needlenose pliers, rectangular jewelers file, pin vise with no. 79 drill bits, hobby knife and (top) a hand-made jig for drilling grabiron holes.

Also added is a trainline (air line) made of .015-inch brass wire supported with four Northeastern lift rings just below the car side. On the same side as the air brake reservoir only, this line is clearly visible (for about 3½ inches in length on the model) as it runs alongside the three hopper outlets. The line bends at roughly 45 degrees toward the center of the car where the ends are CA'd to the underframe near the truck bolster. Insure that the line does not interfere with the swing of the trucks once they are installed.

The offset heap shields for the top of the ends provided in the MDC no. 1536 N&W kit have somewhat squared corners that need to be rounded with a little filing. Perhaps the correct heap shields are commercially available, but I was unable to locate any. Scratchbuilding these would be fairly easy if one is so inclined. One more tidbit of end detail needs to be added, namely three small vertical support pieces for the curved heap shield. These are fabricated from thin scraps of 1x2 Evergreen plastic and glued in place with liquid cement. Installation of a few links of brake chain (see end photo) and coupler cut bars make a nice finishing touch. Since I could not find the *correct* Universal brake wheel in HO, I installed one from the Grandt Line AB brake set no. 5232 that is reasonably close to accurate. This can be easily replaced when the Universal wheel becomes available in the future. You may choose to detail the car even further, such as replacement stirrups, Detail Associates no. 6413 for this car. All that's left is to paint the car black and add decals. When painting black, I prefer to use a weathering black for a lightened effect. **RMJ**

INSTALLING WIRE GRABIRONS

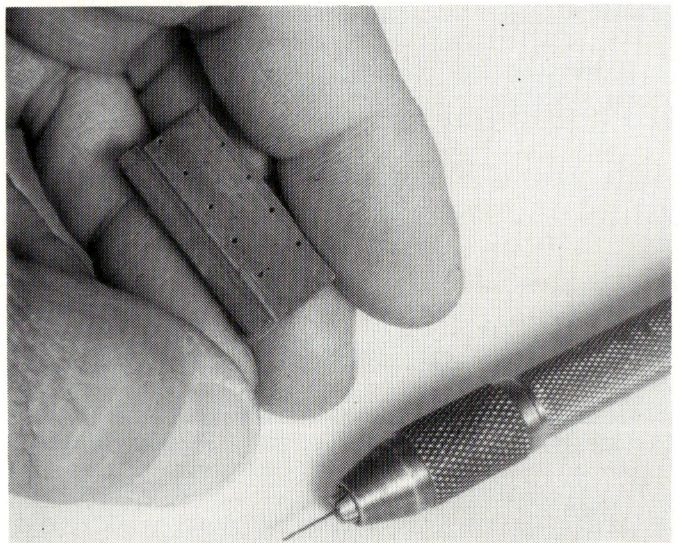

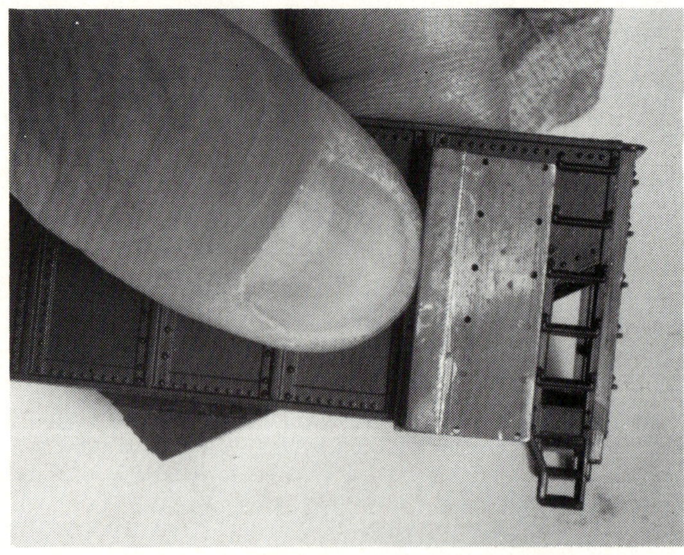

Take the time, right now, to make a jig for drilling handrail grabiron holes as suggested on the Detail Associates no. 2202 grabiron package. I made mine from a piece of .040-inch brass and 1/8-inch square brass tube soldered together, but the same sizes of Evergreen styrene will do as well. Space the holes to match the car you are upgrading — different jigs may be needed to match the spacing on specific models.

Use a chisel-shaped blade (this is a well-worn X-Acto no. 17 blade) to shave-off the molded-on grabirons.

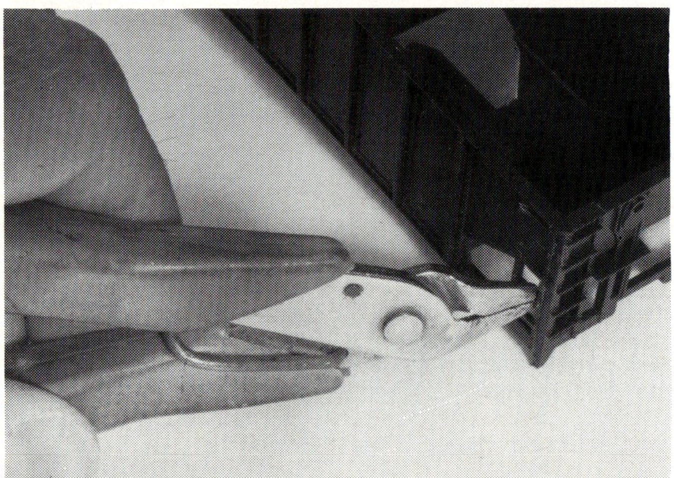

Cut the horizontal posts behind the grabirons from the car with small flush-cut diagonal cutters.

File the edges of the cuts made with the flush-cut diagonal cutters using the rectangular jewelers file.

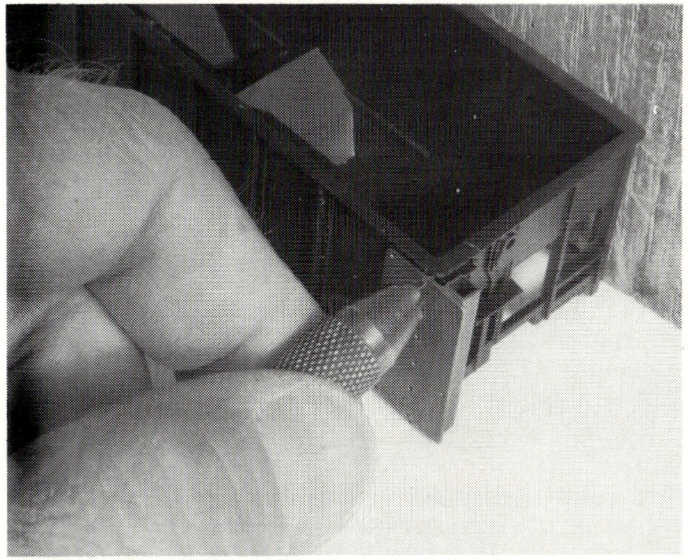

Position the grabiron drilling jig on the end of the car and be sure the jig is vertical. On some cars, you may need to add some plastic shims between the 1/8-inch square tube on the jig and the car end. Chuck the no. 79 drill bit in the pin vise and gently rotate and push the pin vise to drill the holes. The holes on the extreme ends enter the thick sides so you cannot drill through. Drill these holes just 1/16 inch into the sides, using the end of the pin vise to gauge how far the drill has penetrated into the plastic.

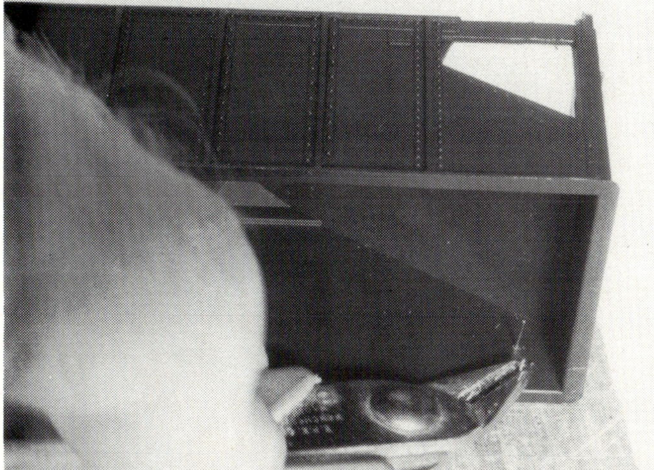

Cut the protruding ends of the grabirons flush with the inside wall of the car with the flush-cut diagonal cutters. Cut the ends from the vertical posts on the bottom of the car as well.

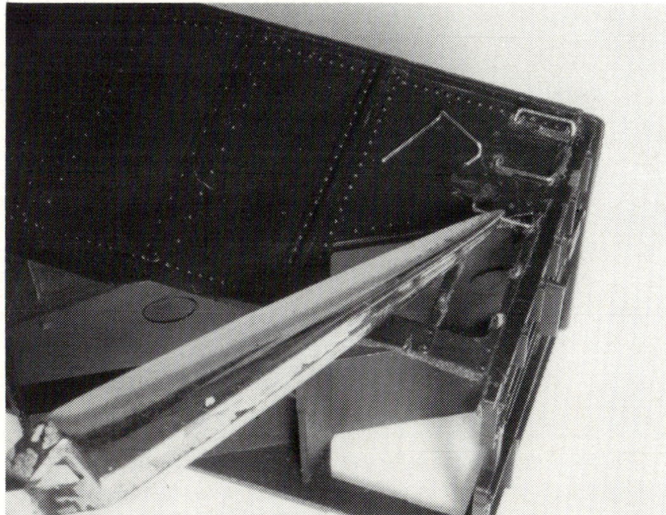

Cut the "outer" leg of the Detail Associates no. 2202 grabirons (the one that will go into the 1/16-inch deep no. 79 hole) short so the grabiron will not bottom out in the shallow end holes. Dip each end in a puddle of thickened hobby-type cyanoacrylate cement (CA) dribbled onto a scrap of clear plastic, then push the grabiron into the car side. Note that the top grabiron on the model, and on the prototype car, is a Detail Associates no. 6210 straight grabiron, so its holes must be drilled slightly closer to the next grabiron. The stirrup steps have already been cut from the bottom edges of this model with the flush-cut diagonal cutters.

INSTALLING SEPARATE END DETAILS

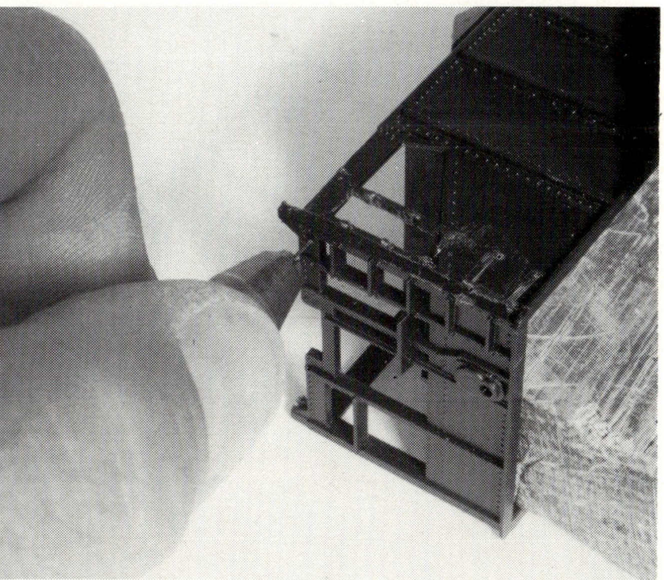

All real railroad cars have coupler cut-bars so the crew can operate the coupler lift pin from the side of the car. To install the Detail Associates no. 6215 coupler cut-bar, drill a no. 79 hole about 1/8 inch in from the outer edge of the end.

Left: Dip the end of the wire eye bolt (from the 6215 package) into a puddle of thickened hobby-type cyanoacrylate cement and push the eye bolt into the hole you just drilled. The lift bar (or cut lever) will be cemented in place with the same cement after the couplers are in place.

Replace the too-thick brake wheels in the kit with a wheel matched to a photo of the prototype car. Here, the Grandt Line no. 5232 AB brake set has a brake wheel that is close. Install a short piece of chain below the brake housing. Precision Scale, Campbell and Builders in Scale make HO-size chain. Use the thickened hobby-type cyanoacrylate cement to install the pieces.

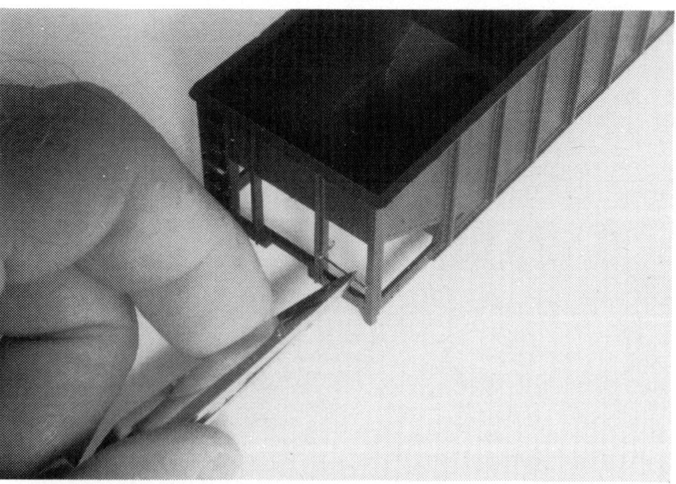

Cut the horizontal bars from the ends and replace them with a piece of .015-inch diameter wire from Detail Associates or Precision Scale. Cut the wire to fit the car and cement it in place with the thickened hobby-type cyanoacrylate.

The prototype for this hopper had offset heap shields on the tops of each end. Add some vertical braces with three short strips of Evergreen HO scale 1 x 2 strip styrene.

Most hopper cars have an external air line that runs down one side of the car. Drill four holes with the pin vise and the no. 79 drill bit, spaced as shown in the photographs.

Use that .015-inch wire for the air line, and cement it in place.

Ed Hawkins finished this model with the stock stirrup steps in place. There are photos of the prototype and the model on the previous pages.

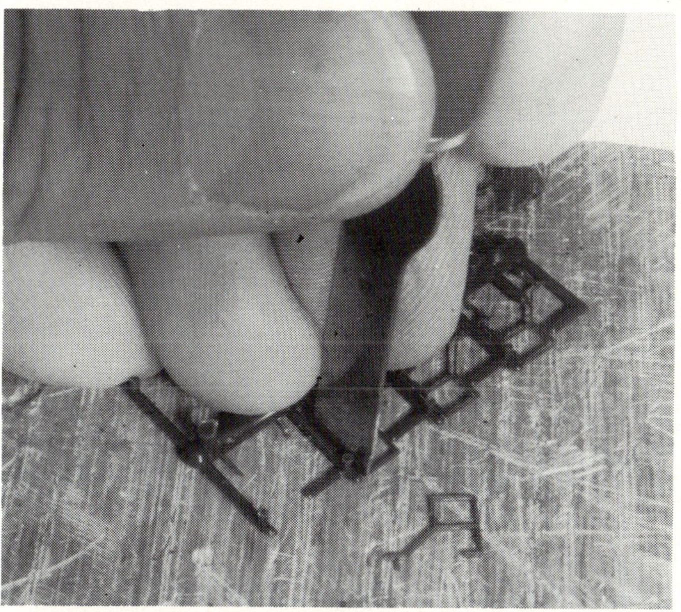

Detail Associates no. 6413 stirrup steps match the steps on the prototype car. Use the X-acto no. 17 chisel blade to carefully slice the steps from the sprue. Support the sprue on a hardwood block while you slice into the plastic.

Use the step itself as a guide to locate the holes for the step mounting pins. Use that same no. 79 drill bit to drill the holes into the bottom of the car side.

Dip the prongs of the step into the thickened hobby-type cyanoacrylate cement and press the prongs into the no. 79 holes.

FOCUS ON FREIGHT CARS NO. 33

Ed Hawkins' MDC (Roundhouse) HO Scale Texas & Pacific Three-Bay Hopper

The prototype photo needed to add the details described on the following pages.

Prototype photos courtesy ACF Industries from the Hawkins/Wider/Long collection
Model photo by Robert Schleicher

Prototype Information

A total quantity of 250 of these 40'6" three-bay cars were produced at the Huntington, West Virginia, ACF plant. They were numbered in series 9600-9849 and delivered to the T&P in March 1952. The cars have 10 riveted vertical ribs and offset, curved peaked ends. The volume capacity is 2,608 cubic feet, and the height is 10'8" from the rail to the top of the car side. Each car came equipped with a Universal brake wheel.

As built, the entire car was painted black with white lettering. The T&P diamond had a white border, red background and black center. In 1966 there were 244 cars still in service, all with original numbers. System renumbering of the Mopac began soon thereafter, and the cars were assigned to the 500300-500549 series. According to the *Official Railway Equipment Register*, 232 cars were still in service by 1976. Amazingly, three cars still wore their original numbers (9737, 9762 and 9799). While I do not have any photographic evidence handy, I suspect remaining cars were repainted box car red and received Missouri Pacific buzzsaws in their later years of service.

Modeling Notes

The basic model that closely approximates the overall dimensions and characteristics of the prototype is produced in HO scale by Model Die Casting. The undecorated version is no. 1485, but the heap shield pieces must be obtained separately. Some decorated kits contain the heap shields, including no. 1536 for N&W.

Some basic modification to the MDC body detail is needed to match the prototype. On the sides, leave all rivet detail except the disgonal row that angles along the slope sheets. These rivets are easily shaved off with a no. 17 X-acto chisel blade. All rivets on the end of the car should be removed, as the prototype cars had welded ends.

The modifications to the model are shown, step-by-step, on the following pages.

Decals

Because no commercially available decals work on this car, Oddballs Custom Decals was asked to consider making a set. I helped the firm by scaling the lettering from the ACF builders photos. Oddballs has done a fine job producing an accurate decal set for this car. While all lettering in the decal set is white, the T&P diamond is white with red background. The center circle is clear, allowing the black paint to show through. The two-color diamond added to the cost of the decal set but makes application much easier than other options. The only detail lacking from the set is the ACF builder's logo. However, the logo is readily available in a variety of other decal sets, should you desire to use it. Builder's logos were often painted out by the railroads after the cars were in service for awhile, unless you are modeling a brand new car, you may want to leave it off.

Some of the lettering on the prototype was only one or two inches in height. On the third panel left of the diamond is "ADJUST BRAKE HERE" in 1-inch letters. On the panel just left of the diamond is 2-inch dimensional data as follows:

Bill of Materials

1 — MDC no. 1485 three-bay ribbed hopper, undecorated
2 — MDC no. 2993 peak ends (Heap shields)
10 — Westerfield 1198 straight grabs (Tichy no. 3021 alternative)
16 — Detail Associates 2202 drop grabs (Westerfield no. 1197 or Tichy no. 3015 alternate)
2 — Detail Associates 6215 out levers
4 — Northeastern eye pins
1 — Brake wheel from no. 5232 Grandt Line AB brake set
Evergreen 8102 1x2 styrene strip
Detail Associates 2505 .015-inch-dia. wire
Detail Associates 2506 .019-inch-dia. wire
Alloy forms chain no. M-1000
2 — Kadee no. 5 couplers
1 — Oddballs Custom Decals for T&P hopper

EXW 10-5 H10-8
CU FT 2608
BLT 3-52

Below this in 1-inch letters is "RPKD HTG 3-1-52" which describes journal bearing re-

packing at Huntington, West Virginia, where the car was being built.

The end lettering is located on the center panel in 2-inch letters as follows:

AB AIR BRAKE
SPRG TRAVEL 2 ½
IW WROT STL WHEELS

In HO, this lettering becomes very tiny and difficult to produce on the decal film with good clarity. Most of your normal commercial decal sets don't bother to provide this level of detail, so I think you will be quite pleased with the efforts of Oddballs Custom Decals.

For anyone interested in modeling this car, the decals are available from Oddballs Custom Decals, 109 W. Gertrude, McLouth, KS 66054. Cost is $1.95 per set, postpaid. Please note: These decals are relatively thin and somewhat delicate. As a word of caution, I found full-strength Solvaset to be a bit much for these decals. However, by mixing with an equal amount of water, the diluted solution worked just fine.

Additional Cars Matching This General Arrangement

Cars of this basic design were also built by ACF for the Chesapeake & Ohio, Central of Georgia and Grand Trunk Western. A follow-up to this article will appear in a future issue, containing photos and roster information. **RMJ**

C&BT CAR SHOPS HO SCALE 40-FOOT BOX CAR KITS

State-of-the-art basic bodywork deserves state-of-the-art detailing. . . this is a kit you can build quickly or one worthy of a few extra evenings to upgrade to "super-detail" standards. Photographs of the real cars appear in Volume II of the Freight Car Models book series.

Richard Hendrickson

The AAR standard 40-foot box car design was officially adopted in 1932, and cars of this type continued to be built new until the early '60s. During that 30-year period, however, the design underwent considerable evolution, and at most times in its history there were alternatives in such basic construction features as roofs, ends and doors, not to mention brake equipment, safety appliances, and other details. As a result, there were many somewhat different versions of the AAR "standard" box car.

The inside height of the AAR box car was increased from 9′9″ to 10′0″ in 1937, and a further increase to a maximum of 10′6″ was approved in 1941. Murphy rectangular panel steel roofs were common on early cars, but other roof styles — notably the Viking corrugated roof — were also widely applied until the mid-'40s, and in the late '40s the improved Murphy diagonal-panel roof was introduced. Running boards were usually wood until after World War II, when steel running boards were mandated by the AAR.

Dreadnaught ends were genearlly used on AAR cars, but these, too, changed over time. Originally they had sharp corners where the ends wrapped around to join the side sheathing, but round corners came in around 1940 with the adoption of W-section corner posts, and both styles of early dreadnaught ends were made in 4-4, 4-5 and 5-5 main rib arrangements, depending mostly on the height of the car. Then the improved dreadnaught end design made its appearance in 1944, with either 3-4 or 4-4 main rib arrangements (depending, again, on the height of the car). A few years later this design was further modified and acquired a rectangular top panel.

There was considerable variety in door sizes and configuations as well. Youngstown 6-foot corrugated doors were almost universal in the '30s, with seam panels varying in width according to car height. By the early '40s, Superior seven-panel doors were becoming a popular alternative, and door widths of 7 feet or even 8 feet were beginning to appear. In the late '40s, the Youngstown door was redesigned, with at least two variations, and in the '50s, Superior doors became available in six-panel and five-panel designs. Even the arrangement of side sheathing and framing was not entirely uniform; the original design called for 10-panel sides, but 12-panel sides with more closely spaced body framing for added strength were introduced as early as 1940 on some Rio Grande cars and became increasingly common after World War II.

In short, though the basic structural design of the AAR standard 40-foot box car remained essentially unchanged, most production lots of new AAR cars were at least a little different in some details from others, even when constructed at the same time by the same builder. Some of these variations were too subtle to be clearly visible, of course, but others had a significant effect on the cars' appearance.

This model of a Santa Fe Bx-50 class box car was painted mineral brown with black roof and underframe and lettered with Clover House dry transfers (mostly from set no.7056-26, with some data and numbers from other sets and 2-foot square heralds from a Microscale decal set for Santa Fe covered hoppers). The model represents its prototype as delivered in September of 1947 from the Topeka shops, except for route cards on the doors and a few chalk markings.

MODELING AAR CARS IN HO SCALE

Since more AAR-design box cars were built during the '30s, '40s and '50s than any other type of freight car, models of these cars are needed in large numbers on most model railroads. For many years, however, the two AAR box car models that were readily available in HO scale were the molded styrene kits produced by Athearn and Model Die Casting, both representing the AAR design as built in the late '30s and early '40s with early style 5-5 dreadnaught ends and corrugated doors (Athearn) or 4-5 ends and (incorrect) six-panel doors (MDC). Other versions of the AAR box cars could only be built by fairly extensive kitbashing.

Furthermore, while the Athearn and MDC kits were "state of the art" when they were first introduced in the '50s, their shortcomings have become increasingly evident with the passage of time. Details such as steps, brake wheels, and running boards are thick and relatively crude; doors are too short with oversize tracks and clumsy, claw-like track slides; underbody detail is sketchy (and, on the Athearn car, located in a mirror image of where it should be). And though their modest prices make these kits a genuine bargain, this has proved to be a mixed blessing because it has discouraged the development of better box car kits at the higher prices that would be required to cover the cost of new tooling.

In recent years, the situation improved considerably with the introduction of plastic kits for '50s-vintage AAR box cars by Front Range. But several of the most common earlier variants on the AAR design remained unavailable in HO scale, including the post-World War II version with improved dreadnaught ends which was built by the thousands in the period from 1944 to 1950 and was owned in significant numbers by most North American railroads.

Meeting this need was the impetus behind the new C&BT Shops AAR box car kits, which are now on the dealers' shelves after almost two years of planning and development. Having started out with some successful plastic kits for East Broad Top narrow-gauge hopper cars, Dick Schweiger of C&BT Shops moved into mainline modeling in a big way by offering kits for postwar AAR cars in a number of different variations, with 6-, 7-, and 8-foot door openings, with both 10- and 12-panel sides, and even in double-door auto car form.

Kit modifications and added details show up clearly on this model of a Santa Fe Bx-48, photographed before the paint was touched up. Small details like the door locks and the defect card holder, though seldom modeled, contribute to the model's overall visual effect even when the viewer isn't consciously aware of them. The running boards and corner grabs will be installed after the roof is painted black, and Kadee couplers and wheelsets will be added when all painting and weathering has been completed.

C&BT SHOPS AAR BOX CAR KITS

The one-piece car bodies in the new C&BT Shops kits are exceptionally well done, with only a couple of very minor shortcomings that are easily corrected. The lettering also deserves praise; in the kits I've examined, it's accurate and complete — except that there's no lettering on the ends, a common weakness of pre-lettered plastic models — and it's located exactly where it should be on the car bodies. In the past, kit lettering has so often been incorrect, if not entirely unprototypical, that it's a pleasure to open a kit box and find that the car class, road number and lettering style correspond exactly with the model.

The doors, too, are accurate and well-detailed, with both postwar Youngstown and Superior seven-panel doors supplied in each kit — and, since they're not intended to slide, the doors are the right height and have tracks of correct size and location. In addition, the placard boards on both doors and ends are separate parts, so they can be installed either in the original locations or in the lower positions to which they were usually moved in the '60s. The running boards can also be left off and the ladders shortened, as was done to most prototype cars in later years, without having to fill any mounting holes.

The underframes in these kits are almost as good as the bodies and include molded-on air brake detail that's the best so far in HO scale. Meticulous modelers still won't be satisfied with anything less than the realism of freestanding underbody detail, but many buyers will be happy with the undersides of these cars just as they come out of the box. AAR-type cast steel trucks molded in black plastic are included, along with wheelsets of a unique and ingenious design. The wheel centers and axles are plastic, made in separate halves and molded integrally into nickel-plated, turned brass treads and flanges. Two halves slide onto a piece of brass rod to form a complete wheelset, a clever design that makes it possible to have self-insulating, non-magnetic HO scale plastic wheels with realistic looking metal treads and flanges. (A word of caution, though; the gauge and axle straightness of these wheelsets need to be carefully checked after assembly, as they tend to have crooked axles and wobbly wheels if put together hastily.)

With so many good things going for them, have the C&BT Shops kits finally satisfied the demand for accurate, well-detailed, yet reasonably priced plastic box cars in HO scale? Unfortunately, the answer is no, at least for the present, because the detail parts aren't as good as the rest of the kit — in fact, they're downright disappointing. At best, such parts as grid-type running boards, steps, and grab irons can't be successfully molded in styrene without making them somewhat oversize, but in this case almost all the parts on the sprue — running boards, ladders, grab irons, steps, hand brake, pla-

This view shows the underside of the Bx-48 model, with Cal-Scale brake gear replacing the molded-on brake equipment provided in the kit. Re-detailing the underbody isn't worth the effort if the car is to be operated on a table-height layout, but it adds a lot to the realism if the car is to be viewed at or near eye level. Note the simulation of the Royal Type F brake regulator and the transverse mounting of the air reservoir, in accordance with standard Santa Fe practice of the '40s and '50s.

card boards, and other bits and pieces — are excessively heavy and clumsy looking.

In addition, some mounting pins don't fit the holes cored for them in the car body, and the two halves of the mold for the detail parts sprue are out of register so that surface details on such parts as ladders and placard boards are displaced noticeably to one side. Some of these detail parts can be rendered acceptable with some careful reworking, but for others the only solution is to either ignore their shortcomings (which isn't easy) or replace them with parts from other sources.

To his credit, Dick Schweiger of C&BT Shops is well aware of these flaws and current kits have thinner roofwalks, grab irons and step. (See "What's New in HO Scale" for a sample). In the meantime, although the new C&BT Shops kits are something less than the ultimate in AAR box car kits, they're well done in many respects and — most important — they're the first kits to accurately reproduce the post-World-War-II version of the AAR design, so their introduction is a major event for those who model any era from late steam to second-generation diesel.

IMPROVING THE C&BT SHOPS CARS

In building the models shown here, I made a number of improvements to enhance their realism. To start with, I added two 1/2-oz. A-Line weights to the steel weights included in each kit, since these cars are — like most plastic models — somewhat lighter than is called for by NMRA recommended practice RP 20.1. I filed off the molding sprue at the center of the roof and filled all the ladder and grab iron holes with Grandt Line .020 styrene rod. I sanded off the parting lines on the ends and cemented narrow strips of .005 styrene at the tops of the ends to represent the roof seams. I also sanded off the parting lines where the ends meet the sides and did a bit of reshaping where the end ribs wrap around the corners, and I scribed seam lines just inside the vertical rows of rivets to represent the joints where the ends lap over the side sheathing.

The corrugated doors were made somewhat thinner by filing and sanding, and I also narrowed their vertical edges, which looked a bit too wide in comparison to the prototype doors. Then, since the narrowed flanges no longer overlapped the door openings, I cemented 4x4-in. styrene strips onto the edges of the openings to support the doors. I substituted Central Valley ladders (from stair/ladder/railing set no. 1602) for the kit ladders and used A-Line no. 29000 stirrup steps instead of the molded plastic ones. The bracket-style grab irons on the sides and ends are Westerfield no. 1198 with Detail Associates no. 2203 nut/bolt/washer castings. Various bits and pieces of styrene were used as necessary to provide mountings for the ladders and grabs, and door locks were made from styrene and wire staples.

The kit running boards were replaced with Overland no. 2156 etched metal box car running boards, using stryene strip stock and wire staples to make the end supports, and the brake steps are pieces cut from an Overland no. 2154 reefer running board (Detail Associates parts 6203 and 6211 could also be used for the running boards and brake step). The hand brake parts are Cal-Scale, and I also added Detail Associates no. 6215 uncoupling levers. In addition, since my rolling stock is intended to be viewed at eye level, I cut and filed off all the molded-on air brake parts and brake rigging from the underframes (a process I simplified by also filing off all the rivet detail, since by the late '40s most AAR cars were being built with welded underframes). I then replaced the brake details with Cal-Scale no. 283 AB air brake sets, fabricating the brake rods from .015-in. brass wire. Collectively, these relatively simple changes greatly improve the appearance of the finished models. ***RMJ***

Note the etched metal brake step and the mountings on the roof for the Overland etched metal running boards. Close-to-scale size of A-Line steps, Westerfield wire grabs, and Detail Associates bracket grab irons and uncoupling levers does a lot to improve the appearance of the model. End numbers and mechanical data were added in the form of decals before the car was lightly weathered to represent the appearance of its prototype after about a year of revenue service.

UPGRADE:

Athearn or MDC HO Scale Box Cars

Scale-height doors, new door guides, separate grabirons, ladders, steps and cut levers and a new roofwalk can make an inexpensive Athearn or MDC box car look at least as well detailed as the McKean Models or C&BT Shops kits. Since the Athearn and MDC models are replicas of earlier era cars, they are necessary additions to most model scenes.

On the previous pages, you've learned how to add interior details. In a future issue of ***Railmodel Journal,*** *you'll learn how to improve the underbody details.*

Martin Lofton

Plan and execute the upgrade of the exterior of the car before beginning the construction of the interior. Suggested changes include: replacing the side ladders and grabirons with Detail Associates or Grandt Line ladders and grabs; creating new roof and cornerwalks from Evergreen styrene or use of commercially available ones in wood from Detail Associates or, to simulate expanded metal roof walls, from Overland Models or Detail Associates; replacing the cast-on power handbrake with Cal-Scale's AB brake set and the addition of cut levers.

Replacement of the too short doors with more prototypical ones is a critical step. Prototype height doors are available from Westrail, Westerfield, Cannonball Shops or McKean Models land in C&BT kits. The door will be open, of course, and this element sets the stage for an open-door box car.

Follow these procedures to install the taller doors once you have finihsed other exterior work:

1. Remove the snap-in top door guides.

2. Place 2x4 styrene strip 12'8'' in length into the cavity of the upper door guide. Add 12'11'' of .010x.060-inch strip on top of the 2x4.

3. At the top of the door guide, just above the .010x.060, add .010x.020-inch strip on its edge.

4. Place the door on the side — partially or fully open — below the .010x.020, and attach with hobby-type cyanoacrylate cement.

5. Add 1x3 strip, overlapping the .010x.020 and the upper lip of the door.

6. Styrene 2x2 strips are cast between the lower door rollers. Add 2x2 strip on both sides of the rollers to the full length of door movement. Use pieces of 1x2 to support the lower guide on the sides of the car. **RMJ**

Modeling Open-door Box Cars

One of the visible hallmarks of many real railroad branchline (and occasionally mainline) operations was the sight of box cars in trains with their doors still open. For those scenes, as well as for scenes at box car clean-out sites (see the article on page 31 of this issue), you'll want to have a few box cars with at least one door open. Open that door, however, and you will also need to do a bit of work on the interior of the car because the interior will be a visible (and noticeable) part of the model.

Martin Lofton

In our hobby, one hallmark of excellence is the carefully constructed model of rolling stock, built by simply improving a basic plastic kit. That kit is usually one of Athearn's or MDC's ubiquitous offerings, because they are readily accessible and — within limitations — easily modified. Numerous articles have demonstrated how the exterior appearance of the plastic kit can be improved to create a more accurate model. Let's add one more technique for improving basic kits: modeling the interior of the car.

*This Santa Fe double-door car has recently seen service hauling grain or a similar bulk commodity; the shreds of the paper door-liner are still visible. The November 1990 issue of **Railmodel Journal** describes how to model those door liners. — Martin Lofton photo*

During the time period of most of our models — late steam and early diesel — box cars made up about 80 percent of all the freight rolling stock of the prototype railroad. Of all the box cars on the road, some meaningful percentage of these cars would have been seen with their doors open. The doors were open for a variety of reasons, from the expected purpose of loading and unloading to simply lax procedures.

Loading and unloading of box cars took place at several locations. The most frequent spot was an industrial siding, where companies loaded their product or unloaded materials for production or resale. In an era when rail transport predominated, industrial sidings commanded the railroad scene from town to country.

The railroads' own freight houses were another common location for the discharge of cargo. In the steam and early diesel era, these loading facilities were located in all towns and cities having a population of 5,000 or more. Where a freight house was not justified, the depot had a selection or annex for handling freight.

Probably the most interesting location for the modeler was the team track. The team track was an outdoor loading and unloading facility. Here, trucks from the local merchants could back up to a box car to transfer crated or boxed cargo. The team track also was frequently the location for unloading of bulk items such as autos, farm equipment and construction equipment, from box cars or flats. In small towns, some bulk commodities, such as coal or aggregate, were unloaded at team tracks.

The freight yard was another location for box cars with open doors. Cars were returned from unloading sites to be redistributed to locations requiring empties. These locations could be in the same vicinity or some distance from the yard, requiring movement of empties.

It was the yard personnel's job to put the box car back into serviceable condition. This included cleaning the car and closing the door. However, just like other procedures, this process could be and was frequently ignored. More and more with the labor shortages of World War II and the period of increasing labor costs after the war, yard employees never got around to this task.

If the car door was not in good repair — difficult to close or not easily latched — the door would be left open. In addition, the process of coupling cars, with its occasionally violent collision of cars, could knock open a poorly latched door.

While not an accepted practice, box cars could be seen rolling cross-country with their doors open. Where else, after all, would the hobo, a frequent sight during the steam era, have found shady accommo-

Composite gondolas (with steel frames and wood side panels) can be detailed with this same procedure. This is one of Sunshine Models' War Emergency cast resin gondola kits with a new interior.

All four of these cars have interiors and, because of the open doors on the box cars, those interiors are visible and well worth modeling.

Finished box car interior panels for (top to bottom): the ends, the right sides, left sides, top of floor and bottom of floor. These parts are also available, as shown, from Sunshine Models (see text) if you'd rather not bother painting your own.

Creating "wood" out of plastic. Right to left: the base coat of Pactra's Acrylic Enamel (for modelers — see Walthers' catalog or ask at a model shop that sells plastic airplane and tank kits). The Evergreen sheet styrene has been scratched with sandpaper to simulate wood grain. Center: Variation on the wood color (for alternate boards) by mixing in a few drops of tan or red. Left: The final wood, weathered, and the "grain" accentuated with a dilute wash of flat black and water.

dations on a hot summer day? An empty car was easily entered and the door left open for ventilation.

The most likely place to see a box car in transit with an open door, however, was the branchline. The branchline was one long series of industrial sidings, team tracks and freight houses. The branch local spent its day hustling cars from yard to loading facility and back to the yard. If the industry or a local railroad employee didn't close the door of the box car, the car would make its way into a branchline freight or mixed train with the doors open. Enforcement of railroad regulations was lax in these out-of-the-way locations. Review of branchline photos from popular railroad books will show a disproportionate number of box cars with open doors.

We modelers need to include this variation of open-door cars on our pikes. Some portion of our box cars are appropriately modeled with the door open for any of the reasons outlined.

We require some way of replicating this open-door box car by modeling the interior, as well as the exterior, of some of our cars. Interior kits produced with similar techniques, pre-painted and ready to install, are available from Sunshine Models, P.O. Box 4997, Springfield, MO 65808-4997. Kit B.1 includes the pre-finished simulated wood interior pieces and B.2 the interior with prototypical height doors. Both come with wood trash and pastels to complete the weathering of the interior. The kits, with materials for two open-door cars, well for $12 and $17, respectively. However, the creation of an open-door box car is within the reach of modelers who have experience in kitbashing to meet specific prototypes, if you'd rather do-it-yourself than buy a kit.

We'll use the standard MDC 40-foot box car to demonstrate the creation of an interior. The MDC and its near duplicate, the Athearn 40-footer, are the most common pieces of HO rolling stock. Most modelers

These MDC (left) and Athearn (right) box cars have been upgraded with separate ladders, steps, grabirons and new, thinner roofwalks plus correct-height doors and slimmer door guides, as described on page 30 of this issue.

have a couple of these cars around that could stand upgrading and therefore are good candidates for this procedure.

Wood interiors can be created in at least two relatively simple processes: with scribed wood or styrene. Each has its advantages. Scale wood obviously looks like fresh wood, but it has some disadvantages. Chief among these is that thin wood tends to warp, either from the paint and stains you apply or from the absorption of moisture from the air. I have several models where, months after completion, the roofwalk or interior has bowed. These problems can be overcome in the interior of a car if you bond the wood well to the plastic shell of the car.

The wood alternative is most applicable to models that simulate new cars, so you may wish to use wood here despite some limitations. There is no special technique needed for wood, except a recommendation to use pastels to add a used look to the wood rather than paints and stains. Simply cutting the required pieces is all that is needed, and that will be discussed later.

Styrene avoids the warping associated with wood, and the material is readily available. However, the styrene requires some unique finishing techniques before it looks like wood. This finishing is different than painting and requires some experimentation.

This is the approach I use to complete the interior of the 40-foot plastic box car using styrene finished to look like wood. The process consists of two major tasks: creating the parts and finishing them to resemble wood.

The Athearn or MDC car kits consist of separate floor and underframe. Retain the floor for support of the shell while making modifications to the exterior. When complete, dispose of the floor and keep the underframe.

While inside the shell, remove the protrusions that accept the top door guides. Use a no. 17 flat blade in a hobby knife to snap off these posts. Also, smooth and paint the roof interior. Some roof interiors were painted the oxide red color, while others received a silver color. Some acquired black sealants and some other colors of primers. Take your choice. Only on cars intended for loading of flour and similar powders did the roof interior receive wood sheathing. Then, the sheathing was plywood and matched the sections of the roof.

Creating the Interior Pieces

The interior floor, walls and ends will be created from Evergreen .010-inch grooved styrene. While the floor boards used for box car interiors varied, the most common dimensions are 1 3/4 x 5 1/16-inch planking. The walls of the car would most likely be 3 1/4-inch tongue and groove of varying thickness of less than 1 inch. These dimensions can be simulated by styrene grooved at .060-inch for the floor and .040-inch for the walls.

For flooring, cut two pieces of the .060-inch grooved styrene to a 39'9" by 9'4" size. To create one floor place the two pieces back to back. Of course, the boards run across the floor, perpendicular to the length of the car.

The .010-inch thickness of the two floor pieces does not fill the distance from the bottom of the door to the top of the underframe on the Athearn and MDC cars. This space offers the opportunity to do some more detailing of the underframe of the car, however. We'll discuss this in a later issue.

Create pieces for the wood interior sides from the styrene grooved every .040 inch. The walls are 9'8" tall. Each segment will be 16'8" long but can be less. The interior of the car can be shorter than the car length and not be noticeable. The wood of the interior sides runs horizontally.

Dry fit the pieces, and trim to fit. The interior sides will need to precisely match the edge of the door opening. Use care in measuring the height of the interior wall pieces, because the bottom edge of the side pieces will serve as a seat for the floor. Assure that the interior side walls match the lower edge of the door opening.

Cut end pieces of the same height as the walls. The wood of the interior end pieces generally was placed vertically but could be horizontal. Fit the wood pieces into the ends between the side segments, and trim to a snug fit. You have now prepared the required parts of the interior — a simple enough job.

Creating Wood Appearance

One needs to create marks in the styrene to cause the eye to see wood grain. This is easily produced by scoring the face of the scribed side with coarse sandpaper of 40 or 50 grit.

If you want to make absolutely clear that this is wood, you can score the boards individually with a sharp hobby knife. However, grain this pronounced is not representative of what one would see when viewing a prototype box car from the same proportional distance. You will likely find that scoring with coarse sandpaper alone is the best.

The finishing of styrene to look like wood is a three-stage process: The first is building a base for application of a wood-like

finish. Second is the finish. Third is the creation of varying degrees of aging or distressing.

The following techniques for creating the appearance of wood on styrene were adapted from Gould's instructions for simulating wood on its 40-foot flat car kit, now produced by Tichy. Through some modifications, the same basic technique works on Evergreen styrene.

Since the Tichy model begins with a deck molded in gray plastic, and Evergreen styrene is white, some modifications are required. First, overspray with gray, such as Floquil gray primer. Then spray with a red. Finally, lightly overspray with Floquil Foundation or Tamiya Buff.

Use medium sandpaper to create breaks in the paint and grooves for the washes you will use next. Use a lighter hand here than when creating grain to prevent flaking the paint. Take the paint down to the point where a slight amount of gray and red begin to show, but don't overdo it.

Now create the wood appearance. After experimentation, I chose Pactra's Acrylic Enamel Flat African Yellow to give the appearance of wood. "Flat African Yellow," you say. That's right. It's closer to tan than the name implies. It has a slight yellow/red tint common in fresh lumber.

Create a wash by diluting heavily. You will want to experiment. The process of finishing is not easily reversed, so use of a very dilute wash will assure that you can observe and modify the wash between succeeding applications. In fact, if you want a bit more red color, then add a few drops of Tamiya's flat red. If you want a faded look, add some light tan.

Begin by applying the wash unequally to the boards. Try to create a difference in the tone of each board by more applications on one and less on another. With a stepwise application of a dilute wash, you will find the styrene approaching the look of a wood that was used but not bleached by sun or water.

Add further variation in the wood. Use the Tamiya or Pactra flat black, and create wash again. Apply this wash to individual boards as you did with the African Yellow. The purpose here is simply to highlight the grain, vary the darkness of the boards and accentuate the joints of the boards.

A dusting of artist's pastel chalks (reduced to powder, by rubbing them over fine-grit sandpaper) will give the wood the look of dirt acquired over years of use. With a hobby knife, scrape a dark brown or gray pastel dust onto the wood. Spread it around with your fingers. The grain will begin to stand out, and the wood will acquire a rough appearance.

Apply additional pastel dust to the floor center line, (near the doors) to simulate the appearance of heavy use. Create the appearance of spills, tire marks and dirty shoes on the floor, you can paint the bottom of the floor flat black or simulate wood and add streaks of weathered black above the wheels.

Finish the exterior of the car before assembly, including painting. By now you will have done your upgrade of the car exterior. Take the car shell to the paint shop. Paint and decal for the road you want.

An interesting idea is to letter the two sides of the car for different railroads. Purists may shun this idea, but it has a long history. It was used in the 1939 New York World's Fair. The designers of that model railroad layout used this technique to provide variety when the same train came back in the opposite direction. Whether you have a layout with a return loop or not, the technique creates a greater multiplicity of car lettering.

Complete your overspray to protect the decals, and give the desired level of weathering to the car surface before proceeding with assembly.

Assembly of the Car

The parts of the box car interior are ready for assembly.

Dry fit the walls and ends, followed by the floor. Check to see that the floor fits snugly into the Athearn or MDC shell and seats on the bottom of the wall segments. The floor top should match the bottom of the door opening, and the bottom should touch the underframe, if you adding stringers.

You will have to forfeit the Athearn or MDC weight. The car ends now are the most logical place to hide weights. Attach 2-3 ounces of weight onto the inside of the ends of the plastic shell. A-Line weights will do nicely. The weights will be obscured by the addition of the interior end pieces.

Start the interior assembly with the walls. Match these to the door opening, assuring that they are also parallel to the car bottom. The walls should be flush with the door bottom. When satisfied, secure with hobby-type cyanoacrylate cement (CA).

Add the interior ends. They will conceal the weights added into the ends of the shell and brace the side walls. Attach them with CA also.

Add the floor, checking for the important match between it and the lower edge of the door opening. Secure it with a few touches of CA or solvent, so it doesn't move when the car is put in use.

Add the underbody frame and detailing. When satisfied, use a touch of solvent at the junction of each crossbearer and the body shell to secure the floor. The car is ready to accept couplers, trucks and air hoses.

Using pastels, touch up the areas of the floor that would have received the most traffic. The door entrance and centerline of the floor are the obvious targets. Add some bits of fresh wood and thin black draftsman tape to simulate the debris from broken crates and tie-downs and metal straps.

Just like modeling cars of different heights and lengths, the inclusion of a few box cars with open doors brings variety to a model railroad layout. Whether you intend to put the car on your pike as a stationary piece or run it on your branchlines, as I do, you'll find you just perked up your layout. **RMJ**

UPGRADING

Athearn or MDC 40-foot Box Car Underframes

The Visible Details

Athearn uses this same underframe beneath all its HO scale 40-foot box cars (and reefers). Here's how to add the details that are visible on the prototype when seen from the side (not the bottom). There's more information, on upgrading the exterior of Athearn (and MDC) box cars and on installing interior details, in the January 1991 issue.

Martin Loftin

Here's an option by which you can add that ultimate touch of underbody detailing: the stringers, diagonal braces, spacers and air line. Refer to the accompanying diagram that identifies these elements of the underframe.

Stringers are longitudinal supports between the floor and crossbearers of the steel underframe. They run the distance between the body bolsters. Most 40-foot steel boxcars used four stringers of Z-shaped steel, though some used two. Stringers were spaced equidistant between the center sill and side of the car. The stringers can be simulated with scale 1x2-inch styrene strip placed across the crossbearers from one body bolster to the other.

On a steam era 40-foot box car underframe, diagonal braces ran from the pivot point of the trucks to the corners of the car. These braces generally were constructed of flat steel strip of 4- to 6-inch width. The strip

Replace the Athearn floor with a sheet of scribed Evergreen Scale Models .020-inch-thick styrene (as shown in the January 1991 issue) if you want to simulate the car's wooden flooring.

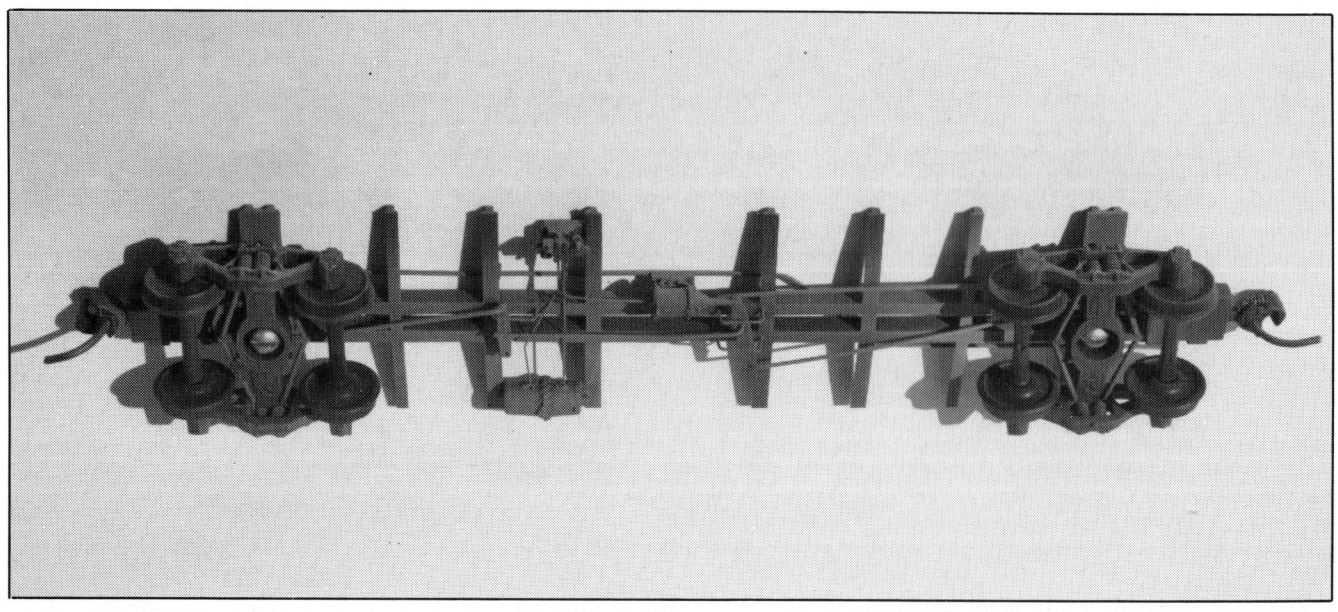

All of these added lines are visible when you look at a model box car (or reefer). It only takes a few hours to add them.

would have a shape, such as a shallow hat section, stamped in it for rigidity. These diagonals can be simulated with scale 1x4-inch styrene strip.

Also, wood was applied between the floor and underframe above the two beams of the center sill. Similarly, wood was applied between the body bolsters and the floor. These wood pieces are best simulated with more 1x2-inch Evergreen styrene strip.

An air line transports the air from car to car. It runs the length of the car between the floor and the underframe. However, it crosses the centerline of the car near the middle of the car in an elongated "S" shape. The line runs close to the center sill, at approximately the width of the Athearn or MDC coupler box. The air line will reach the end of the car at the point where you'll be adding the air hoses — to the right of the coupler as you face the end. Simulate the air line with .020-inch plastic rod or .016-inch brass wire.

Follow these steps to add the detailing to the underframe:

1. Add the air line. Secure it to the underframe with solvent or hobby-type cyanoacrylate cement.
2. Add stringers to the car underframe. Place them on top — between frame and floor — of the underframe.
3. Add the diagonal braces.
4. Add the wood spacers on the center sill and body bolsters. Leave notches or spaces where the air line travels.

Completing the Underbody

You will have a highly detailed boxcar when finished. In fact, the bottom of the floor of the car will have the appearance of wood. So, you will want to create a similar level of detail on the underbody.

If you will not be using the Athearn trucks, clip off the pins at the bolsters and smooth to accept Kadee, Cape Line, Tichy or other improved trucks.

The basic requirement to complement your highly detailed car is a brake set of independent parts. However, there is more to an underbody than better brake parts. If you plan to include the stringers, diagonal braces and air line, proceed as described above. If not, proceed to construction of the new brake system.

Remove the cast-on brake parts, and build a brake system of individual parts onto the Athearn or MDC frame. Use the Cal-Scale instructions or refer to car drawings for the layout of the major brake parts. Join the parts with air lines. Slater's and Grandt Line's .010-inch plastic rod will suffice for this. Straight brass grabirons will provide brake lever hangers, and a 14-inch piece of scale 2x2-inch styrene strip will provide a pivot point. Use brass wire of about .0125-inch diameter for the brake rods.

Your basic underframe construction is complete. Paint the frame with its brake system and air line black.

One final touch is interesting. If you have seen an overturned car, you probably have noticed longitudinal marks on the bottom of the floor above the wheels. When the rails are damp the moving wheels kick up soil and ballast dust from the rail onto the bottom of the floor, just like auto tires. This is a cake of gray limestone and dirt mixture. Simulate the effect with four parallel lines of heavy wash with a gray tone on the bottom of the floor above the wheels, decreasing in intensity the further from the wheels.

Test fit the frame to the floor. The floor will match the bottom of the door opening. Do not attach the floor and frame yet.

Prepare two sets of Cal-Scale air hoses by placing the air hoses in their brackets. You'll add them later, as a final step. **RMJ**

Most photographs of prototype box cars are taken from a low enough angle so at least some of the brake lines and components are visible. These are the features you may want to duplicate on your models. — Photo from the collection of Howard Ameling.

Ed. Note: *This model is similar to the one-piece C&BT Shops kits with 4/4 improved Dreadnaught ends like the prototypes shown in the October and November 1989 issues. The Athearn and MDC cars are based on somewhat earlier prototypes.*

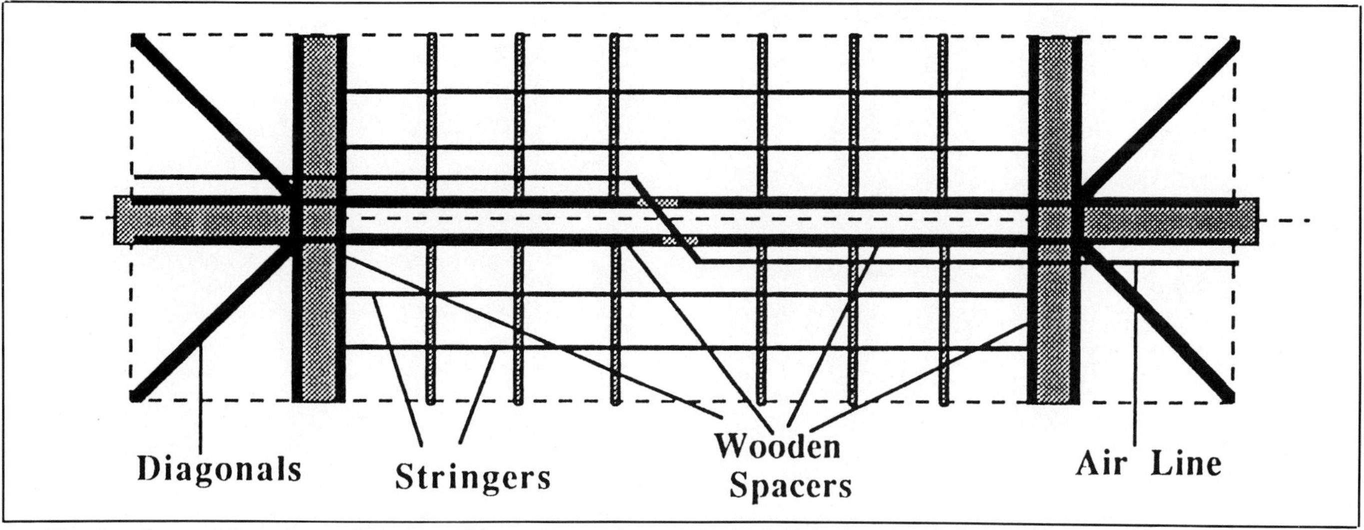

The locations of the wire and styrene strip components on a typical 40-foot car underframe. Not to scale.

Upgrading . . .

HO, N or O Scale Freight Car Kits With Etched Metal Roofwalks

The roof is the first part of most models to be seen, so that's the place to begin adding details to upgrade any model freight car.

■ SKILL LEVEL

The **wrong** way to do it: The top car has an unweathered plastic roofwalk. The bottom car has one of the more realistic etched metal roofwalks, but too much cement was used in installing it, so the "see-through" effect has disappeared at each roof rib.

The top car has an etched brass roofwalk from Detail Associates with none of the open rectangles filled with glue. The bottom car has a weathered plastic roofwalk, but only a random few of the holes have been filled in with black paint.

To replace a plastic roofwalk, first remove the roofwalk itself. Cut the mounting pins from the bottom of the roofwalk (or use the pins in Detail Associates roofwalk kits), and cement them into their original holes. When the cement sets, file the plug to match the shape of the roof.

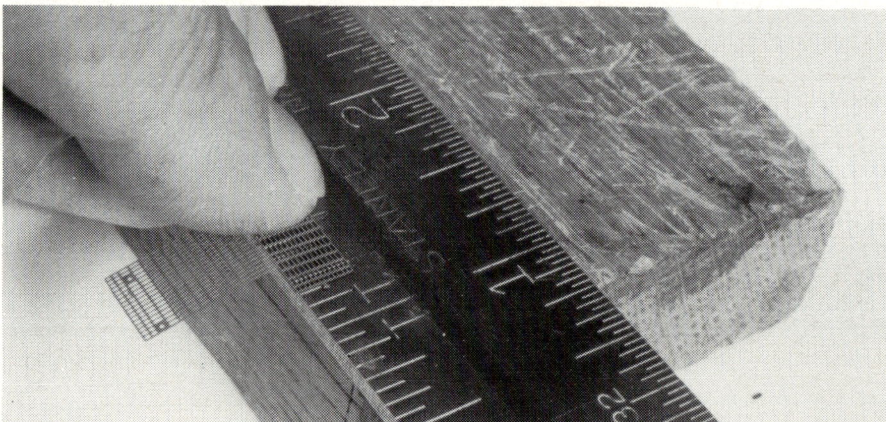

Gently bend the end walks over the edge of a steel ruler to match the slope of the roof.

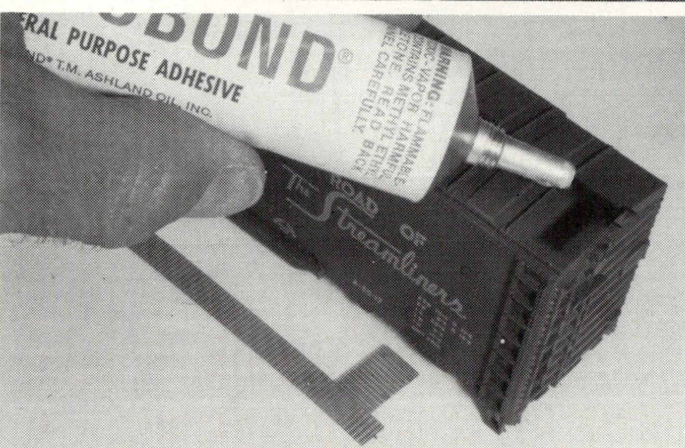

Use Goodyear Pliobond or Walthers Goo to install the etched metal roofwalk. Run a **thin** bead of the glue across each roof rib where it will contact the etched metal roofwalk.

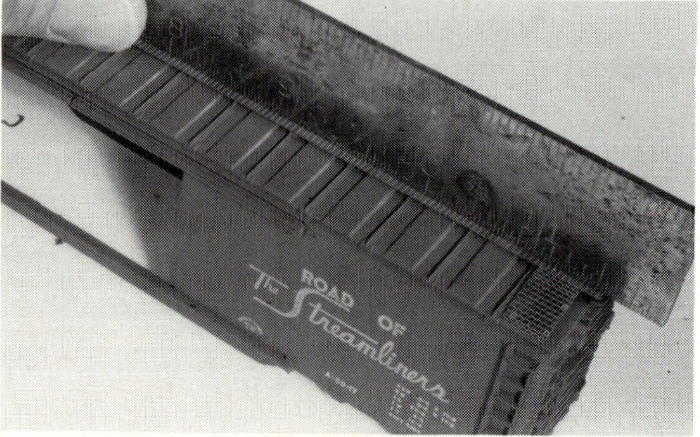

Use that steel ruler to hold the roofwalk flush with the roof until the cement sets. If you have one of these ⅛-inch-thick rulers, it will balance in place on the roofwalk.

Bill Wright

Steel roofwalks provided a much needed anti-slip advantage over the traditional wooden roofwalks on freight cars. A wooden roofwalk, whether it had much of the paint peeled and missing to reveal raw wood or was freshly painted, was as slick as ice when it got wet. The expanded or punched metal roofwalks provided a better grip for brakemen's shoes in the rain, and the open design prevented the formation of most ice.

Modelers seem to feel that the wooden roofwalk is a relatively modern device, an opinion fostered by the inclusion of simulated wooden roofwalks in most of the popular Athearn and MDC plastic box cars and reefers. The real railroads, however, were abandoning the wooden roofwalk by 1940, and by the end of World War II, they had virtually vanished from new cars and any cars rebuilt after that time. If you are modeling any era from about 1945 on, then only a small proportion of your rolling stock (half or less of models of prototypes built prior to 1941) should have wooden roofwalks.

Athearn and MDC do provide simulated metal roofwalks in some kits, particularly the 50-foot plug-door-style cars. These types of plastic roofwalks are also included in most covered hopper kits from these firms, as well as kits from Eastern Car Works, C&BT Shops, McKean and Walthers. If you sand down the overscale thickness of the plastic, then fill in the rectangles with thinned black paint, these roofwalks can capture some of the appearance of the open-grid on the real cars.

One of the most obvious features of the metal roofwalks on real railroad cars, however, is that you can see right through them to the car roof below. Some kits, such as the Eastern Car Works, McKean and Walthers covered hoppers, do have openings right through the plastic, but the webs are so thick that the "see-through" effect of the prototype is lost from any viewing angle but directly overhead. The only way a modeler can duplicate that "see-through" appearance is to install one of the etched metal roofwalks, produced in HO scale by Detail Associates and Overland Models, in O scale by Des Plaines Hobby, P&D Hobby, Precision Scale, and Locomotive Workshop, and in N scale by Plano Model Products (2701 W. 15th St., Suite 113, Plano, TX 75075) and J N J Trains, PO Box 1535, Ottumwa, IA 52507.

Drill no. 78 holes for the corner grabirons and eyebolts in the Detail Associates or Overland kits. On some Overland roofwalks, the grabirons and support brackets are already soldered in place. Overland offers this style for most types of HO scale covered hoppers as well as box cars.

We are also attempting to identify what type of roofwalk each prototype car used, since there are variations in the style of the metal roofwalks; some have rectangular openings, some have round openings, and others have diamond-shaped openings. The style with rectangular openings is available in HO, O and N scales from all of the roofwalk suppliers. So far, however, only Overland offers alternate styles and only in HO scale. The series of articles on 40-foot box cars by Ed Hawkins, Pat Wider and Ray Long that has appeared in **Railmodel Journal** and is reprinted in **Modeling Freight Cars, Volume II, The Box Cars** includes specific roofwalk styles, and that trio's series of articles on the 34-foot ACF-built covered hoppers also includes roofwalk identification. We'll have more in future issues of **Railmodel Journal** on identifying specific roofwalk styles and **on** which specific cars were fitted with which roofwalks, wherever possible. **RMJ**

How YOU can do it BETTER:

Assembling Cast Resin Kits

Learn how one of the designers and manufacturers of cast resin kits assembles his own products. The techniques of course, apply to any kit made of resin, regardless of manufacturer.

Martin Lofton

Two recent trends in model railroading have coincided to encourage the modeling of prototypically correct freight cars. The first is an increasing interest in modeling faithfully a specific prototype car, and the second is the development of cast car parts. Interest in prototype accuracy in freight cars has created demand for kits of cars that cannot be mass-produced. The existence of casting technology, in turn, has reinforced the interest in prototype fidelity. The result of these two trends is a proliferation of short-run kits of cars which would not otherwise reach the marketplace.

The modest market demand for unique freight cars does not warrant the expenditure of money to build the tools for plastic injection-molded cars, such as those by Athearn, MDC and Walthers models. The investment in tooling runs into the several tens of thousands of dollars, even with the new technologies in injection-molding. The investment in the "tooling" for cast kits is only a fraction of the amount of injection-modeled kits.

The Bx-33 is similar to the Bx-36, but with recessed ends and the famous curved map used by the Santa Fe during the mid-point of the rebuilding of USRA double-sheathed box cars.

Injection-Molded Kits

In the injection-molding process, a "negative" of a part is cut into a metal tool or mold. In the cast kit process, silicone rubber captures the features of a master — or positive — of the part. The cost of executing cast kits, however, is substantially greater than the production of large numbers of injection-molded kits, because considerably more hand labor is required in the production process. In sum, the casting technology is well suited to the production of short runs — a few hundred to a thousand or two — of unique cars with modest market appeal. The injection-molding process is ideal for the mass market.

Cast Resin Kits

The rubber mold process has another set of advantages and disadvantages. Rubber molds accurately capture parts details. However, the casting process has been largely limited to creation of parts with flat backs,

The Bx-36 with "Buy War Bonds" decals, created from Sunshine Models kit 9.7.

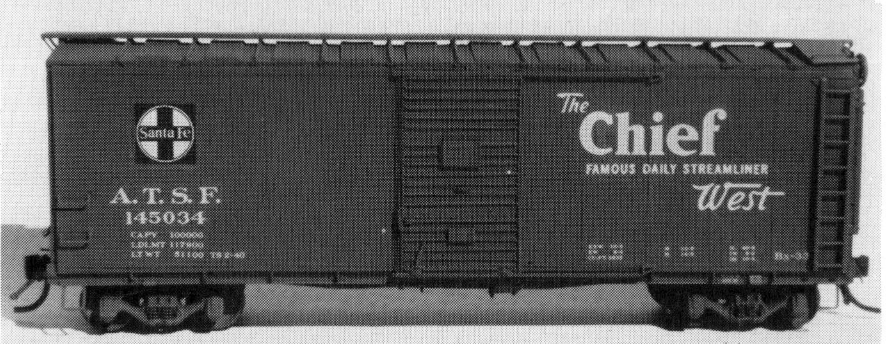

On the opposite side from the famous Santa Fe maps was a slogan about the road's streamliners. The maps and slogans varied by car numbers and dates of rebuilding, as described in the Sunshine Models discussion of the prototype.

The end of a Bx-33 is typical of the Sunshine Models Santa Fe rebuilds.

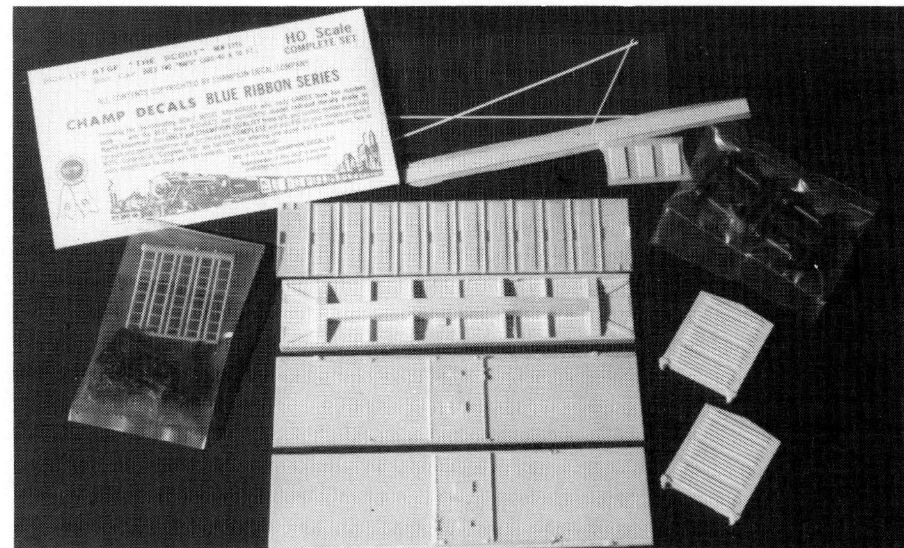

Sunshine Models no. 9.7, a kit for the ATSF Bx-36, includes the major castings — roof, sides, ends, underbody — and detailing parts and decals. Trucks may be ordered separately. This is typical of the contents of cast kits.

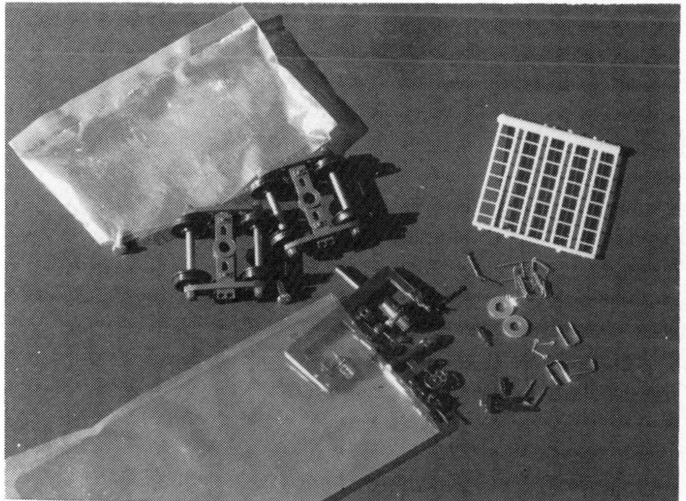

Detailing parts in the Bx-36 kit include brake system parts, ladders, stirrups, grabirons, washers, air hoses and brackets. Trucks which match the prototype will be added by Sunshine Models at the modeler's request.

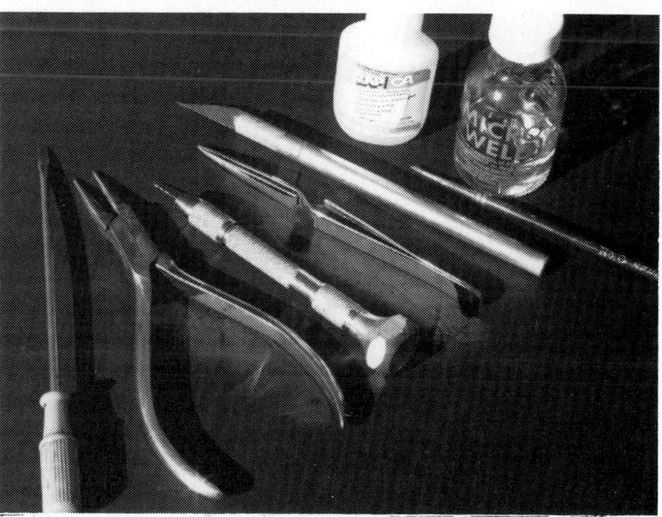

The tools required to build the Sunshine kit are modest. Powered tools, such as a power drill, speed the process but are not essential.

such as the side of a box car. Parts with severe undercuts — or the full carbody, typical of the plastic kits — are difficult in the casting process.

Cast kits differ from plastic injection molded kits in another important respect. The cast kit is, in fact, a kit, not the packaged, pre-painted model typical of injection-molded "kits." Thus, the cast kit largely appeals to the modeler who has both an interest in prototypical accuracy and model building.

A cast kit is in most respects a reproduction of some individual's scratchbuilt model. The master maker for a cast kit is executing his model in parts which may be reproduced by the casting process. The cast kit, then, makes available to the modeling public the scratchbuilt cars of some skilled individual. The modeler can create a distinctive model without much of the time and pain of scratchbuilding. This is the essential value of the cast kits.

Cast kit manufacturers provide the modeler with the major components of the car in the form of castings, as the name implies. The kits typically contain additional detailing parts from the casting process or from commercial parts makers. In most cases, decals — proprietary to the kit — are included. And detailed instructions, including a prototype history, are part of the cast car kit. Construction, then, is the operative word in cast kits, while assembly is the appropriate description of most of the familiar pre-packaged and lettered plastic car kits.

The construction of a sample car will describe the process of constructing the cast kit. A useful example is a kit from Sunshine Models. The kit of the Santa Fe Bx-36 steel rebuild of the USRA double-sheathed 40-foot box car is one of the easier kits to build and is used here.

Santa Fe Prototypes

As is typical of this type of kit, considerable time is spent in the instructions discussing the prototype history of the car. The purpose is not just to contribute to the modeler's knowledge about the prototype but to establish the variations in design and lettering, use of the car in service, longevity, etc. These facts are essential to proper construction and operation of the car.

"The Santa Fe had the largest number of steel side rebuilds of USRA double-sheathed box cars. Some 2,608 rebuilds were on the roster in 1948 in five classes of cars — Bx-28, 31, 32, 33 and 36. The Santa Fe rebuilds lasted for many years after their construction at Topeka in the late '30s and early '40s. Some can be found in company service even today.

"The Santa Fe rebuilt their Bx-2 box cars to a design which is similar to the 1937 AAR design. To increase the car height, the original 5/5/5 Murphy ends received two additional ribs at the top to create a 2/5/5/5 pattern. All cars got Murphy paneled roofs, 10-section sides, trapezoidal side sill brackets and Youngstown ribbed doors. The cars retained their fishbelly underframes.

"The last three classes of Santa Fe rebuilds were 10′ 4″ IH, while the first two were 10′ IH. This kit enables you to build

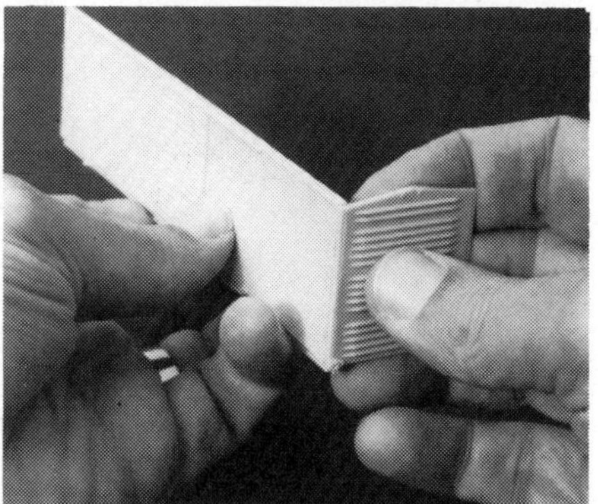

Construction begins with the assembly of the major castings. An end and side are attached with cyanoacrylate (CA).

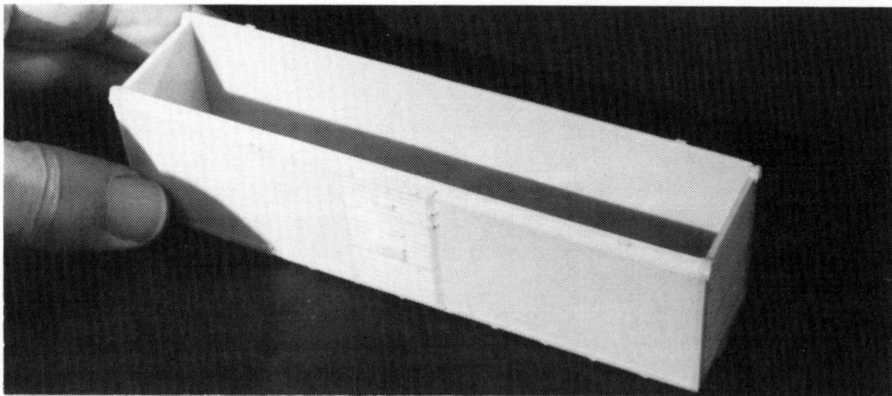

The assembly of major castings creates a box outlining the carbody.

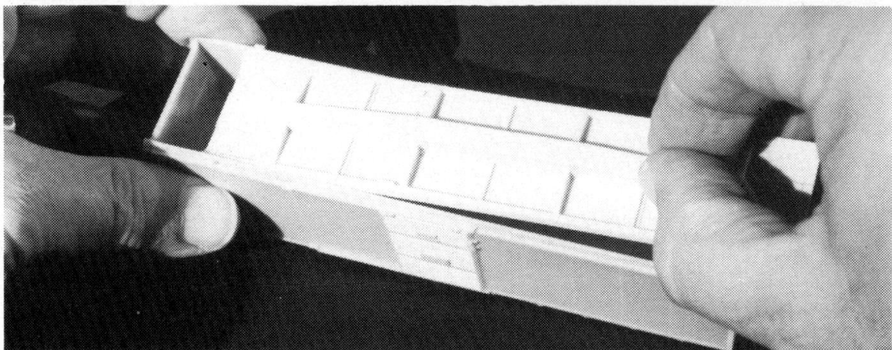

A one-piece underbody casting is sanded to a tight fit within the box formed by the sides and ends.

Before securing the underbody casting to the body, the modeler creates a similar sized piece from .040-inch styrene sheet included in the kit. To this he adds a ridge pole. This assembly creates upper body strength and provides a base for the roof.

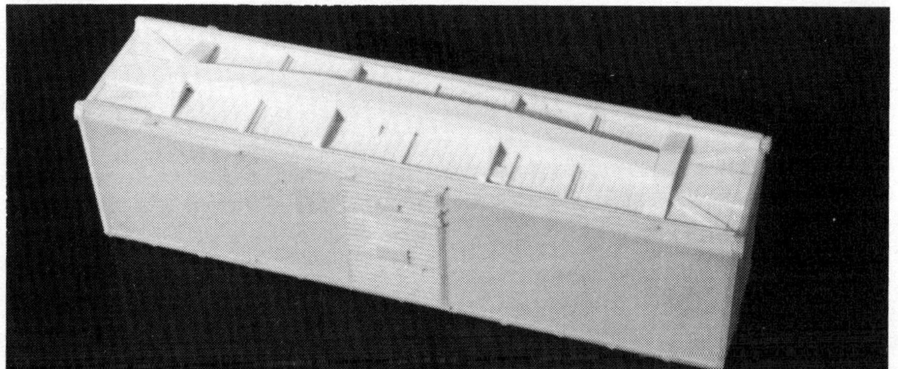

the taller cars. The 10′ IH cars were largely indistinguishable from a distance. There is more space around the two ribs added to the ends and in the area where the sections of the doors are joined. In addition to the above characteristics, the Bx-36 had full-width ends and no corner notch. This made the Bx-36 unique among double-sheathed rebuilds — along with the Wabash 10′ 4″ IH cars.

"The Bx-33 was a 50-ton car. It was equipped with 'Bettendorf' cast steel sideframe trucks. The Bx-32 and 36 were 40 tons with Andrews trucks.

"The Santa Fe rebuilds of USRA double-sheathed cars are important not only for their reconstruction of older cars — a common practice on the Santa Fe — but because the later rebuilding took place during the development of the famous map paint scheme. The rebuilds became a test bed for the map designs.

"When the first rebuilt cars came off the line, the famous map emblem was not used. The Bx-28, Bx-31 and their first few Bx-32s received a simple "Santa Fe" box herald on the left side, a scheme associated for years with ATSF box car lettering.

"In January 1940 the Santa Fe began to design and apply the famous map scheme to box cars and reefers. From then until 1941, the road experimented with various styles of maps, finally settling on a straight line map with the 'Ship Santa Fe all the way' logo.

"The Bx-32 rebuildings were completed in early 1940. Beginning with car 148034, the class received the rare curved map, classified as style number two of map heralds by the historians. These cars were one of only three series of box cars to receive this distinction. The only new cars to receive the curved map were the early segment of the Bx-34s from Pullman.

"By the time of construction of the Bx-33 cars, the first straight map herald without the word 'ship' in the logo was being used. We have learned, however, from an enclosed Howard Ameling photo that the first few Bx-33s got the curved map. Car 145036 sported the curved map, but we don't know how deeply into the numbers the curved map went.

"The Bx-36 cars received the straight map herald, style number 4. The two straight map styles — numbers three and four — are distinguished by the addition of the word 'ship' in script before 'Santa Fe' on style number four. It became the Santa Fe standard for seven years.

"The map was placed on one side only, the 'L' or left side. The right side featured a slogan advertising the Santa Fe's prime passenger trains. An appropriate slogan has been included with each kit decal set.

"When the map design was dropped in 1947, the rebuilds began to appear with 'ship

The underbody is attached to the box formed by the sides and ends with CA. This process squares the carbody and adds strength.

and travel Santa Fe all the way' slogans as they returned for repairing. However, the map paint lasted for many years.

"The Bx-36 was unique in another respect. Some 368 of the cars were chosen by the Santa Fe to receive the logo 'Buy War Bonds' in 1942-43. This period-specific lettering lasted at least into the early 1950s when they were spotted and probably lasted into the mid-1950s before all cars were repainted."

Assembly

The cast parts are best attached with hobby-type cyanoacrylate cement (CA). It is a strong adhesive and dries quickly. However, it can easily attach a part where it is not supposed to be, including your fingers. Be careful. Place a few drops of CA on a plate of glass, and use a wire to transfer small amounts to the areas to be joined. Wear safety glasses.

1. — The first step is to join the sides and ends. First, wash the castings in warm water and soap. Clean the flash from edges.

Creation of a "square" box is a critical step in a top quality model. Sight and "square-up" the box as you proceed. The alignment between the sides and ends at the top of the car is the most critical. Dry-fit the sides and ends to assure this alignment.

Flow CA onto the edge of one side and add an end. Before the CA sets up, place the two pieces against a square to assure a 90-degree angle. Continue around the perimeter of the car until you have created a box.

2. — *Dry*-fit the floor. Sand the length to fit. If you need increased width, shim with styrene strip. Develop a *snug* fit. Do not attach until later.

3. — Cut and sand the piece of .040-inch styrene sheet until it fits snugly into the top of the car. Cut the cast ridge pole to the inside length of the car or less. Dry-fit the subroof and ridge pole. When satisfied that the parts create a support for the roof and assure straight sides, attach with CA, beginning at each end. Sight down the ridge pole to assure no sag or bulge. Now secure the subroof in the center of the car.

4. — The cars need about 2 ounces of weight if using plastic trucks and 1 ounce if using metal trucks. Slide the floor into place, aligning the coupler pad with the bottom of the ends. Attach with CA.

5. — The roof is cast in one piece to assure matching ribs, and it must be divided. Using a sharp X-acto knife, score the roof down the center line. Bend the roof to conform to the roof line of the ends. Recheck the fit and make any modifications necessary. Attach with CA, starting at one end and moving along the car on each side.

6. — Temporarily mount the trucks. Measure a point on the body bolster equidistant between the sides; don't guess.

Detailing

7. — Add the ladders. The ladders stood about 1 inch from the carbody and were held by unique brackets. Refer to diagram no. 1 and photos:

a.—Cut 10 pieces of .010x.040-inch styrene strip to 8 scale inches in length and trim to a trapezoid.

b.—Cut four 6-inch trapezoids from the .010x.040-inch strip.

c.—Cut the two end ladders to six rungs.

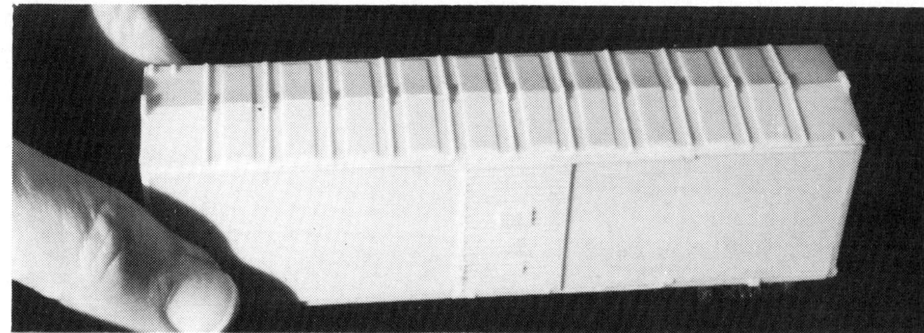

The carbody is completed by scoring the roof casting down the middle and fitting it over the ridge pole. The roof is secured with CA around the boundary.

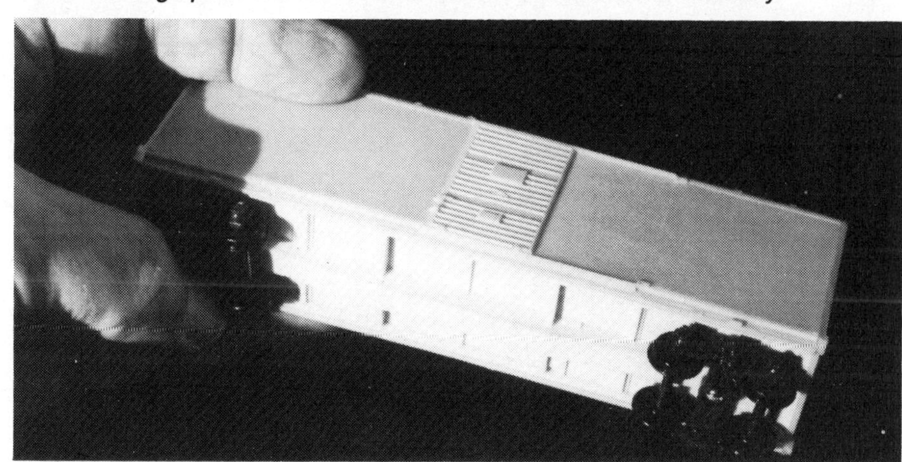

The underbody is prepared for trucks and the trucks test-fitted.

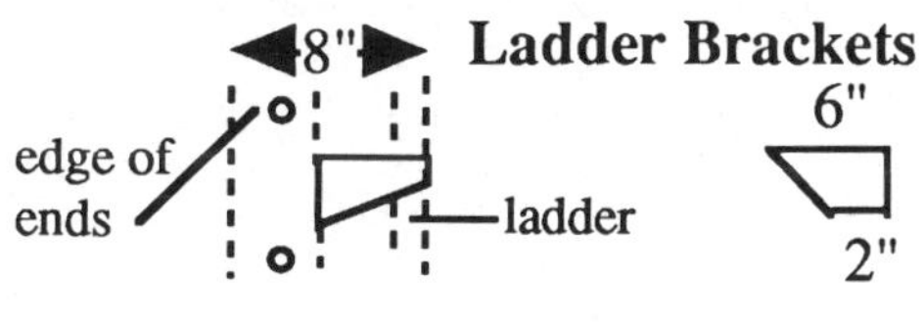

Diagram 1

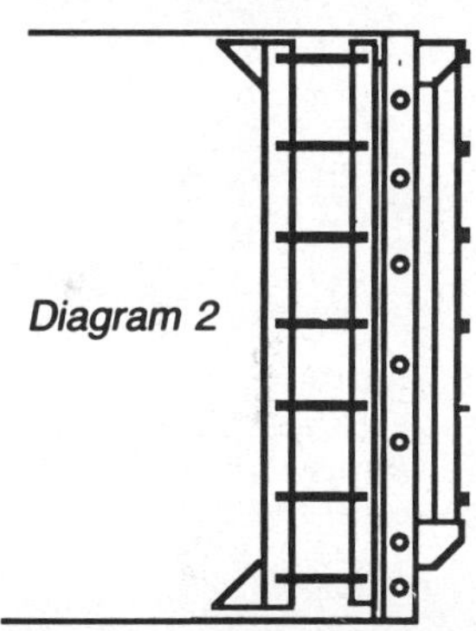

Diagram 2

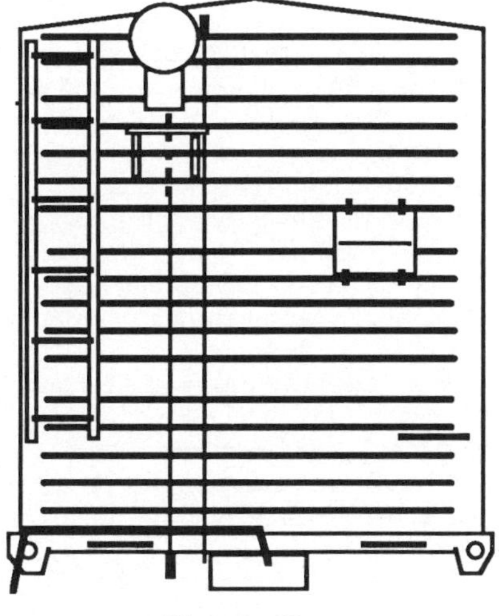

Diagram 3

The "B" end of the carbody is detailed, according to Diagram 3, using the parts included with the kit — ladders, power hand brakes, steps, vent and vent line, actuating rod, couplers, air hoses, cut lever, etc.

Diagram 5.

Viewed from below

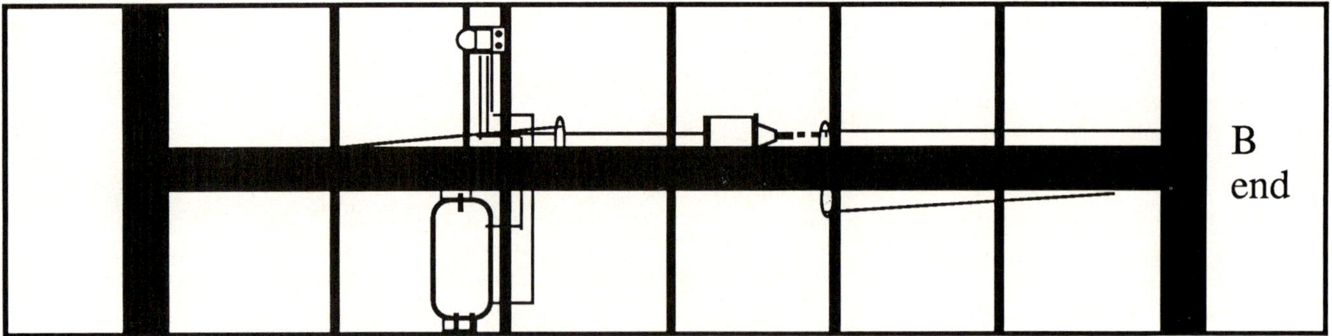

Cut four diagonal corner braces from .010 x .040-inch styrene for the lower sills of the ends.

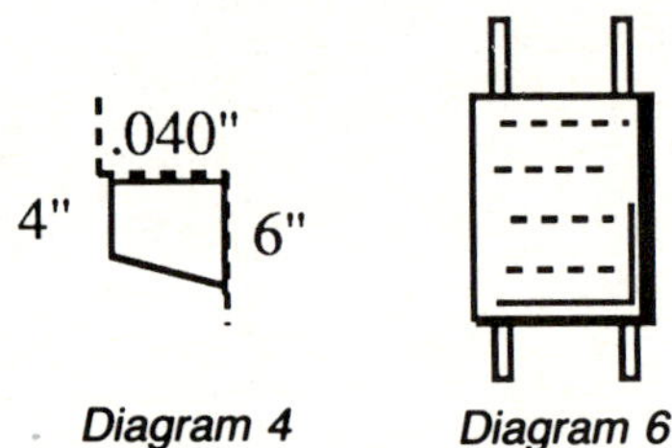

Diagram 4

Diagram 6

Ladders are commercially available plastic ones, attached with brackets shown in diagram 1 with rungs aligned according to diagram 2.

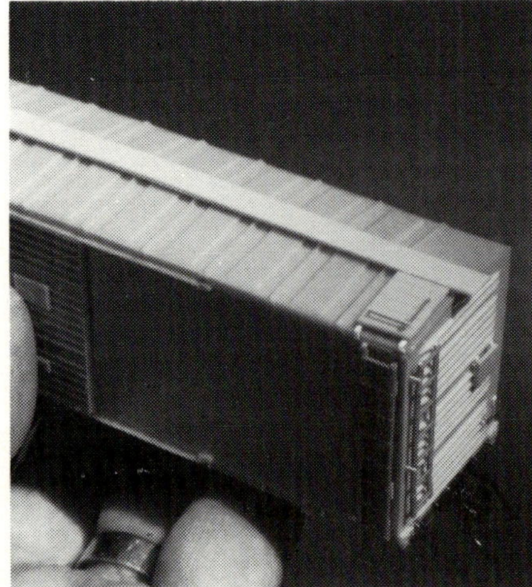

Corner walk and running boards are added. In the case of the Bx-36, during much of the late steam and early diesel era, the roof would be painted black and mineral red running boards added later. Assemble the corner walks according to diagram 6.

d.—Add the extra rung to the side ladders, making them eight rungs in height.

e.—Attach the 8-inch brackets into the corner cap or notch — three for the side ladder and two for the end ladder. (For the Bx-36, which had no corner cap in which to insert brackets, shorten the brackets and mount on the face of the sides and ends.)

f.—Add the 6-inch brackets to the side at the top and bottom of the sides. These pieces mount flush on the sides of the car, partially under the side ladders. See diagram no. 2

g.—Mount the ladders with solvent.

8. — Add grabirons. See the end diagram, no. 3:

a.—Place a tab of .010x.040-inch strip to the right of the fourth rib from the bottom of each end.

b.—Add a grab in the fourth rib and tab.

c.—Add grabs in the end sill on either side of the coupler.

d.—Mount two eyebolts for top-mounted cut levers.

e.—Add two grabs on the left of each side, 2 and 4 scale feet from the bottom.

9. — Add trapezoidal side sill brackets under each junction of the side sections.

a.—Cut 16 6-inch lengths of .010x.040-inch styrene. Trim one corner at a 30-degree angle. See diagram no. 4

b.—Add short brackets under door guide.

10. — Add the Type A stirrups. Drill .020-inch holes in the bottom edge of the side casting. Bend the stirrups outward by 30 degrees before mounting.

11. — All ATSF cars used AB brake systems with Ajax power hand brakes. The ATSF used perpendicularly mounted air reservoirs. Refer to diagram no. 5. Remove the trucks and finish the underbody brake system:

a.—Add the three major AB brake parts according to the diagram.

b.—Add three 4-inch strips of scale 2x2 to the side of the center sill to accept the brake levers.

c.—Cut the brake levers to 6-inch stubs and add above the 2x2s with solvent.

d.—Use .010-inch plastic rod for air lines.

e.—Use .015-inch brass wire for rods.

f.—Add the couplers and air hoses.

g.—Replace the trucks.

12. — Detail the ends using diagram no. 3. The careful modeler will notice that the modeler in our example made a simple, but important mistake in haste. Notice that the brake details have been added to the "A" end of the car, not the "B" end. Don't let this happen to you. Follow the instructions!

a.—Select the "A" end of the car. Add the power hand brake between the first and second rib from the top.

b.—Add the brake vent to the right.

c.—Add the brake step on the fourth rib from the top.

d.—Add the bellcrank in the bottom edge of the end casting, directly under the power hand brake.

e.—Run .010-inch plastic rod from the brake vent to under the end next to the coupler.

f.—Run brass wire from the end of the power hand brake chain to the bellcrank.

g.—Add the brake wheel.

h.—Add end tack boards.

i.—Add diagonal braces under the brake step using .010x.030-inch styrene.

j.—Add top-mounted cut levers.

13. — All ATSF rebuilds used an anti-skid material on the roof that was black but contained granular material which gave it a flat, rough and dark look. Wash the car and paint the roof.

14. — Add the roofwalk and corner walks:

a.—Create 90-degree corner grabs in each corner walk from brass wire and eyebolts. The corner grabs are 19 inches on a side. Insert into the corner walks, and secure with CA.

b.—Smooth the back of the corner walk.

c.—Add two lengths of .010x.030-inch strip under each corner walk. See diagram no. 6.

Painting and Lettering

15. — Before painting:

a.—Cut four 24-inch diagonal braces of .010x.030-inch styrene strip.

b.—Use doubled-over household tape to place the roofwalk and corner walk and styrene strip on a painting board.

c.—The ATSF painted the entire car "mineral brown," which is closer to a true brown than most roads' box car red. The trucks were this color, also. In Floquil colors this means a 50/50 mix of Box Car Red and Rail Brown.

16. — Wash the car thoroughly with dishwashing liquid and a toothbrush. Let dry. Mask the roof and paint the car, roofwalks, corner walks, strip of styrene and the metal trucks, if purchased.

17. — Mount the roofwalk and corner walks. Add diagonals under the roofwalk ends.

18. — Correct Champ decals have been included in the kit. Decal using the photos and Table 1. Before using the decals, read the Champ notices carefully.

The map decal goes on the side opposite the power hand brake, the slogan on the same side as the power hand brake.

A small "L" goes to the left of the door by the handle on the map side, the "R" on the other side. When the cars were repainted after 1947 — which could be years later — the map was replaced with "Ship and travel Santa Fe all the way," and modelers may wish to post-date the model with these decals.

The Bx-36 was an 80,000-pound car, using Andrew trucks. The dimensional data in the set is abundant. Use the data that features 10′ 4″ IH and 3837 cubic feet capacity.

The "Buy War Bonds" decals, proprietary to the kit, are added to the left of the door on both sides of the car. The lettering is centered in the space of the left two panels — centered both vertically and horizontally. Only certain cars were given the "Buy War Bonds" lettering, and those are specified in the kit, courtesy of Richard Hendrickson and the Santa Fe Modelers Organization. The numbers shown in the accompanying photos are authentic ones. Selected other numbers are shown in Table 2.

Finally, you will have enough remaining Champ decals to finish at least one more car.

19. — The plastic trucks, provided as an add-on to the kit, have red sideframes in conformity with ATSF standards. They should be weathered, however, to give them the apporpriate look and blend their color with the car sides. Remount them or other trucks now.

The Bx-36 is a useful example of how to build cast kits. One does, in fact, *build* such a kit. The chief attraction of the cast kits, such as the sample Sunshine kit, is the availability of reliable reproductions of the prototype car in HO scale. The modeler invests perhaps four hours in construction and one more hour in painting and lettering the cars. For this he gets a model that is distinctive from the mass-produced kits. He begins to populate his layout with cars that are as distinctive as the strings of freight cars that were on the railroad he is modeling. **RMJ**

An assembled carbody is sturdy and details are secure using the techniques described in the article. It is ready for the paint shop.

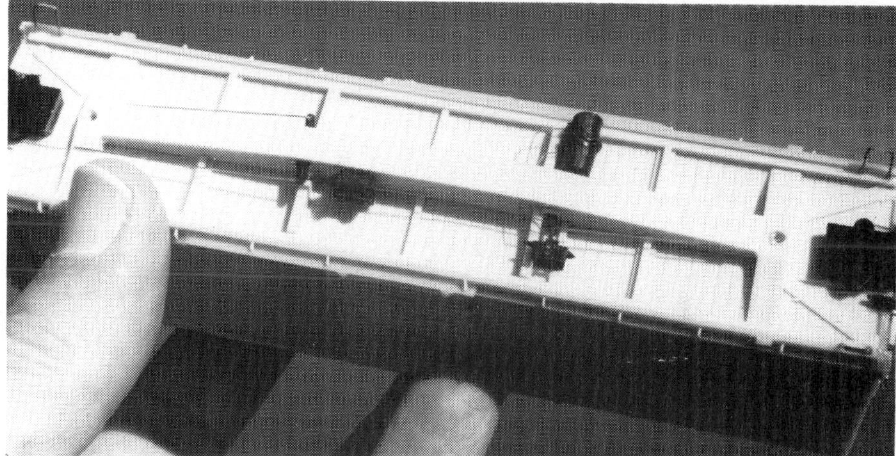

The underbody is detailed using the parts in the kit. In this case, the brake equipment is matched to the Santa Fe layout according to Diagram 5.

Table 1
Slogans Applied to Bx-36 Box Cars

The slogans that appear on ATSF freight cars — on the opposite side from the map — vary by car number. You may be interested to know the assignment of ATSF slogans to the Bx-36 class by car number when the cars were new:

Numbers	Slogans
148400-148549	Scout
148550-148699	El Capitan
148700-148849	Super Chief
148850-148999	Chief
149000-149149	Grand Canyon
149150-149934	(data incomplete)

Of course, the most precise information for lettering your model is a photo of the car during your period of interest. That's how we selected the slogans for each kit.

For this and other information on Santa Fe lettering, see the *Santa Fe Railway Painting and Lettering Guide, Vol. 1, Rolling Stock,* compiled by Richard H. Hendrickson. It is available through the Santa Fe Modelers Organization, Inc.

Table 2
Select Car Numbers Bearing "Buy War Bonds" Slogan

148413	139425	148439	148476	148501	148515
148618	148627	148710	148720	148739	148776
148795	148823	148865	148907	148907	148958
148999	149028	149053	149090	149115	149151
149178	149217	149266	149299	149332	149366
149394	149427	149450	149488	149527	149899

Assembling Etched Brass Kits

You can use the same materials and techniques the Koreans do in assembling imported brass models. The Car Shop, Gloor Craft and Precision Scale have offered etched brass kits for rolling stock in HO scale; N scale of Nevada has an etched brass N scale tank car; and dozens of O scale brass locomotives and cars are offered by Des Plains Hobby, Locomotive Workshop, Central Locomotive, Babbit, Precision Scale and P&D Hobby. Here are some of the methods professional modelers use to assemble brass kits . . . .

Robert Schleicher
Photos and research by Dave Lawler, the Car Shop

SKILL LEVEL

Hardware stores and electronics supply stores (like Allied Radio or Radio Shack) sell small clamps and self-clamping tweezers that can make assembling a brass kit easier. A small square (Walthers sells them) can be used to check that all the corners really are assembled at 90-degree angles.

Three small electronics clamps are being used here to clamp the angle along the bottom of the side while the soldering is accomplished. The clamps are just as useful if you're using five-minute epoxy for assembly rather than solder.

The imported brass model freight cars and diesels are assembled from sheets of brass that have the rivets, window frames and other surface details etched into the surface of the metal. The etching process is simple: The areas that are to stand out are covered with paint, and the brass around them is eaten away with acid. Thus, the surface is etched. Today, brass imports are often etched to as many as three different depths and on both sides of the sheet.

The etching process can produce weld lines, panel seams, rivets, wood grain and similar surface texture details when the brass is only etched part way through. Using sophisticated, multi-level techniques, a bolt head, for example, can be etched in one dip into the acid and the washer around the bolt head etched in the second dip. If the brass is held in the acid bath for long, it will be eaten through, and that is how most windows are created in brass diesel locomotives, in steam locomotive cabs and in cabooses and passenger cars.

Most modelers may not be aware that there are kits available that contain primarily etched brass parts. It is a relatively inexpensive method to produce a kit, since the ''dies'' are merely drawings that are transfered to the brass. Etched brass kits are very common in England but rare in America: at present, only the Car Shop, 2361 Northland Ave., Lakewood, OH 44107, offers etched brass kits of American and Canadian prototype cars, but Gloor Craft, N Scale of Nevada and Precision Scale have offered etched brass kits in the past. A photograph of the parts in the Car Shop's cylindrical covered hopper kit appeared in the November 1991 issue with two examples of the finished kit and its prototype.

If you like to solder, use that method to assemble the etched brass kits. The soldering techniques in the November 1989 and the September 1991 issues of **Railmodel Journal** for assembling trackwork will work as well in assembling any etched brass kit. You can also use thickend hobby-type cyanoacrylate cement with ''kicker'' and/or filler for the corners, or use five-minute epoxy. The completed model will have the same appearance regardless of which of the three techniques you use for assembly.

The Car Shop pre-forms the tricky parts, like shaping the curve for the cylindrical covered hopper (you must tighten the curve into a cylinder, however) and bending the sloped roof center seam in most caboose kits. Each of the parts must be cut from its sprue with a sharp hobby knife or diagonal cutters. Leave just a trace of the waste metal so you can file the edge smooth with a flat jeweler's file. The inside edges of the window and door openings and their frames must also be filed smooth.

The metal in some etched brass kits is covered with a protective layer of laquer to prevent tarnish from forming. Remove that coating with thinner and a rag. Any edges to be soldered or cemented must be clean along all points where the solder or glue will cover. Use a stiff wire brush, a wire brush fitting for a motor tool, or simply scrape the surfaces with a hobby knife. It's also wise, with any kit, to go through a complete ''dry run'' with the kit assembly instructions so you know which parts fit where and in what sequence. Most kits, including all the Car Shop kits, give specific step-by-step instructions for the particular car that kit will build.

The photographs illustrate the assembly of the Car Shop's Canadian National wooden caboose. The assembly steps are virtually identical for the firm's CP, C&O, DL&W, W&LE, USRA, NKP, N&W, NH, B&M and Pennsy wooden caboose kits, as well as for the NH, B&M, W&LE, NKP and N&W steel cabooses. There are only minor variations in the sequence needed to assemble the Car Shop's express car, silk and tea car or the cylindrical covered hopper.

The Car Shop's instructions include a small photo of the finished car and drawings showing the step assembly, floor-mounting, cupola roof grabiron placement and end railing and ladder positions. The photographs in this article are only described in the instructions, so the photographs should make assembly of any of these kits a bit easier.

When you go through the ''dry run'' assembly, note where the parts will join so you can clean and roughen those joining surfaces. Also note where the grabirons and other wire details are located so you can drill the holes for those parts **before** you begin assembling the kit. Notice, too, where the inner window and door pieces fit, and trim any edges that will interfere with the assembly of the sides and ends of the carbody or cupola.

If you are using solder to assemble the model, you may want to consider soldering only the major components of the body and cupola, using thickened hobby-type cyanoacrylate cement or five-minute epoxy to attach the details like fascia trim, grabirons, ladders and piping. This technique minimizes the chance that you might heat some part enough to loosen a major solder joint. There isn't room here for a short course in soldering; the articles in the November 1989 and September 1991 issues contain all the information you will need. Remember, though, on a kit with this many parts, that

Four scraps of ½-inch plywood can be used to make an all-purpose jig to assemble any corner. Be sure the edges of the plywood are perfectly square and smooth. Clamp the blocks together with two clamps and use the third clamp to hold the side. Use tweezers to hold the end in place while you apply solder (or five-minute epoxy) down the inside of the joint.

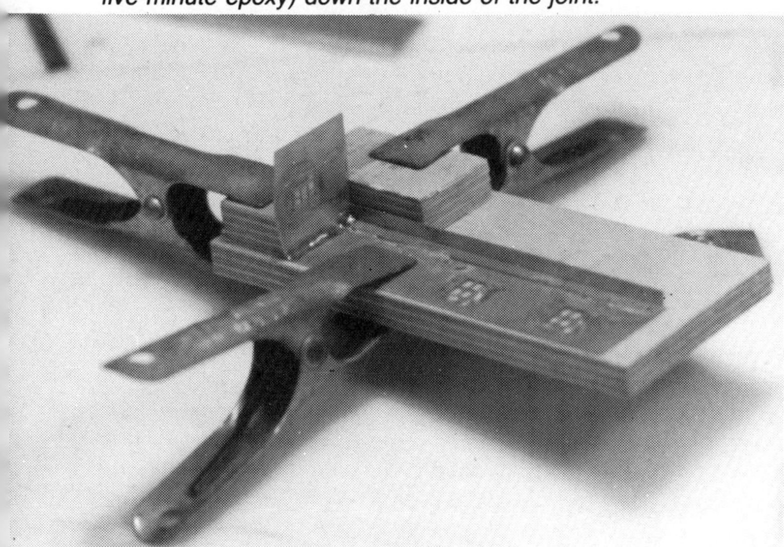

A ¼-inch square piece of basswood can make it easier to clamp the fascia strip to the top of the sides; the wood will place an even pressure on the strip, leaving both of your hands free to hold the soldering gun or iron and the solder.

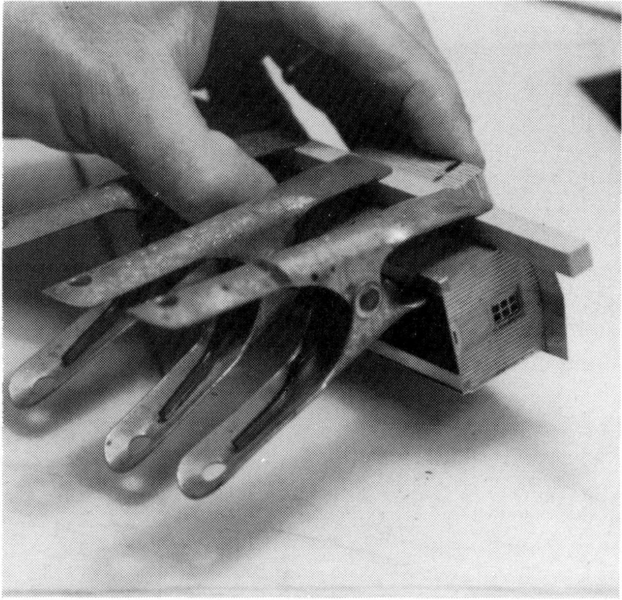

you can use higher melting point 50/50 lead/tin solder for the major joints and lower melting point 80/20 lead/tin solder for later parts to minimize the risk of unsoldering earlier joints. Wadded-up lumps of wet facial tissue make fine heat sinks to keep the heat in the area you are soldering and to insulate previously soldered joints nearby. Walthers sells Tix or Sta-Brite soldering flux as well as solder. When the soldering work is complete, wash the model in thinner and let it dry before you apply any additional details with cement or before painting.

Small blocks of wood can also be used to clamp the doors and windows inside the walls while they are soldered in place.

The Car Shop kit is designed so the cupola is assembled after the roof is soldered to the carbody.

Use the ½-inch square wood to clamp the fascia strips under the eaves of the roof while you apply solder. These pieces will be a bit easier to apply, without the danger of unsoldering earlier joints, if you simply use five-minute epoxy to hold them in place or, if you want to solder, use the lower melting point 80/20 lead/tin solder.

There is a special satisfaction that you'll feel only after you've assembled a brass model. Somehow, the seemingly unmovable quality of metal makes the model seem more substantial than a wooden, plastic or resin model (because it is more substantial) and the feeling of accomplishment is greater. I feel like I've conquered the ultimate challenge in modeling when I finish one of these metal models. In truth, however, they are really no more difficult to build than many cast resin kits. **RMJ**

The Car Shop includes instructions for applying small metal angles so the floor can be removble for adding lights, interior detail or window glazing. Test-fit the floor before adding step, end or underbody detail.

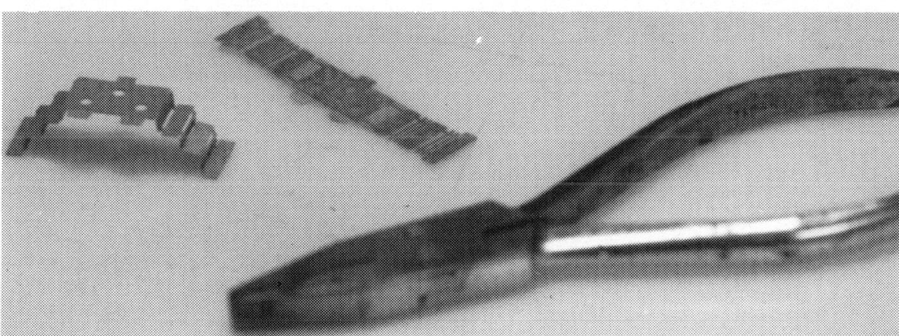

The steps are one of the few parts that must be bent to shape in the Car Shop kits. Use wide or duckbill needlenose pliers with jaws just a bit narrower than the width of each step tread. Solder the steps to the floor, and add the end details, grabirons and underbody details as described in the kit instructions. The instructions include references to magazine articiles that provide locations for the underbody details and painting and lettering schemes for each kit.

The finished model has the look and feel of an imported brass model for a small fraction of the price. The Car Shop kits do not include some of the fine cast details like poling pockets, marker light brackets, coupler pockets and such; those can be added from the brass parts sold by Precision Scale, PIA, Overland or Custom Finishing.

The Big Boxes, part I

Modeling Plate C 60-foot Auto Parts Cars

Alternative prototypes for Mark Ala's conversion techniques on Con-Cor HO scale 60-foot box car kits

This Cotton Belt car was built by Gunderson in October of 1965 as part of SSW series 63200-63309. The circle with the C inside indicates that the car exceeds Plate C, while a square with the C inside signifies a car that conforms to Plate C. To model this car, remove the rivets, use two of the doors from the Front Range Products 50-foot box car kits and add a full-length lower sill. — Photo courtesy Gunderson

Decals — HO Scale: Microscale 87-219 plus 87-258 or Herald King B572. Microscale 87-1 data decals include the circled C.

An ACF Industries builder's photo of one of the cars built in December of 1969 as part of Western Maryland series 495975-495989. Although barely discernable in these photos, the ACF cars have three panels to the right of the door that are inset about a half-inch. The cars also have the characteristic ACF side sill — ACF Industries photo

Decals — HO Scale: Herald King B270 (for a 40 foot car) or Champ HB306 — both plus Microscale 87-1.

*This car's construction is virtually identical to the Western Maryland car, but the details on the door are a bit more visible. This is the **only** car that appears in the Rock Island listings — a class of **one**? It was built in April of 1970. — ACF Industries photo*

Decals — HO Scale: Herald King B545 or Microscale 87-20, both plus Microscale 87-1

*A double-door version of the ACF Industries Plate C "Auto Parts" car. This dark blue car is part of N&W series 600928 and 600929 (yep, **two** cars!), built in October of 1968. The double-sliding-door cars had those characteristic (and nearly invisible) ACF inset panels to both the right and left of the door openings. — ACF Industries photo*

Decals — HO Scale: Champ HB364 or Microscale 87-81, both plus Microscale 87-1.

*David Casdorph's 94-page **60-Foot Auto Parts Boxcars** book was the inspiration for this new series on modeling the cars. This issue of the **Journal** includes modeling techniques to duplicate the smallest of the cars, those that conform to or slightly exceed the Association of American Railroads (AAR) "Plate C" clearance dimensions. That's the car Con-Cor has duplicated in HO scale. Later, we'll show you how to model the larger "Plate E" cars in both N and HO scales. Casdorph's book is an essential resource for those modeling today's freight cars. It's $19.95 postpaid from **Freight Cars Journal,** P.O. Box 2480, Monrovia, CA 91017.*

Four of Mark Ala's 60-foot auto parts cars (he's done a dozen).

The Evans cars are the prototypes, it seems, for the Con-Cor kits. This car, however, has six-panel sliding doors similar to Mark Ala's C&NW model. The car is part of SLSF number series 9200-9205. — James Eager photo, circa May 1985

HO Scale Decals:
Herald King B-464 (or Microscale 87-149) plus
Walthers 934-69120 for 60-foot markings.

An ACF Industries Plate C car with double plug doors similar to the Con-Cor kit. The side sill, however, has a different shape. This car is part of Conrail's X-59 class in number series 218764-218814, built in 1964. They were originally Pennsylvania Railroad class X59 cars. — James Eager photo, circa March 1984

HO Scale Decals:
Herald King B700 (or Microscale 87-161) plus
Walthers 934-96120 for 60-foot markings.

Gregg Drawbaugh submitted this photo for use in the "Readers' Roster" section, but the car happens to be a near perfect prototype for the Con-Cor model (leave the wheelbase, rivets, sills and doors alone and repaint). Herald King's catalog suggests a mix of 10 parts Floquil 110035 BN Green and one part 110154 Vermont Green. The car is part of number series 912-916. — Gregg Drawbaugh photo taken March 10, 1988

HO Scale Decals:
Herald King B-193, Microscale 87-446.

The Conrail Car

The doors from two of the Front Range 50-foot cars were cut apart to produce a taller door for the Conrail car. It retains the stock Con-Cor lower sill and short wheelbase frame. The decals are Herald King B-700.

The Rio Grande Car

This is the most difficult conversion of the lot because the kit's sides must be cut to remove the doors completely. The double plug doors from the MDC FMC 50-foot car no. 1981 (the undecorated kit is no. 1980) were cut from that body and inserted into the openings in the sides of the Con-Cor 60-foot body. Again, Mark added .030x.030-inch door guides and .040x.188-inch lower side sills from Evergreen styrene strips. The decals are Herald King no. B-40.

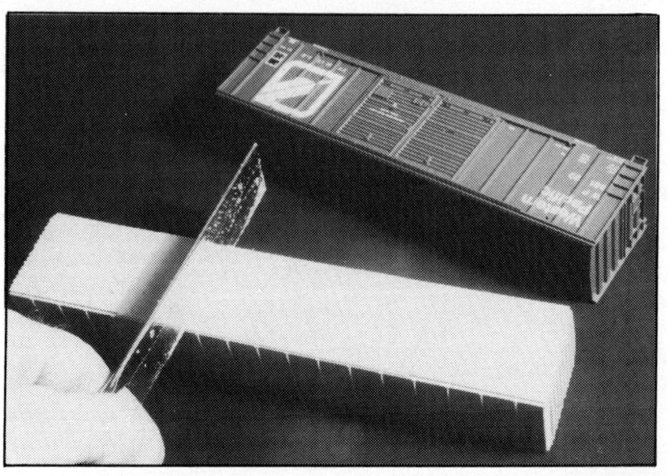

Con-Cor 60-foot Auto Parts Box Cars

Mark Ala converted the Con-Cor (ex-Robins Rails) HO scale 60-foot box cars into four alternative styles, and here's how . . .

Robert Schleicher
Models by Mark Ala

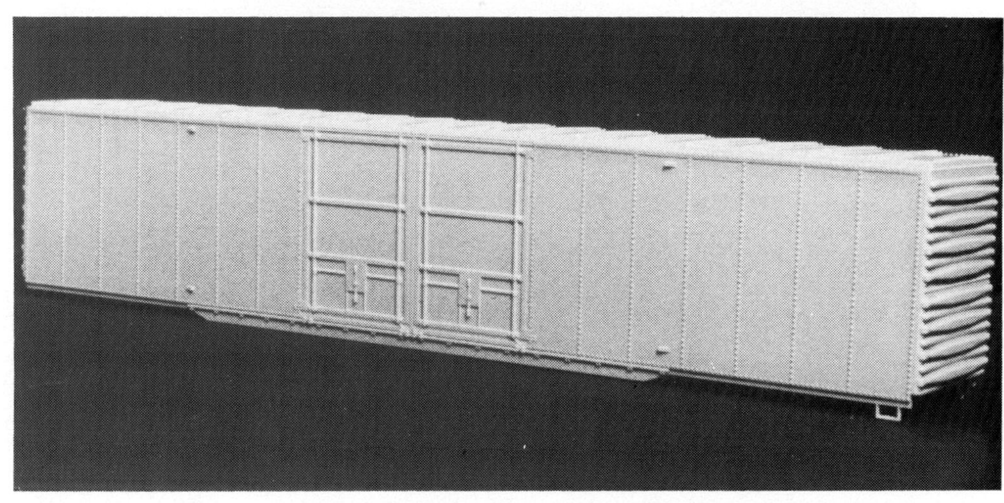

These are the kinds of models that members of the Railroad Prototype Modelers group hope to encourage. Mark Ala's models have appeared at several of the RPM get-togethers, and they always attract special attention.

Some of the RPM gatherings include clinics on both prototype equipment and modeling techniques. Mark has NOT presented this information as a clinic; consider **Railmodel Journal's** presentation, then, on behalf of the Railroad Prototype Modelers group, as a way of encouraging you to attend and, yes, to participate in the next possible RPM get-together . . .

Virtually all of Mark Ala's 60-foot auto parts box cars are modified Con-Cor (ex-Robins Rails) HO scale plastic kits. The out-of-the-box model duplicates the relatively rare cars with riveted sides, so that's the first detail to change on Mark's models. There are thousands of these 60-foot Plate C cars, but only a relatively few have doors that match the kit, so that's another of the changes Mark makes to the models. Even fewer share the lower side sill shape of the stock kits, so Mark alters the side sills too. Finally, while some of the cars had trucks positioned on the 41′3″ centers of the Con-Cor kits, many of the cars had the trucks hung further outboard on about 46′3″ truck centers; Mark has duplicated both styles on these cars, with the Conrail having a stock kit wheelbase and the D&RGW, GTW and C&NW cars having modified frames with the longer wheelbase.

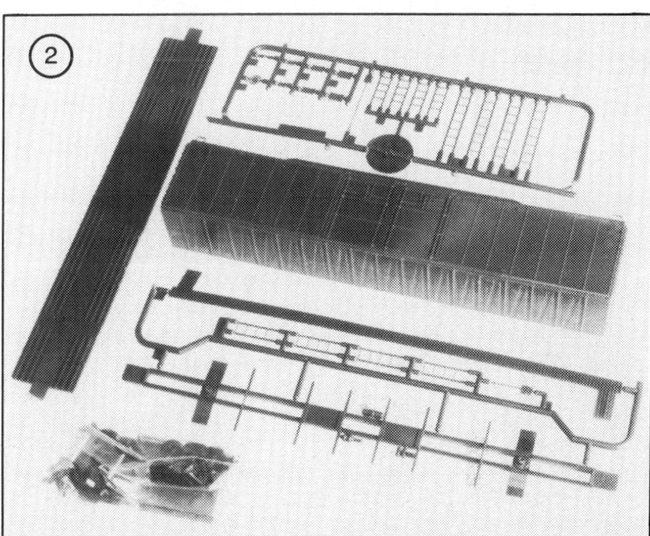

Con-Cor's parts for the 60-foot auto parts box cars are molded in black plastic with small holes to attach the ladders. The original Robins Rails cars were molded in grey plastic — we used one of them for the photographs.

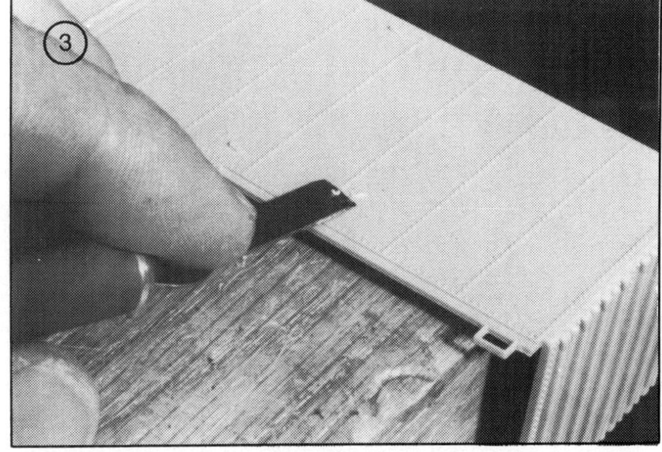

Use a no. 17 X-acto blade to shave the rivets from the sides. Use the same blade as a chisel to remove the door detail if you are going to use alternate doors.

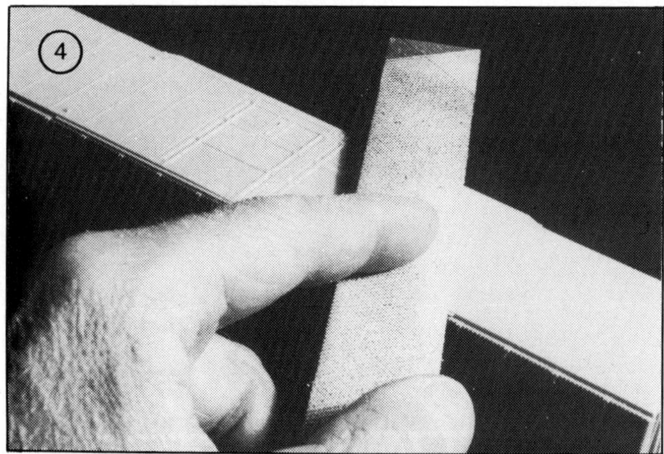

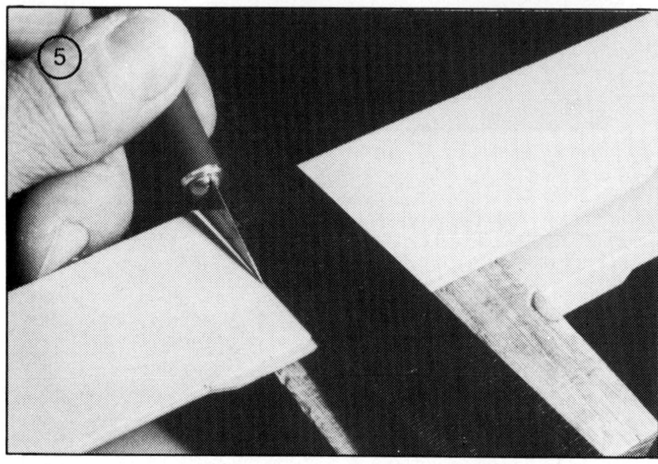

Use a no. 11 X-acto blade to slice the panel lines down the sides. Match the spacing of these lines (simulated panel weld seams) to the photos of the protype you are duplicating. Some are spaced a scale 3 feet part, but other cars have odd/even panel sizes and, sometimes, fewer panels (wider-spaced lines). After you have sliced the panel lines, shave off the small ridge that the knife leaves on each side of the slice as it "plows" the plastic. You may need to go back again and gently reslice the lines. These steps are critical if you want to avoid the "sliced butter" look of just running a knife down the plastic. Use the same techniques to add the lower (horizontal) seams.

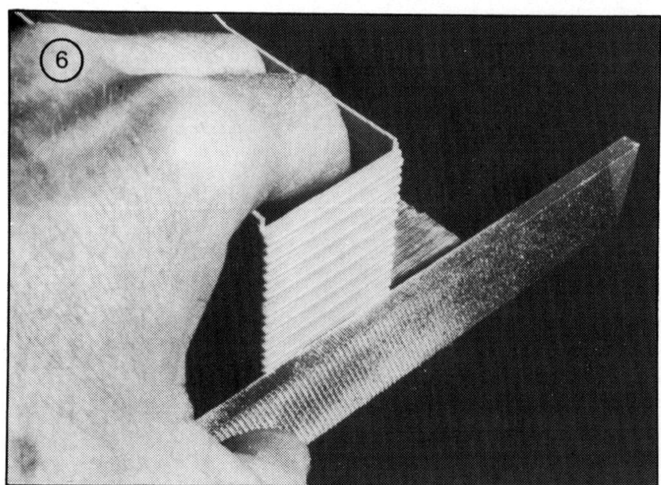

Many of these cars do not have the top rib molded into the model (to match the Evans prototypes). File the rib flush with that mill (or Formica) file. Protect the adjacent rib with a strip of masking tape (not shown).

Use a medium-cut mill file (or a Formica-shaping file) to finish smoothing off the sides so no traces of any rivets or door details remain.

New Lower Sills

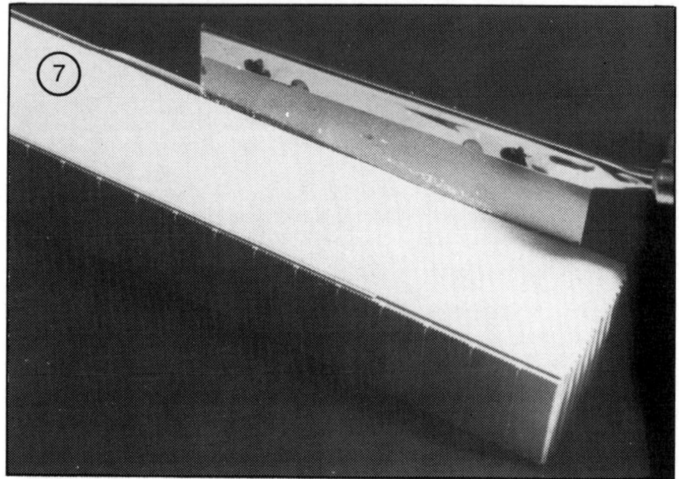

Use a razor saw to slice the lower sill flush with the bottoms of the ends. If you saw at a small angle, as shown, the cut will be easier to keep straight.

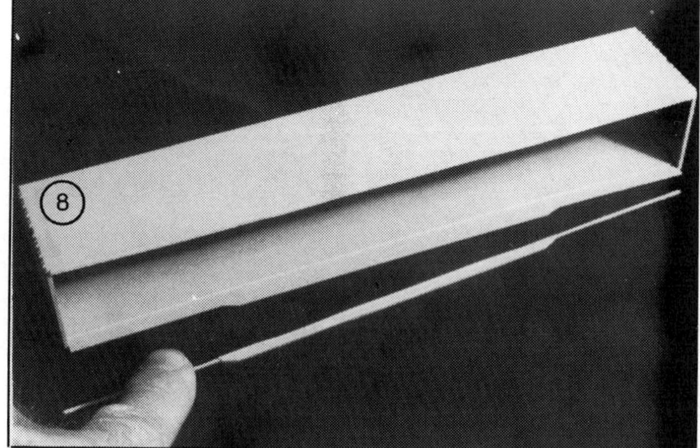

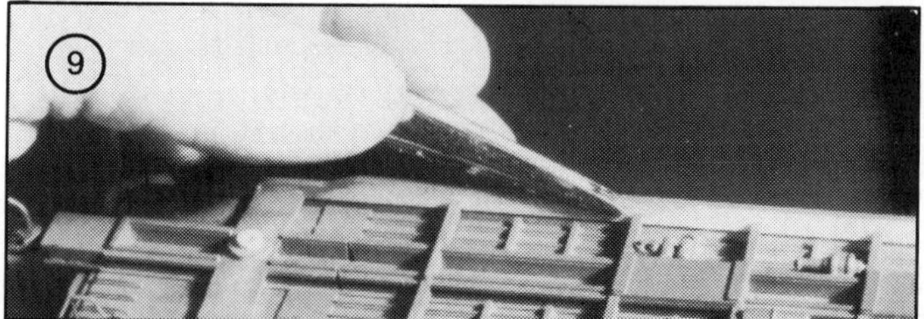

Cut new side sills from Evergreen HO scale .040x.188-inch styrene strips. Use prototype photos as a guide in shaping the strips.

Short Truck Center Frames

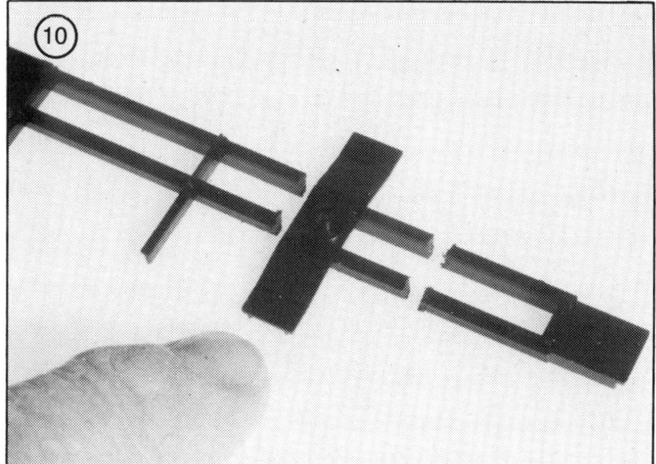

Use a razor saw to cut the underframe just at the outside edges of bolsters, with the second cut a scale 5 feet further toward the center of the car.

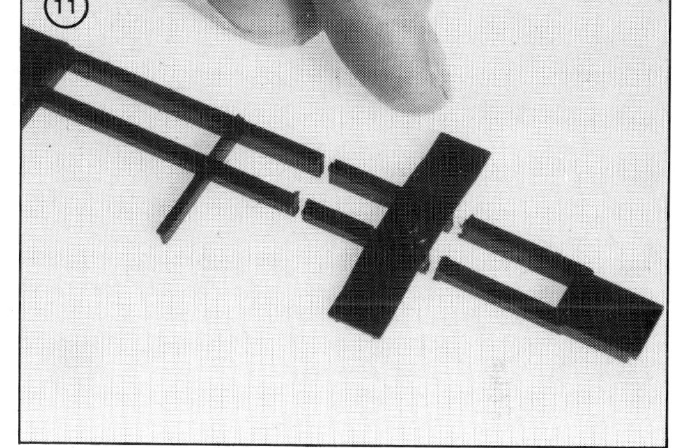

Rotate each of the just-cut bolsters 180 degrees into this position. File away any burrs and reassemble the frame using liquid cement for plastics. The resulting truck center-to-center dimensions should be an HO scale 46′3″.

Completing the Conversions

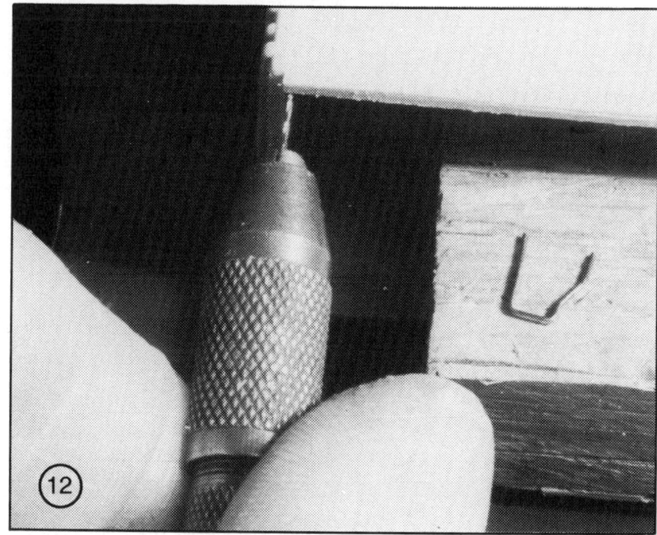

Mark used A-Line "style C" stirrup steps at each corner. Use a pin vise to hold a no. 75 size drill bit to drill the holes for the steps in each corner of the car.

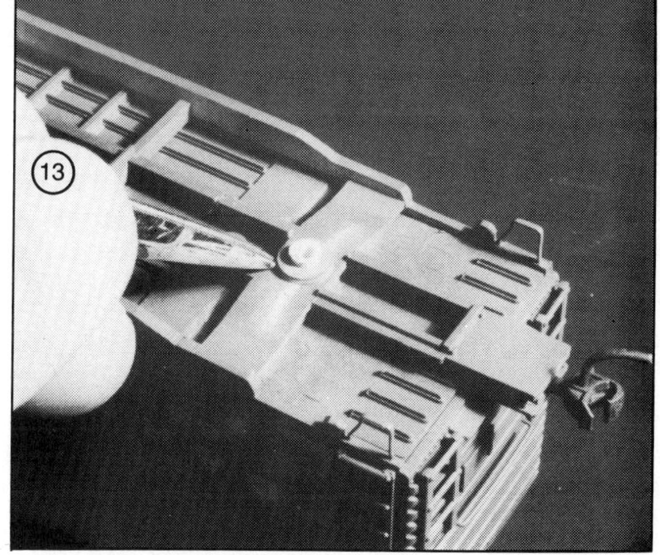

Some of the kits ride a bit too low, so you may need to add a Kadee washer to the bolster. Use the Kadee coupler height gauge to be sure the coupler height is correct if you do add spacer washers. Mark adds enough A-Line weights so the car weighs 5½ ounces.

The C&NW Car

Mark built new doors from Evergreen .010-inch-thick sheet styrene with HO scale 1x3 strips cemented in place. Use thickened cyanoacrylate cement for the thin strips. The door guides are Evergreen .030x.030-inch strips. The full-height ladders were matched to a photograph of the full-size car. The decals are Herald King B-22. Walthers has some decals for 60-foot cars with the proper reporting marks (but no "Plate C" in a square) in Wabash set 934-96120 (for white).

The Grand Trunk Car

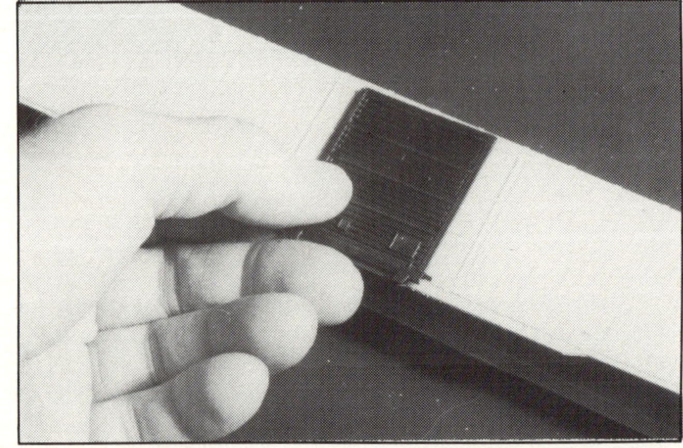

Mark used a door from the Athearn 40-foot Hi-Cube car (door no. 12028 — from kits 1950 through 1956) with Evergreen .030x.030-inch strip door guides and a new lower sill. The decals are Herald King B-110.

Athearn Kit-Conversion 86-to-60-Foot Auto Parts Box Car

Or build it in N scale from the Arnold 86-foot model

If you're modeling any era after 1964, you'll want one of the fleet of Plate E 60-foot auto parts cars. Photographs of the real cars appear in Volume II of the Freight Car Models book series.

Bill Deuroun

These big and bulky box cars are certainly some of the most "railroad"-looking pieces of rolling stock on today's railroads. These cars have proportions that, to many modelers, seem to be more pleasing than, say, a 40-foot car or one of the huge 86-foot "Hi-Cube" cars. This 60-footer, though, is a car that you must build, because there's nothing like it in a kit.

There have been two injection-molded plastic 60-foot house cars in HO scale: a nice ready-to-run mechanical refrigerator with a 10-foot plug door imported by Pemco nearly a decade ago (and long gone), and the kit produced by Robins Rails. The Robins Rails car is now being molded by Con-Cor with some upgrades and improvements. but it is one of the relatively low Plate C cars with an overall height similar to the Athearn or MDC Railbox cars.

The Plate C cars are a maximum of 14′2″ tall at the eaves, while the prototype for this kit conversion is a whopping 15′8″ — much taller than the Railbox cars, about the same height as the flat-roofed 50-foot "Hi-Cube" cars from MDC but a scale foot lower than the 40-foot "Hi-Cube" cars from Athearn and Bachmann and Athearn's 86-foot "Hi-Cube" models. This conversion involves removing the necessary amounts from the center and ends of the Athearn model to match the dimensions of the prototype. Once that material is gone, you can use a plug door, a Superior-style panel door or a variety of double plug doors. In fact, it would be even easier just to remove the extra 12 feet or so from each end of the Athearn model to build a double-plug door car and leave the doors alone. Unfortunately, I have not seen a car with doors that wide. The techniques shown here will allow you to duplicate most of the cars shown in David Casdorph's *60-Foot Auto Parts Box Cars* book by simply removing some of the width from an additional pair of doors or, if you want a Pullman-Standard car, building up ends from PS-1 40-foot box car models from Cannonball, Walthers, McKean or Front Range. **RMJ**

Before . . .

. . . and after. *Most 60-foot auto parts cars have the proportions of a standard 50-foot box car, but they're about 20 percent bigger in every dimension except width. Compare this kit-converted car to the Athearn 86-foot "Hi-Cube" (actually what the railroads call a Plate F) car and the Athearn Railbox (a Plate C car). This particular 60-foot auto parts car is a Plate E car. The ends and side sill are spotting features for cars built by ACF Industries.*

The conversion requires one Athearn no. 1974 undecorated 86-foot Hi-Cube box car kit, a pair of Athearn no. 12028 doors from the 40-foot Hi-Cube box car (or a complete no. 1950 kit to get the doors), plus Cal-Scale (now made by Bowser) no. SC-301 Hydra-Cushion car detailing set (for the extended drawbars and ladders), A-Line 29002 stirrup steps and Detail Associates no. 625 couple cut-bar levers. We did not replace any of the molded on grabirons or railings, so you may want to add some .012-inch Detail Associates wire for that purpose. We also used a strip of Evergreen .020x.156-inch styrene for the lower sill and strips of HO scale 4x4 for the extended door guides, with A-Line self-adhesive lead weights and Kadee no. 7 short shank couplers.

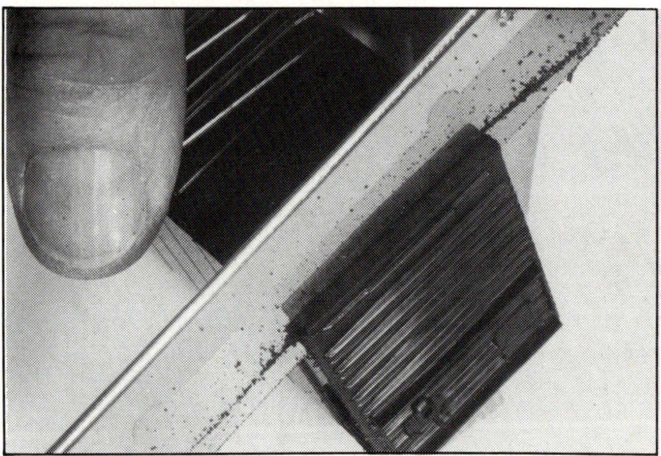

Use a razor saw to slice into each corner of the roof just inside the vertical row of rivets up the sides. Use those slices as guides to cut across the roof (so the cut is straight), then slice down the sides to remove the ends from the car.

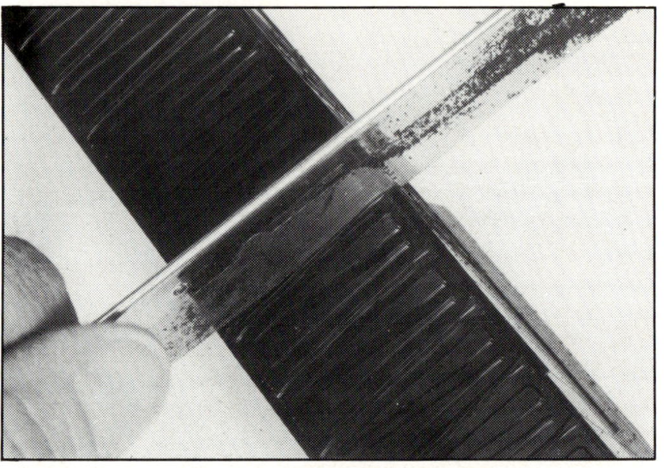

Remove a scale 17 feet from the exact center of the car. That's the width of five of the roof panels. Count out 2½ panels from the car's center and cut just ***outside*** *the roof rib. When the body halves are joined later, the seam will be along the center of that roof rib. Cut across the roof first, then down each side. I would suggest you mark all the cuts we've made on the body with masking tape and compare your proposed cuts to the photos to be sure you're making them properly.*

The center portion of the car can be discarded because we have sliced into the doors, making each of them unsalvagable, The cuts, however, minimize the modifications needed to the door slides.

The ends of each side have unusually recessed panels for the ladders and grabirons. Remove these panels ***plus*** *a scale 14 inches of the adjacent panel. That extreme end panel of each side (right and left) should be a scale 2 feet wide. All the other panels are a scale 3 feet wide. Again, start the cuts in the upper corners, cut across the roof, then down each side.*

Measure 12 HO scale feet from the outside top corner of the roof, and lightly slice a line along the lower edge of the body. Use a razor saw to remove that portion of the lower edges of the body. Repeat the same cut on both halves of the body.

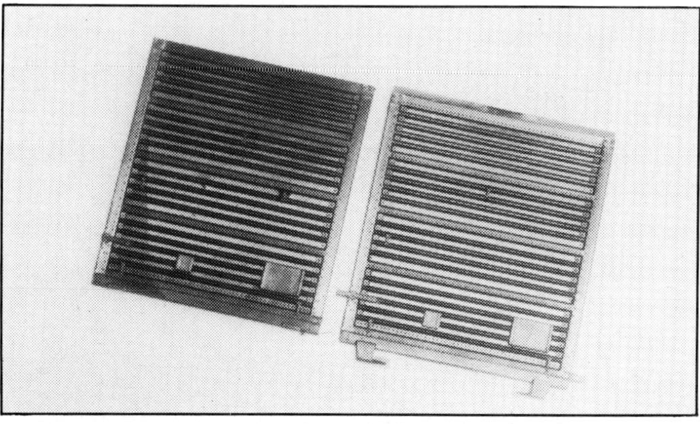

I used the no. 12028 doors from the Athearn 40-foot Hi-Cube car as-is, even though they have one less rib in the top panel and a slightly taller bottom panel than the doors on the full-size car. Their overall height is about right. Do, however, remove the two lower door slides, and saw off the thin upper strip that was supposed to slide in the Athearn door slide. Use a razor saw for the cuts.

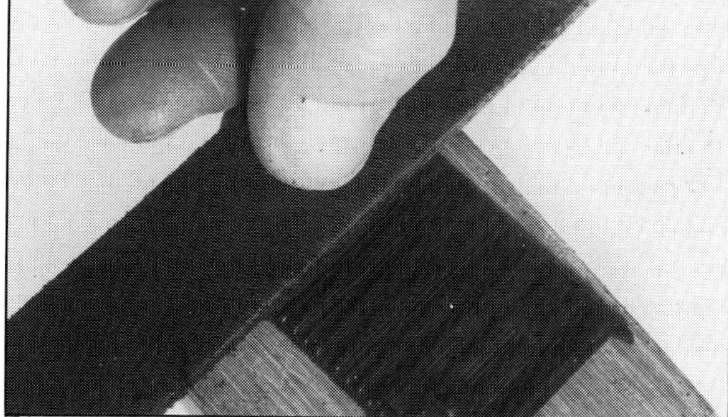

I used that Formica file shown in the April 1989 issue to remove the upper rectangular rib and just the one top tapered rib from each end. The remaining thin tapered rib (that's thick at the ends) must remain untouched.

Use the razor saw to remove a scale 11 inches from that just-filed top panel of each end. Cement the thin top section to the bottom section of each end.

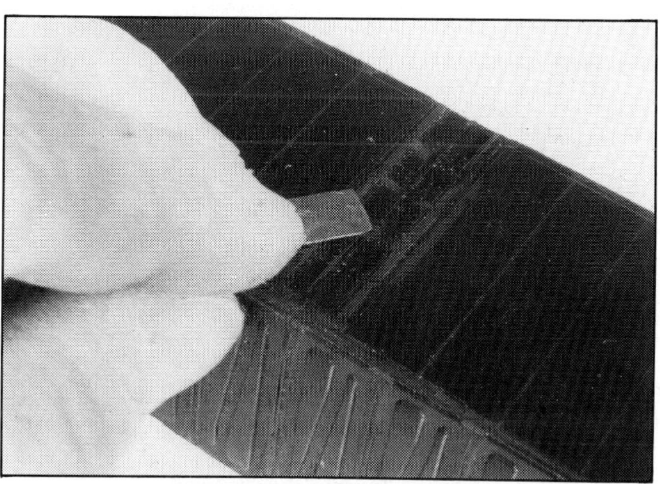

Cement the ends to the body after filing all the joining seams perfectly flat with a medium cut mill file or that Formica file. Use liquid cement for plastics and work the joints back and forth while they are wet to create a paste-like seam along each joint. When the cement dries, scrape off that seam and most joint lines will be invisible. If there are gaps, use automobile body spot putty to fill them, and file it smooth after it dries.

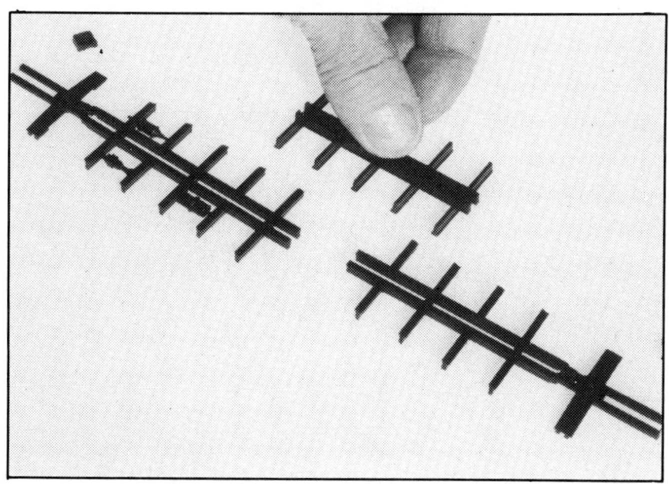

Remove a scale 18′9″ from both the underframe and the floor to produce a truck wheelbase of a scale 46′3″ to match the prototype cars. Remove the rectangular pads from the extreme ends of the frame.

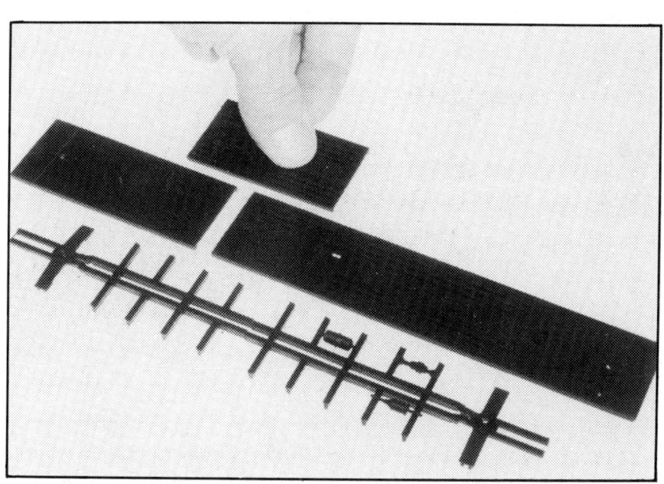

Test fit the floor into the body and mark the amount that needs to be removed from each end of the floor so it will fit snuggly inside.

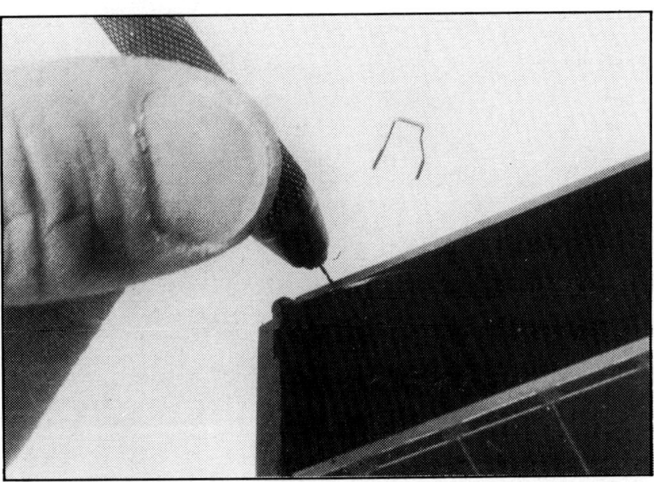

I drilled holes for the A-Line no. 29002 stirrup steps in the bottom edges of the body sides just before I cemented the floor in place. Use a no. 74 drill bit in a pin vise to drill the holes.

Drill a no. 50 hole in the ends of the floor to mount the Cal-Scale SC-301 coupler pockets.

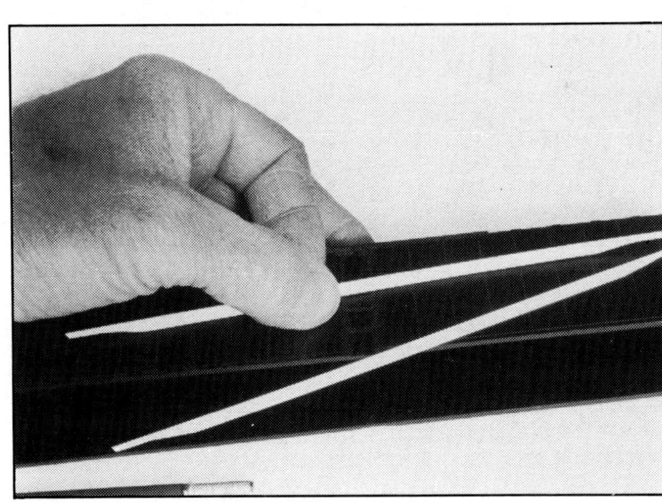

I used one of the Front Range Products 50-foot HO scale box cars as a guide in shaping the lower sills since it is based on an ACF prototype. Slice the outline into the sides of the Evergreen .020x.156-inch styrene and use the scribe-and-break technique to remove the excess material from the ends of the strip. The center portion of the strip can remain as-is. The overall length of these new sills is 50 feet. If you are modeling the cars built by the Baltimore & Ohio, that thin (about a scale 9-inch) portion should extend all the way to the end of the car.

I added four ounces of A-Line self-adhesive weights on the floor before installing it in the car. The two halves of the floor can be cemented together, with liquid cement for plastics, after the weights are in place. The floor, frame and side sills can now be cemented to the body.

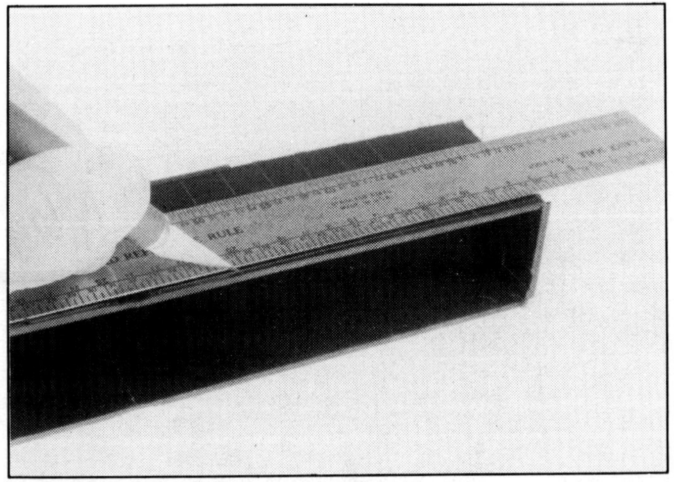

Gently scrape the lower 9 inches of the weld seam detail from the bottom of each weld seam using a hobby knife. Next, lightly slice a line a scale 9 inches up from the bottom of the side with a steel ruler to guide the knife. That simulates the seams on the full size cars' lower sills.

REPRINTED FROM RAILMODEL JOURNAL — February 1990

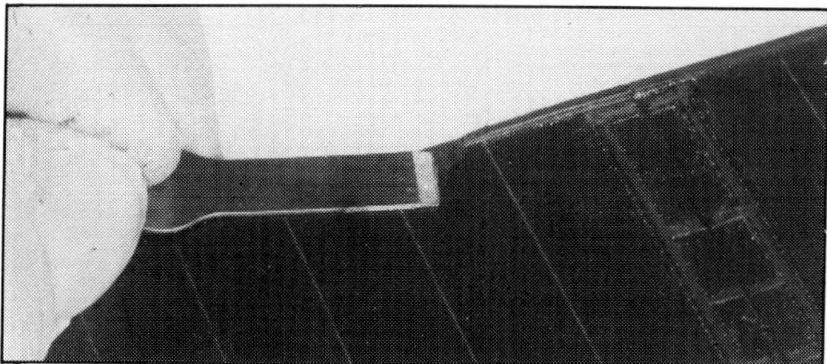

Install the doors directly over the center of the car. Use the no. 17 blade to carefully shave away the excess door sill to the left of each door.

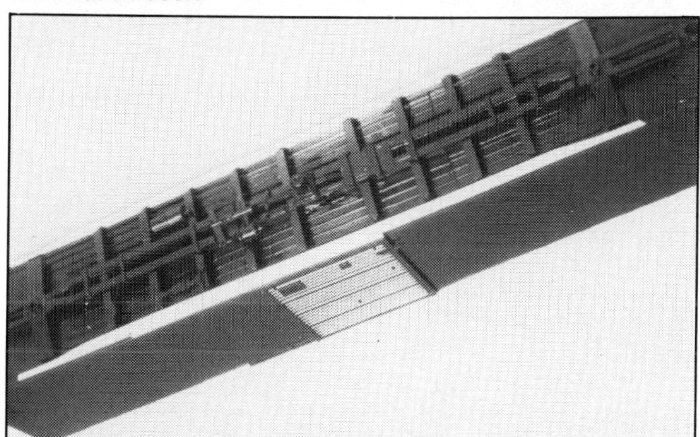

Assemble the shortened underframe, then install the Cal-Scale Hydra-Cushion pieces over the frame. I cut the valve and cylinder from the Athearn underframe and repositioned them as suggested in the Cal-Scale instructions. I also trimmed the low-hanging round post nearly flush with its bracket on the Cal-Scale center frame cover. Kadee no. 6 couplers will fit the Cal-Scale pockets without extending too far out the ends if you cut the tabs from the sides of the no. 6 couplers. Kadee no. 5 couplers drop right in.

Check the coupler height of the finished car before you attach the coupler pockets with 2-56 screws from the Athearn kit. This is the shape of the lower side sills (the white plastic) used on ACF-built cars; the B&O-built cars would have the strip extending all the way to the ends as shown on the prototype photos in this issue.

Extend the upper and lower door sills to a scale 10 feet beyond the right of the door with the HO scale 4x4 strips of Evergreen styrene.

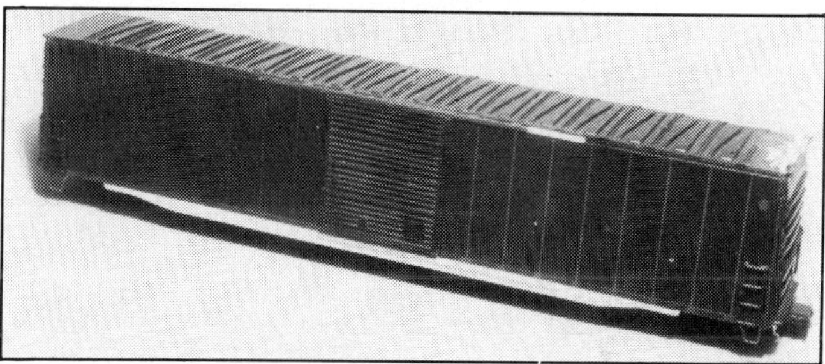

I elected to leave the ladders and grabirons on the ends just as Athearn molded them, but I did install new side ladders from the Cal-Scale Hydra-Cushion kit. The coupler cut levers are Detail Associates no. 6215 installed in no. 76 holes.

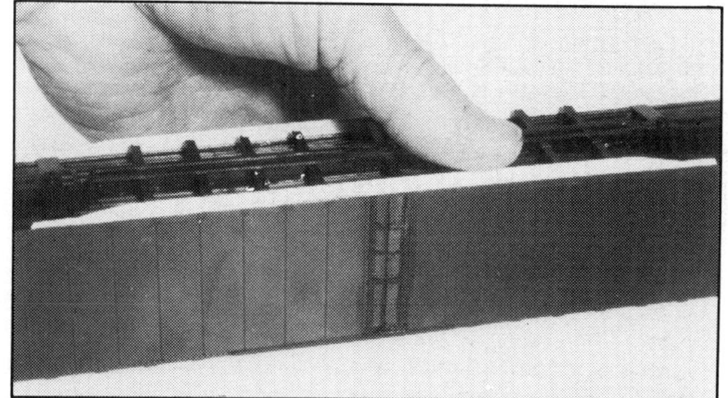

I used Floquil RR50 dark blue paint with Herald King no. B140 decals and ignored the errors in the dimensional data. I also scraped away the "C" in the square "Plate C" decal so it could pass for the proper "Plate E" marking. I could not locate any 60-foot box car decals for a Plate E car; let us know if you locate some.

CREATE YOUR OWN KIT: "FLAT" KIT-CONVERSIONS, part I:

General American 50-foot Box Car Kit-Conversion

"The Green One" — to Use the Decals in This Issue

Apply those HO scale GAEX decals to a stock Athearn no. 5050 kit, to a Details West 800 kit (with a new door), to the old Walthers (ex-Pacific HO) kits . . . or to the dead-accurate kit-conversion on these pages.

Apply those N scale GAEX decals to the Con-Cor 50-foot car. Buy the S DeSignS S scale prepainted and lettered Pacific Rail Products S scale kit from S DeSignS c/o Don DeWitt, 37 Snow Dr., Mahwah, NJ 07430.

Robert Schleicher

Modelers are a tough lot to satisfy. The more you learn about the hobby, the more accuracy you expect in your models. The hobby manufacturers have done an incredible job of creating kits and components, and most of them are accurate. Still, there are at least 100 times more prototype freight cars and locomotives than there are kits. If you want an exact replica of a particular prototype car or locomotive, then the odds are that you're going to have to modify a kit.

Kit modifications range from something as simple as erasing the number and changing it to match a prototype photo (then applying equally realistic weathering) to a complete kit rebuild. In **Railmodel Journal,** we try to be consistent in referring to simple kit alterations as "upgrades" and to more complex kit alterations as "kit-conversions." A typical upgrade might include adding wire handgrabs, a Detail Associates or Overland Models etched roofwalk, stirrup steps, coupler lift bars and Kadee couplers — all alterations made to the model on these pages.

This particular kit conversion, however, is about as complex as possible, just short of a complete scratchbuilding project like that described by Al Westerfield in the December 1989 and January 1990 issues. In those articles, however, Al wanted a few dozen replicas; this box car is unusual enough that you'd likely want only one or two.

The "Flat Kit" Society

As an editor, I receive dozens of requests from readers for specific kits to recreate specific freight cars. The more experienced readers often suggest that they would be willing to build a kit like those sold by firms such as Central Valley, Tichy, Eastern Car Works (ex-E&B Valley) or the now out of production Walthers (ex-Pacific HO) 50-foot box car kits in injection-molded plastic or the cast resin kits produced by firms like Westerfield or Des Plaines Hobbies (ex-Storzek). These kits have one thing in common: all the parts are flat pieces with separate roofs, sides, ends and floors. They are the alternative to "one-piece"-style bodies like those in Athearn, Walthers (improved Train Miniature), McKean, C&BT Car

The end rib shapes and sizes, the side panels and rivets, the roof pattern and the door shapes on this car are all near-perfect matches for the General American 50-foot box cars built in 1950 and illustrated in this issue — but it took three kits to do it!

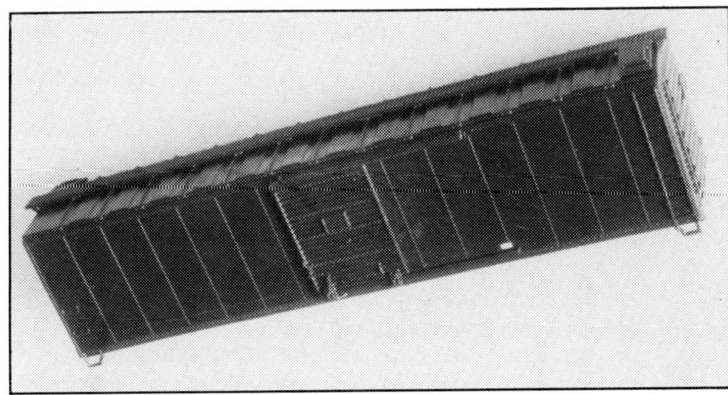

1 — The easy way to reproduce the General American 50-foot box cars in HO scale is to use the Athearn no. 5050 undecorated kit with dark green paint (see text) and the decals from this issue. The proportions will be right, and you can add the "upgrade" details we applied to our "flat kit" conversion car to give the model a superdetailed look.

3 — You'll need two C&BT Car Shops kits. The no. 1500 undecorated kit has the 12-panel sides, an 8-foot-wide door opening and 4/3/1 interim improved Dreadnaught ends with a rectangular top rib. Cut the first body just outside the furthest molded panel and rivet lines as shown by the cards inserted in the cuts. Use a razor saw for the cuts, cutting first across the body, then over the roof, and finally along the upper edge into the rivets at the edge of the roof (to leave the full height and thickness of the sides intact). Remove both ends from this body, too, by making the cuts at a 45-degree angle into each vertical corner.

5 — Leave a bit of excess plastic on the sides when you make the cuts to leave room for filing-to-fit. The sides will include three pieces: the short ones from the second body and the door and center section from the first body. The combined length of the three side pieces must be a scale 6 inches shorter than the Front Range or McKean 50-foot roof (shown) to leave room for the ends with the roof extended the full length of the car. Test-fit all the parts (as shown in later photographs) to be sure you leave the sides long enough to match the needed length of roof. It's the roof that determines the precise length of this model.

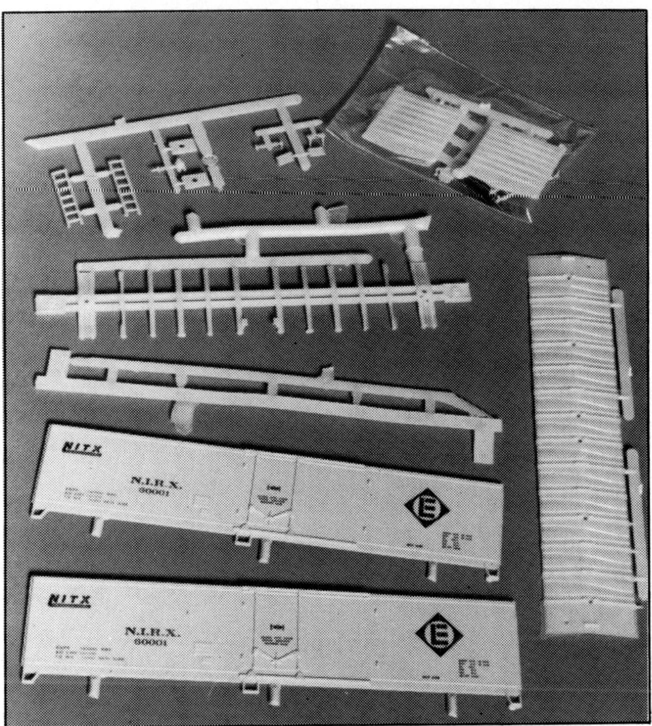

2 — Walthers no longer produces these ex-Pacific HO "flat kit" 50-foot plug door box cars. The kit would be an alternative starting point for a kit conversion to match the General American cars because the roof pattern, the number of side panels and the number of end ribs are correct. The shape of the end ribs and the height of the sides, however, is not accurate. Instead, create your own "flat kit" — it won't be much more difficult, and the resulting model will be nearly perfect.

4 — The three extreme right and left panels on each side will be needed from the second body. Make the cut into the corners at a 45-degree angle to make it easier to hide their joint with the ends. It would be possible to leave the ends in place, but it will be nearly impossible to remove the roof without removing the ends. The ends can be cut, at the same 45-degree angle, from the first body to leave a bit of "file-to-fit" plastic on all the parts. Again, a pair of cards have been inserted in the cuts to show you their locations and angles.

Shops, Con-Cor, Details West, Front Range, MDC or Mantua kits.

The advantage of the "flat" kit is that the molding dies to produce the parts are less expensive to cut than the dies for the "one-piece" kits. The dies for a flat kit have a simple top and bottom. Dies for the one-piece kits have a top, a bottom and at least two "slides" or side dies to mold the details into the sides as well as the tops and bottoms of parts. Some body dies have as many as six or eight slides, and those molds are extremely expensive for a manufacturer to produce. The molds that produce those Athearn or Atlas or Bachmann models are multi-slide molds.

What do you, the modeler, care about flat kits? The production methods influence the price. You can purchase one of the flat kits for about $10 to $20. If that same model were produced as a one-piece body, the price would be twice as much. That sounds totally illogical when compared to an Athearn model that sells for $5 or so, half the price of the flat kit. The difference lies in the number of kits that can be sold. Athearn, MDC, Walthers, Con-Cor, McKean, C&BT Car Shops, Details West and firms like them sell enough kits of common cars that they can amortize the cost of their expensive production dies or molds over many thousands of kits. There are just not enough sales for the more exotic models in most "flat" kits to make them appealing to enough modelers to sell enough kits to keep the price down. Like it or not, the reality of the economic world of model railroading is that the more exotic models are going to be both more expensive and more difficult to build.

The box cars in this issue are examples of the type of kit that might be produced as a "flat" kit. You can apply those decals to an out-of-the box Athearn no. 5050 box car and have a model that reproduces the proportions and appearance of either the 1950- or 1955-built General American box cars very effectively, indeed. Most of you will likely use the decals in just that manner, simply painting the Athearn undecorated model with a mixture of one part Floquil no. 10 Engine Black to 20 parts Floquil no. 183 Reading Green and applying decals. Some of you might upgrade the Athearn model by adding individual grabirons and ladders,

6 — The Front Range or McKean roof is designed to rest inside the body, but the C&BT Car Shops sides are a bit too thick. Use a cabinetmaker's formica file (ask a kitchen tile shop) to smooth the upper edges of the roof and to remove about 1/64 inch of the thickness of the sides where the roof will fit.

7 — The Front Range or McKean 50-foot roof runs all the way to the end of the car, so the C&BT Car Shops ends must be shortened to match the thickness of the 50-foot roof (right). Use the formica file to remove the material. Remove material from the back of the tops of the ends so the end is only about 1/32 inch thick so the 50-foot roof's aligning ridge can fit inside the end as it does on the Front Range or McKean kits.

8 — Cut the two C&BT Car Shops 40-foot floors so they fill the distance between the ends — it's about the same as the length of the modified and lengthened 50-foot sides, but test-fit to be sure the floor is the proper length when the two pieces are butted together. Use liquid cement for plastics for all the joints, thickened hobby-type cyanoacrylate cement to attach the small parts.

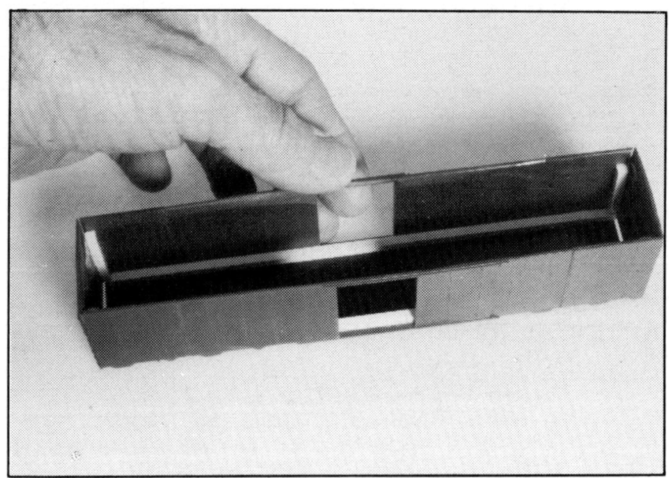

9 — The inner braces are optional, but they make assembly a bit easier. I simply cut some 1/8-inch-square strips of Evergreen styrene a scale foot or so shorter than the car's interior for the floor-to-side braces, and similar vertical pieces for the end-to-side braces.

perhaps a Detail Associates or Overland Models roofwalk, and Kadee couplers.

Very, very few modelers, however, will care enough about the rivet patterns, the roof rib patterns, the end rib shapes and the door corrugations to want to go to the trouble of creating their own flat kits as described in the photos and captions. If, however, you want an accurate model of the 1950-built General American box cars, you must know that there is not a single detail on that Athearn kit that matches the prototypes (except for the general proportions). At a glance, the finished model looks better than the Athearn kit — but only because of those added detail parts items you can add to that Athearn kit with ease, compared to the kit conversion shown.

*10 — The A-Line (Proto Power West) self-adhesive weights should be installed **before** the roof is cemented in place (I forgot and had to slip them in through the doors). Add enough to bring the total car weight up to the National Model Railroad Association RP20.1 "Car Weight" Recommended Practices of ½ ounce per inch of body length plus one ounce.*

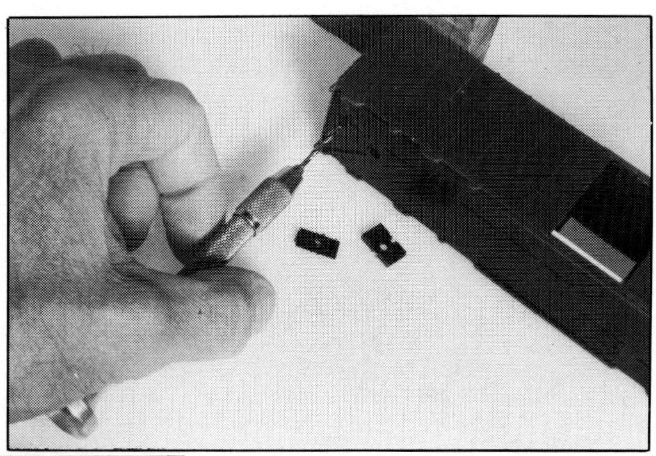

11 — Drill the floor with a no. 50 drill bit, then thread the holes with a no. 2-56 tap to accept Kadee no. 5 coupler pockets at each end. Trim the side loops from the Kadee pockets.

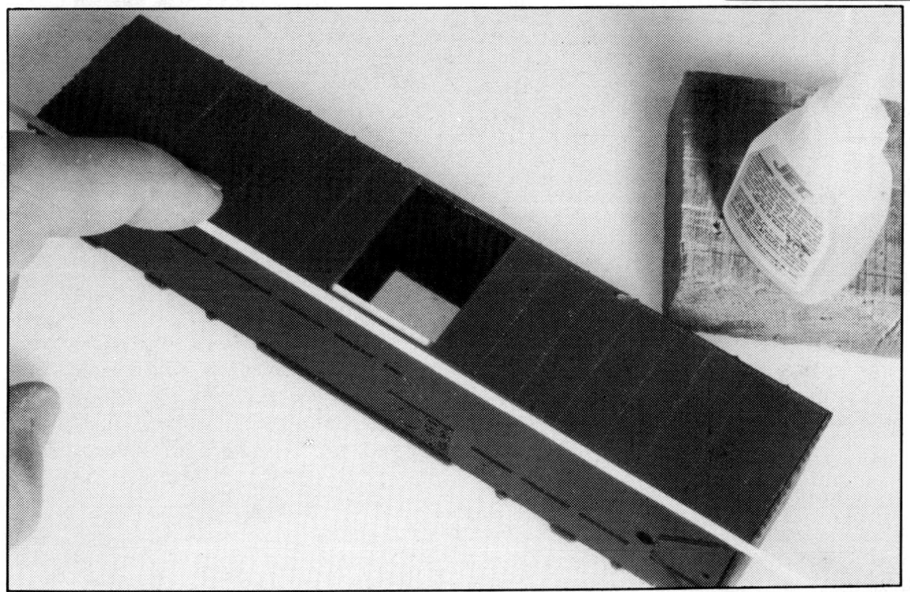

12 — Gently file the outer faces of the lower tabs along the bottom edges of the sides with a flat jewelers file or the edge of that formica file to remove about .010 inch of plastic. Cement a new straight lower side sill of Evergreen .010x.080-inch styrene strip to the tabs with thickened hobby-type cyanoacrylate cement (plastic cement will pock or pit the .010-inch styrene). Trim the ends of the strip after the cement dries.

13 — Cut the two C&BT Car Shops 40-foot underframes as shown, then remove the coupler pockets from the two longest ends (upper right and lower left in the photo). Cement those two parts in place to produce a scale 41-foot bolster center-to-center distance. Center the three-beam piece on the underframe, then fill in the remaining gap with the longest chunk of frame. Add the Kadee no. 5 coupler pockets to fill in the ends of the frame.

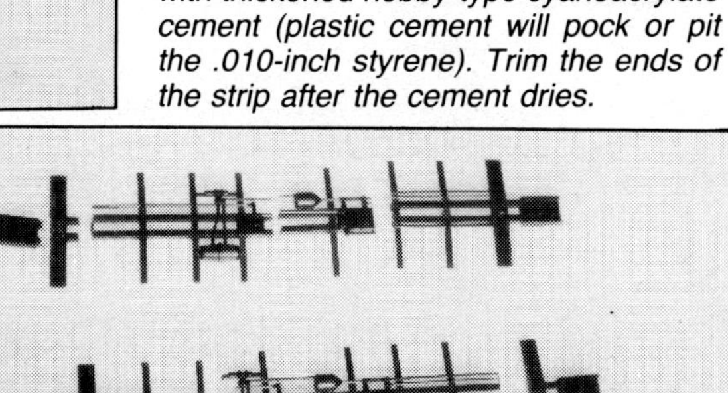

The 1955 version of the car would be even more difficult because the same reconstruction methods would be needed to produce sides from two C&BT Car Shops 40-foot kits plus the roof and ends from a Details West 50-foot car. Then you'd have to produce the horizontal rivet band that is on the sides of those 1955-built General American cars — that's why we opted for the 1950 version for this kit-conversion article. The 1950-built cars seem to have lasted in service as long as the later cars, and, for a time at least, both carried the same paint schemes to match the decals in this issue. These cars were later sold to the railroads, by the way, and repainted in a variety of colors. We'll feature those prototypes in a subsequent issue for those modeling an era later than about 1965.

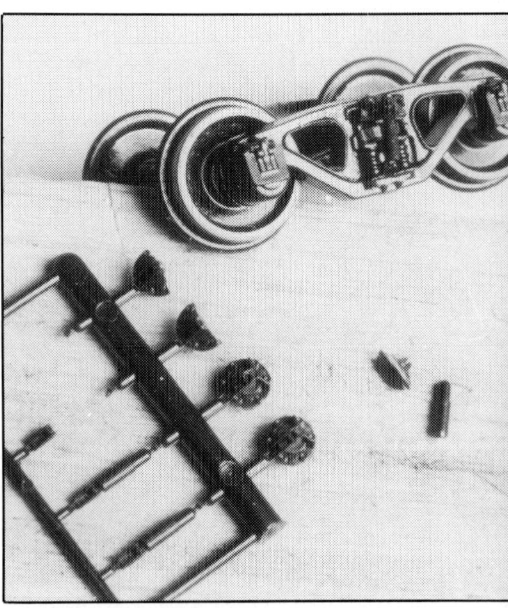

14 — There are no HO scale versions of the Chrysler trucks used on these General American cars. You can, however, simulate them with either C&BT Car Shops or Athearn (shown) trucks with Detail Associates no. 2802 EMD snubbers cemented to the truck spring faces with thickened hobby-type cyanoacrylate cement. Cut the top of the snubber and slice the round bracket in half, then mount the flat face against the top of the truck. The modified parts are shown loose and installed on the truck. We'll have more information on these trucks in part II of Richard Hendrickson's trucks article in a later issue of ***Railmodel Journal.***

15 — If you are going to produce an accurate body, it only makes sense to add the same types of "upgrade" details you'd want on a stock kit. This model has Overland Models' no. 2158 etched stainless steel roofwalk and Detail Associates number 6209 plastic bracket-type grabirons, 6412 stirrup steps, 6215 coupler lift bars, and a single 2202 wire grabiron on the bottom corner of each end, with .015-inch wire for the brake line. The small tack board for the "P.R.R." lease logo (there's a choice of seven others on the decal sheet in this issue — see previous article for the appropriate car numbers) is a 2-scale-foot piece of that .010x.080-inch Evergreen styrene strip. The ladders are from the Front Range kit, as are the doors and larger tack boards.

16 — Paint the car a mixture of one part Floquil no. 10 Engine Black to 20 parts Floquil no. 183 Reading Green. The decals, of course, are those bound into this issue of ***Railmodel Journal.*** *These decals are extremely thin so they'll cover the rivets like paint. Use plenty of water on the car side to float the decal. Position both decal and paper as perfectly as possible, then gently pull the paper from beneath the decal so you don't need to move the decal after it is off the paper. Several applications of decal-softening fluid (like Micro-Sol, Solvaset or Decal-Set) will make the decals cling like paint.*

Create-Your Own Kit, part II: "Flat" Kit-Conversions, part II: The Basic Cutting Techniques

These are the methods and tools used to make easy-fit parts for a "flat" kit-conversion like the General American/Evans 50-foot box cars in this issue and the HO model in the March 1990 issue.

Robert Schleicher

For some modelers, the thought of taking a saw to a kit body is simply ridiculous. Why destroy a kit to make it into another kit? If you're particular about the surface details of your models, the simplest method of capturing the details you need to recreate a prototype is to "steal" those details from a kit — in other words, to use a kit to make a kit.

The General American/Evans 50-foot green box car on page 16 of this issue was constructed using the parts and methods illustrated in the March 1990 issue of **Railmodel Journal.** That article, however, merely illustrated where the parts were to be cut and assembled, not specifically "how." Here's the "how."

The "secrets" of cutting and fitting plastic parts lie in the tools more than just the techniques. You'll need a very sharp razor saw l ike that sold by X-acto, Gyros or Zona; some type of vise or clamp to hold the parts steady while you saw; a medium-cut mill file to smooth the joints, and a 4-inch steel square (like General Tools' no. 2704) to check the alignment of the parts as you fit them. I've used the Panavise-brand no. 301 swiveling-head vise, mounted on the Panavise no. 310 surface plate, for nearly a decade. The swivel head allows you to move the work rather than the saw or file, so you are holding the saw or file in the proper position regardless of the angle of the cut. I use the surface plate to suport the parts of, say, a three-piece side like that on the General American/Evan box car kit-conversion while the cement dries on the butt joints. I also have a 3½-inch-long piece of 1x4 hardwood (walnut, I think) mounted in the jaws of the vise. I hold the plastic parts onto the block of wood — I do **not** actually clamp the parts in the vise because that would ruin the precious surface details I'm taking for the new "kit."

The mill file is a critical tool because it can make the final fitting easy — if you have the proper tool. There are two choices, the first being a medium-cut machinist's mill file with one thin smooth edge and with both pairs of edges parallel (no taper or curve). Tile and linoleum supply shops also sell a file used for Formica and other tile countertops. This file has both pairs of surfaces parallel, one blank side, a rough set of teeth

Clamp a 3½- to 5-inch iece of 1x4 hardwood (get it from a cabinet shop's scrap barrel — but ask first) into the jaws of a swivel-head vise like this Panavise. Rotate the vise head so the work is parallel to the saw cut you'll be making (see later photos). Use your fingers to hold the model onto the block of wood — they'll act as a perfect "soft" clamp to avoid surface damage to the model. Try to butt the model against the vise jaws, too, so they'll help to keep it from shifting while you saw. Hold it this way to make a vertical cut up the side.

For most models, it is best to make an angled cut into the corner to produce a mitered joint. You can cut straight across the side or end and file the backside of the part at a 45-degree angle, but, with practice, you can save a lot of filing (and sometimes make better use of the leftovers) if you cut at a 45-degree angle as shown.

For a mitered joint at a corner, simply file the back corner edge of the parts with the formica tile file held at a 45-degree angle to the surface of the part as shown.

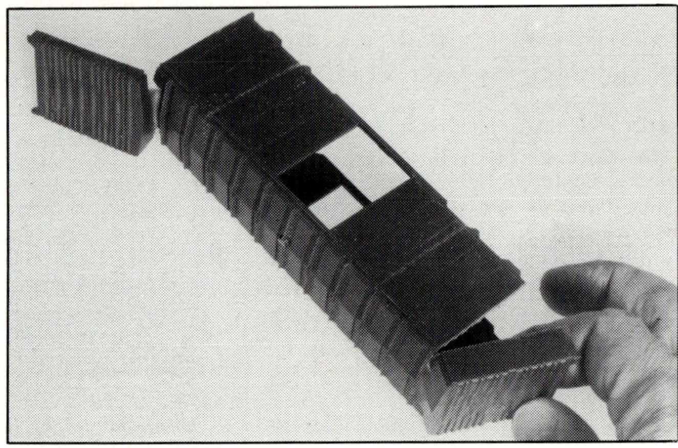

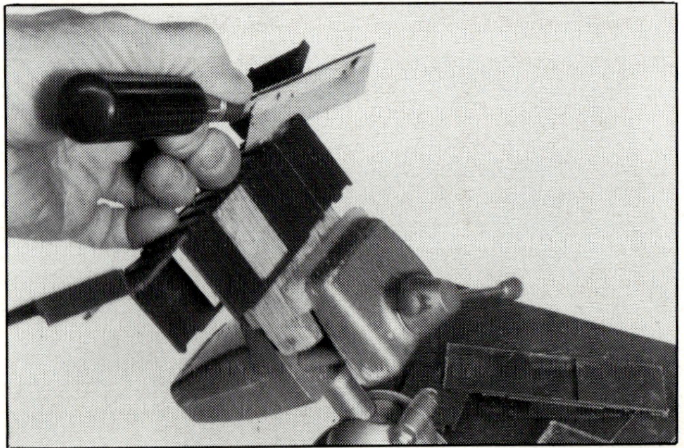

The sequence of cuts needed to remove a panel from the side of a 40-foot box car to make the 50-foot kit-conversion shown in the March 1990 issue: First, the ends are cutoff by sawing up the sides (1/64 inch toward the end from the line you want as your final seam). Next, the end is removed by sawing across the roof. The remaining ends can then be either bent upward as shown or just removed completely. The final cut is made at about a 45-degree angle into the notch along the joint between the car sides and the car roof.

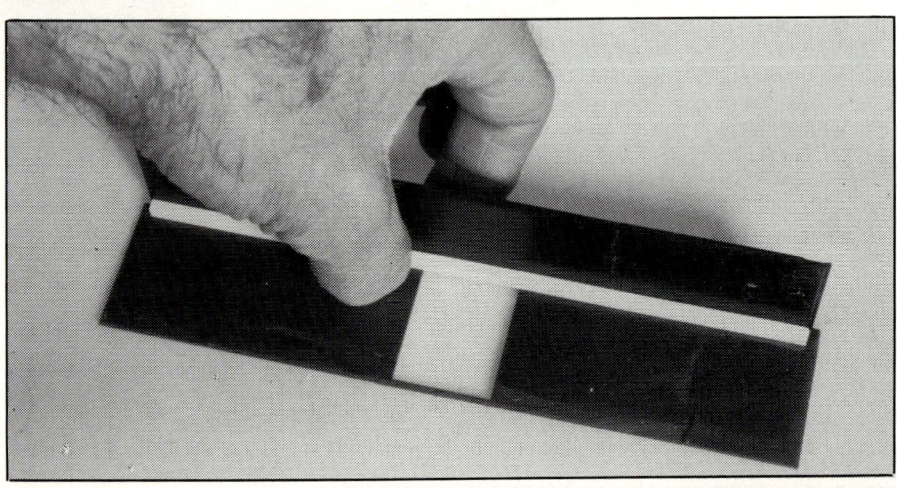

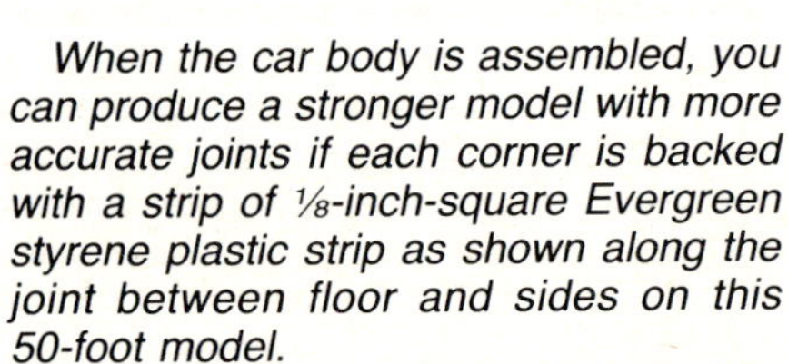

When the car body is assembled, you can produce a stronger model with more accurate joints if each corner is backed with a strip of 1/8-inch-square Evergreen styrene plastic strip as shown along the joint between floor and sides on this 50-foot model.

To complete the removal of the end, simply cut across the roof. Note, though, that the car body is held in a different position over the 1x4 block of wood.

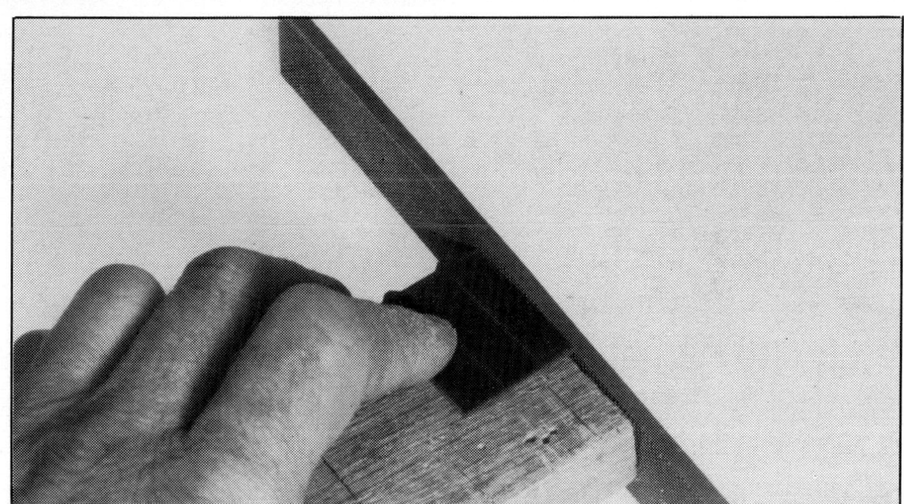

Use another scrap of 1x4 wood to hold the parts while you file. Here, you can hold the part in the vise or lay it along the edge of a table. Use the block to help "aim" the file so it is perfectly vertical to the cut. The Formica or tile file is an excellent tool for this work.

Use a small (4-inch) machinist's steel square to check the angle of the filed edges so they are precisely 90-degrees at each corner. Hold the part and file up to a light so the light can help show where the part needs to be fit. There's a misfit edge nearest the corner of the square on this part — the remaining portion of the side must be filed about 1/64 inch more to make the cut edge straight. Try to leave 1/64 inch or so of excess material outside any cuts to allow for just this type of file-to-fit work.

on one large side and a medium-cut set of teeth on the other large side — that's the file you'll see in the photos.

Finally, a word about cement: Use the liquid-type cement for plastic, not tube-type. On some large structures where the cornr details are relatively crude, it's okay to use the tube-type cement for its ability to fill in small gaps and dips in the surfaces. For a model like this box car, however, you want a near-perfect seam, and the liquid cement will create it. I usually use Testors Liquod Cement for Plastics because it is relatively mild and thus won't destroy details if I do dribble some out of a seam. The seams or joints, however, must fit perfectly, with no visible gaps when you hold the parts up to a light to check the fit of the seam. Apply the liquid cement to both surfaces, then quickly press the two joining surfaces together tightly and gently move the two pieces back and forth against each other, rubbing the cement into the joint. The rubbing action should be directed along the length of the seam. The object here is to allow the liquid cement to dissolve the plastic, then to use that dissolved plastic as a seam-filler. Press the joints tightly enough so a thin bead of cement-softened plastic squeezes out of the seam. Leave it. When the cement dries, you can shave off the bead with a hobby knife to leave a filled and smooth joint. One final tip: Paint the finished model with a thin coat of light grey or beige paint of the same brand you will use for the final color. That coat will accent any gaps or errors, and you can sand them, shave them or fill them with automobile "spot" body putty. **RMJ**

RAILROAD PIGGYBACK FLATS AND TRAILERS, Part III

B&O 50-FOOT TOFCEE FLATS AND TRA

Prototypes for the models on the following pages

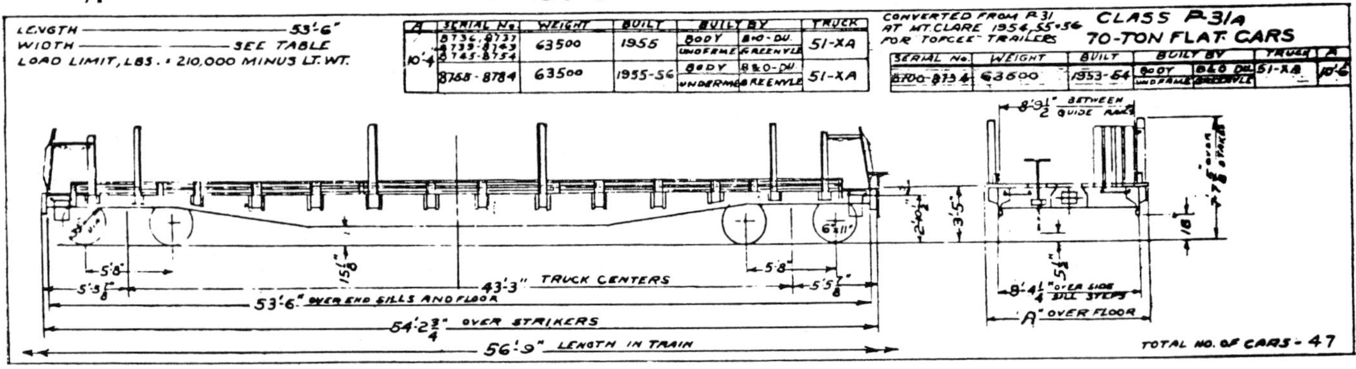

The Baltimore & Ohio equipment diagram for the P-31a class flat cars. Note that the cars are 53'6" over the end sills — about 3 scale feet longer than the Athearn HO scale, Atlas N scale or Con-Cor N scale models. The Con-Cor and Westrail HO scale models are the proper length, but both vary in detail from this prototype.

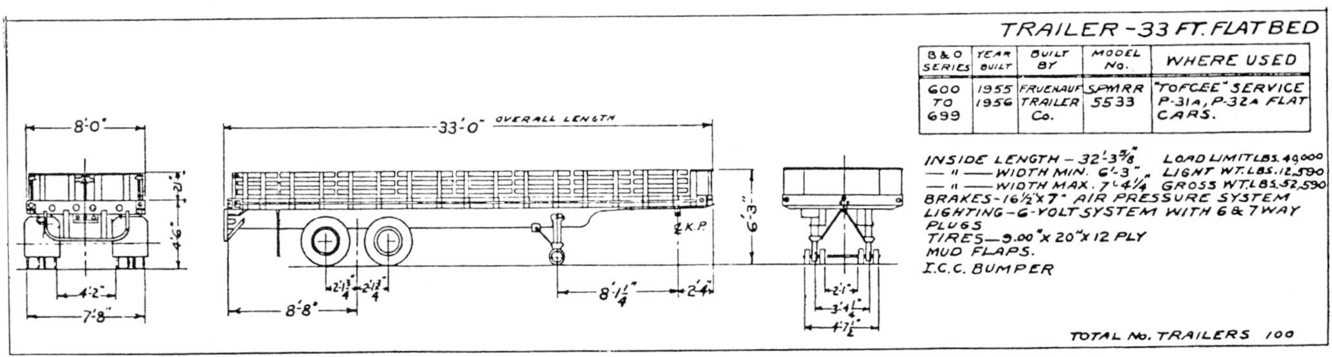

B&O equipment diagram for the (probable) flatbed trailer shown in the photograph.

The prototype for Gregory La Rocca's Athearn kit-upgrade on the following pages: the Baltimore & Ohio Railroad's class P-31a flat car no. 8724. The prototype was built on a Greenville Car Co. underframe in the B&O's DuBois shops in 1953-54 as a standard P31 flat car. The cars were rebuilt, reclassified and renumbered in 1955. Photo taken on August 9, 1955, near the Mount Clare grain elevator.

LERS

Photos and drawings: B&O Historical Society, courtesy Gary Schlerf

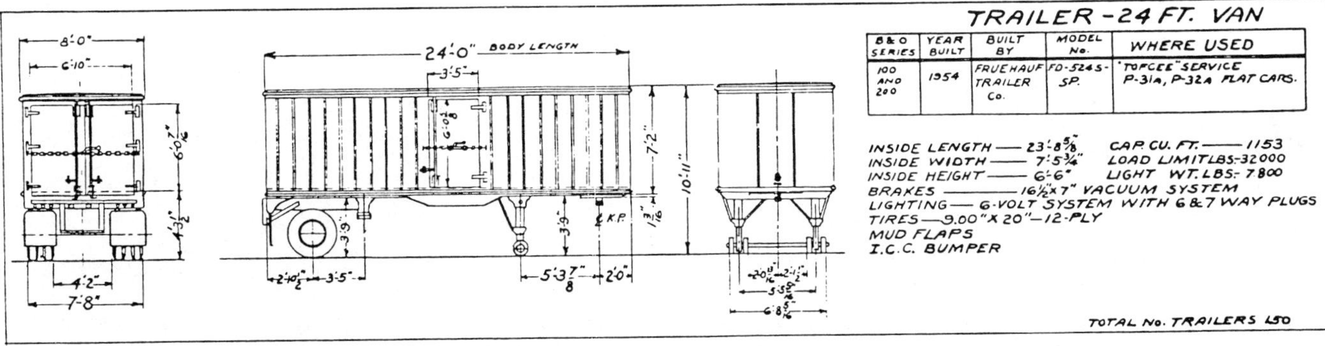

B&O equipment diagram for most of the trailers shown in the 1955 photograph.

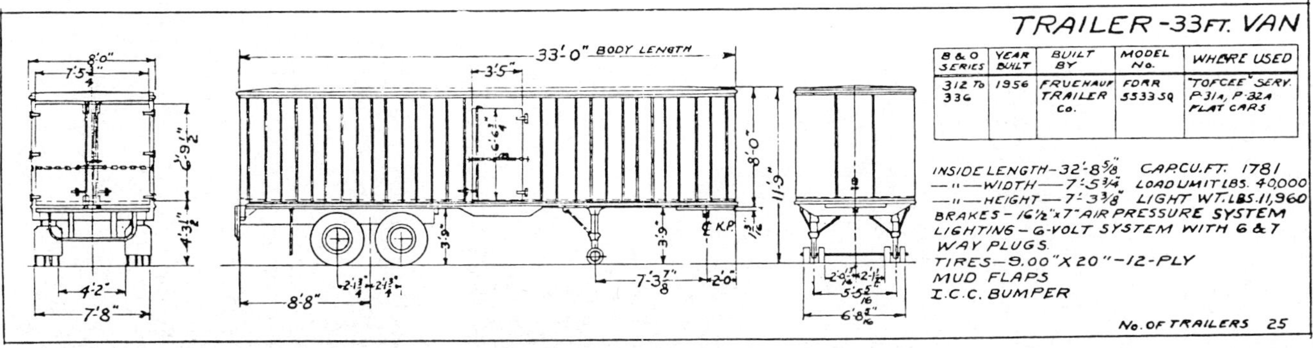

B&O equipment diagram for the trailer that is closest to the Athearn HO scale model and the Atlas N scale models (in length, at least).

Super Details: Athearn Piggyback Flat Cars & Trailers

Rebuilding the Athearn flat car, the easy way, to represent (if not duplicate) the fifties-era flat cars and trailers

Article and photos by Gregory M. La Rocca

When I originally set out to build replicas of B&O's P-31a Tofcee (for TOFC-Trailers On Flat Cars) flats, I had every intention of doing accurate models. However, the more I studied the prototype photos, and all the little doodads and gewgaws on the car, the more I decided that I *didn't* want to build accurate models. The problem is, like so many of us, I'm trying to build a layout, a freight car fleet, a passenger car fleet, and a steam and diesel roster all at the same time. Add to that the fact that I have enough kits and ideas stock-piled to last several years, and you can understand why I began leaning toward building a representation of the prototype, one which would invoke the feeling of the P-31a, without going through the intricacies of modeling it rivet-for-rivet. The photos show the "quick and dirty" model which resulted.

A few words about the prototype. Like many roads, the B&O in the early Fifties (1953 through 1956, to be exact) converted AAR 53′6″ flatcars over to Tofcee service by the addition of tie-down equipment. As you can see in the prototype photo on the previous pages, the tie-downs were much more elaborate than today's use of a fifth wheel support; generally, two chains each were attached to the front, back and sides of each trailer, which was supported by a jack under its fifth wheel. The chains in turn attached to eyebolts in the car deck for the front and back, and onto rails (which allowed them to slide into exact position) fastened along the car sides. Some roads used cables with turn-buckles in place of chains. In the case of the B&O, the side "rails" were more elaborate than most, consisting of two pipes welded to angle iron in the stake pockets, with four taller irons spaced along the car's length. Needless to say, securing each trailer to the car took much time and labor, and by the late Fifties/early Sixties, today's simpler system came into use.

Since I had the cars lying around, I started with Athearn's 50-foot piggyback flat car. To build my models, the first step was to fill in the mounting slots left from the Athearn trailer hold-down system. If you aren't recycling old cars, I suggest you start with Athearn's regular 50-foot flat, or, better yet, the old Revell (now Con-Cor) or Westrail 53-foot flat. At any rate, the fill-in pieces are Evergreen 4x8-inch styrene, cut to length and welded in place with lacquer thinner. While waiting for these fillers to dry, remove the side-mount brake stand by judicious cutting and filing. I proceed as follows: First, saw horizontally from behind, using a X-Acto no. 213 blade. Then, remove the side detail with a X-Acto no. 17 chisel blade.

Simulated Wood Decks

The deck boards are cut back using a file. Finally, I cut lines in the boards with the edge of a razor saw. After being allowed to dry a day, the fillers had lines scribed in with the edge of the razor saw, and then the whole deck was distressed using a stainless steel brush.

Deck Rails

Next, two 46-foot-long pieces of code 100 brass rail were attached to the deck, three boards in from each end, using hobby-type cyanoacrylate cement (CA). I suppose code 70 or even code 55 rail would be better, but I wanted the top of the rail to be as high as the piping, supported by the angle, would have been on a B&O car. Besides, I have lots of code 100 sitting around from my old layout.

Tie-Downs

I don't know what purpose the taller side posts served. They apparently were not used to tie the trailers in place. Perhaps they were meant to catch trailers that were tipping over, although they don't seem massive enough or tied in place well enough (or tall

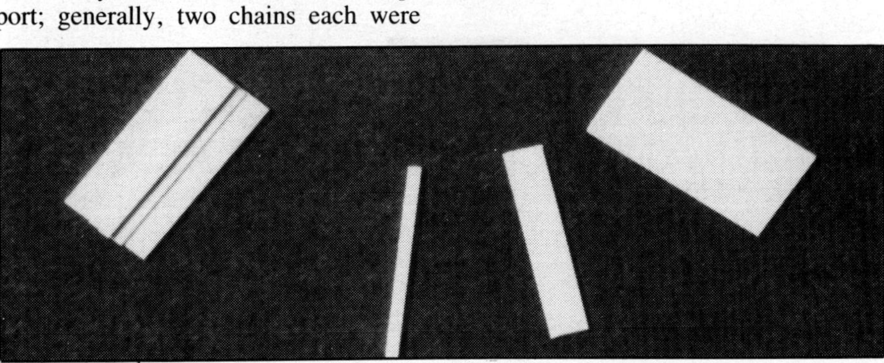

Construction of the bridge plates (see text for material sizes).

Close up of B end of car showing bridge plate and brake gear and wheel mounting.

Close up of the B end of the car, with shadows emphasizing the bridge plate construction.

enough, for that matter) to be effective. The only other cars I can recall that had these were the Pennsy's Truc-Train flats, although they were removed by the time those cars were conveyed to Trailer Train. The two shorter posts at the car ends were used to mount a chain whose other end mounted to the bridge plates to keep them up during train movement.

The posts are Plastruct 3/32-inch Ls. The eight main posts are 5 feet long, and the two bridge plate supports are 4 feet long. I found I had to file the ends slightly before they would fit in the stake pockets squarely; they are secured with Plastic Weld, although, I would use CA if building these again; I kept knocking the danged posts loose all during the construction and painting! Note their locations from the photos. The diagonal on the bridge plate support is a piece of 1x3 inch, 3¼ feet long, mounted with the bottom edge between the third and fourth rivets, and the top about 1 foot down from the top of the support.

Bridge Plates

The bridge plates are made from three pieces each: a main piece of .020 inch, 4x2½ feet; a strip of 1x12 inch, 4 feet long, centered on that; and a piece of 2x4 inch, 4 feet long, centered on top of the second piece. (See photo.) All were centered by eye. The bridge plates were glued to the end of the car, with their outer edge even with the inner edge of the rail. It turns out that the P-31a's had two types of bridge plates, with the Athearn (from the 85 foot Tofcee flat kits — available separately as part no. 20025, Trailer Hitch Set) being right on for the second type. So, feel free to use that one if you wish.

Brake Wheel

The final assembly is the brake wheel. Its gear is made from a piece of 6x6 inch, 1½ feet long, glued on the car end flush with the left grabiron. Note that it should extend below the lower edge of the end sill. The staff is .020 inch brass, 2½ feet long. The brake wheel came from the scrap box.

Henry Ford would have loved the paint scheme on these cars: black. I used Floquil Engine Black. The lettering is from Champ set HG-120, B&O long gondola, which actually is very useful for any oddball B&O car. Weathering is Polly-S, thinned with rubbing alcohol and airbrushed on.

B&O 8769, a P-31a piggyback flat, is an HO scale model built from an Athearn flatcar. Although not an exact duplicate of the prototype, the model follows the major features of this car, and captures its "flavor," while being fast and easy to build, leaving the author time to do everything else needed to build a miniature transportation system.

The finished, unpainted model. Uprights consist of Plastruct angle, the diagonals, bridge plates and brake gear are Evergreen styrene strip, and the rails are code 100 rail. Note the white rectangles on the deck along the far rail; these are the filled-in holes where the Athearn piggyback hold-down system snapped in place.

No, the trailers are not accurate for B&O. They are Athearn's, modified by cutting-off the forward axle, and lettered with Walthers decal set 934-26880. Note that the "Tofcee Service" slogan is actually the reverse of the prototype; it has orange letters on a blue background, whereas the prepainted Athearn trailers have the correct blue letters on an orange background.

So there you have it. A car which captures the effect of the prototype, but without the tears. Someday, I'll redo these cars, accurately. But until then, these will do. **RMJ**

Two of the finished cars side by side.

Con-Cor Pennsy G-31

(Continued from Page 44)

file and sand smooth. Form grabs from .020-inch brass wire, and cement in place (after drilling holes) on left end of each side of car, per photo.

Grabs, End: To each end of car, add two Detail Associate no. 6210 grabs and a cut lever.

Trucks: Trucks are Athearn Bettendorf with Kadee wheel sets.

Brakes: Cal-Scale AB brake detail parts were also added.

Painting and Weathering:

Paint: Pennsy freight car color, obtained by mixing a 1:1 ratio of Floquil Zinc Chromate Primer and Box Car Red.

Weathering: Pastel chalks sealed with Testor's Dull Cote spray.

Decals:

Middle Division HNM-3 Name and Numbers with 16-inch letters;
Middle Division HKY-1 Shadow Keystone;
Plus pieces of various Champ sets for dimensional data.

Bill of materials:

Con-Cor 54-foot mill gondola kit.
Athearn 50-foot box car underframe.
Kadee no. 5 couplers and boxes.
Athearn Bettendorf trucks.
Kadee freight car wheel sets.
Detail Associates no. 6207 freight car ladders.
Detail Associates no. 6210 grabirons.
Cal-Scale no. AB283 AB brake set.
A-line style "A" stirrup steps.
.020-inch brass wire rod.
4x10-inch scale styrene strips.
BB shot.

Modeler's Note:

To retain rivet detail of the shortened lower side sill, shave the rivets off the bottom of the original side sill before removing it from the car, and then reapply these rivets individually to the modified side sill. PRR classes G-31A, G-31B and G-31K can be modeled by shaving off all rivets to simulate welded cars.

References:

The Keystone, Vol. VIII, No. 8, December 1980.